THE NEW TESTAMENT

KNOWING CHRISTIANITY

A series edited by Dr. William Neil to provide for thinkin[g] laymen a solid but non-technical presentation of what th[e] Christian religion is and what it has to say.

The first titles are:

KNOWING CHRISTIANITY

The New Testament

by

A. R. C. LEANEY

M.A., D.D.

*Professor of Theology in
the University of Nottingham*

HODDER AND STOUGHTON
LONDON SYDNEY AUCKLAND TORONTO

To
Violet Clare Leaney
in love
and gratitude
from her son
Alfred Robert Clare Leaney

Editor's Preface

To judge by the unending flow of religious literature from the various publishing houses there is an increasingly large demand on the part of ordinary intelligent people to know more about what Christianity has to say. This series is designed to help to meet this need and to cater for just this kind of people.

It assumes that there is a growing body of readers, both inside and outside the Church, who are prepared to give serious attention to the nature and claims of the Christian faith, and who expect to be given by theologians authoritative and up-to-date answers to the kind of questions thinking people want to ask.

More and more it becomes clear that we are unlikely to get any answers that will satisfy the deepest needs of the human spirit from any other quarter. Present-day science and philosophy give us little help on the ultimate questions of human destiny. Social, political and educational panaceas leave most of us unpersuaded. If we are not to end our quest for the truth about ourselves and the world we live in in cynicism and disillusionment, where else can we turn but to religion?

Too often in the past two thousand years the worst advertisement for Christianity has been its supporters and advocates. Yet alone of all the great religions it has shown that a faith which was oriental in origin could be transplanted into the western world and from there strike root again in the east. The present identification of Christianity in the minds of Asians and Africans with European culture and western capitalism is a passing phase. To say that no other religion has the same potentialities as a world-wide faith for everyman is neither to denigrate the God-given truth in Buddhism, Islam and the rest, nor to say that at this stage Christianity as generally practised and understood in the west presents much more than a caricature of its purpose.

Perhaps the best corrective to hasty judgment is to measure these two thousand years against the untold millions of years of man's development. Organized Christianity is still in its infancy, as is the mind of man as he seeks to grapple with truths that could only come to him by revelation. The half has not yet been told and the full implications for human thought and action of the coming of God in Christ have as yet been only dimly grasped by most of us.

It is as a contribution to a deeper understanding of the mystery that surrounds us that this series is offered. The intention is to build up over the years a library which under the general title of 'Knowing Christianity' will provide for thinking laymen a solid but non-technical presentation of what the Christian religion is and what it has to say in this atomic age.

The writers invited to contribute to this series are not only experts in their own fields but are all men who are deeply concerned that the gulf should be bridged between the specialized studies of the theologian and the untheologically minded average reader who nevertheless wants to know what theology has to say. I am sure that I speak in the name of all my colleagues in this venture when I express the hope that this series will do much to bridge the gap.

The University,   WILLIAM NEIL
Nottingham

Author's Preface

This book is not primarily an introduction to the study of the New Testament; it is intended rather to be a description, so that the reader can discover what the books of the New Testament are about as well as the problems connected with discovering their origin. I have therefore approached most of the books as though the reader knew nothing about them at all; but in the case of the gospels I have assumed that he has some knowledge or that he will be willing to look up passages. In the case of other books, and very especially in the letters of Paul, I have tried to take the reader through a rough outline of his life and at the same time of the development of at least the main lines of his thought. So here I have quoted a great deal, and I record my gratitude for permission to use in these extracts the New English Bible, second edition © 1970, kindly granted by the Oxford and Cambridge University Presses.

The final chapter might seem to be misplaced at the end of the book; but it will mean far more to the reader who has read the other chapters and act in some ways as a kind of summary. But if the reader would like to know why the author thinks the study of the New Testament relevant for a modern man, by all means let him read that chapter first. The author would like however to make clear that he does not worship the great modern idol of relevance, but regards all knowledge as a proper pursuit for its own sake. Just how 'relevant' is Keats's *Ode to a Nightingale* or Sibelius's Violin Concerto? And if they are not objects of knowledge, how relevant are the history of Herodotus or the archaeological researches into the construction of Stonehenge? Yet the New Testament can boast of being relevant in the sense of being worth study, and relevant as many other studies emphatically are not, in having something to say about man and to man; for it opens to us the possibility of a new approach to the problem of Jesus, who he was and what is his true significance. If that does not interest you, do not bother to read on.

9

I would like to record here my thanks to Mrs. Pamela Hutton whose much appreciated services to our department and to myself have included the patient and willing typing of this book.

The University of Nottingham,   A. R. C. LEANEY
The Feast of the Conversion
of St. Paul, 1971

A TABLE OF DATES

Date	Event	Literature
B.C.		
168	Desecration of Temple by Antiochus Epiphanes and Revolt of Maccabees	
165		Old Testament Book of Daniel
c. 150– A.D. 68		Literature of Qumran ('Dead Sea Scrolls')
c. 135– 100		1 Maccabees
c. 100		2 Maccabees, 1 *Enoch*, *Testaments of XII Patriarchs*, etc.
c. 70–6	Rabbi Hillel	
37–4	Reign of Herod the Great	
31	Battle of Actium ensures supremacy of Octavian (Augustus)	
c. 30		Wisdom of Solomon
A.D.	Birth of Jesus (exact date unknown)	
6	Census of Quirinius (Acts 5:37)	
14	Death of Augustus Tiberius emperor	
26–36	Pontius Pilate prefect of Judaea	
c. 29	Crucifixion of Jesus	
c. 32–35	Conversion of Paul	
37	Caius Caligula emperor	
41	Claudius emperor	
49	Paul in Corinth	1 and 2 Thessalonians
51–52	Gallio arrives in Corinth	
54	Paul arrives in Ephesus Nero emperor	

Date	Event	Literature
54–58	Paul in Ephesus	1 Corinthians, Galatians, 2 Corinthians, Colossians, Philemon
58 or 59	Paul in Corinth	Romans
	Paul arrested in Jerusalem	
59	Paul a prisoner of Felix and Festus in Caesarea	
60 or 61	Paul arrives in Rome	
61–64		Philippians
62	Murder of James, brother of Jesus	
64	Death of Paul and Peter in Rome	
66	Jewish Revolt	Gospel of Mark
68	Death of Nero	
	Vespasian's campaign in Judaea and destruction of Qumran	
69	Vespasian emperor	Hebrews (?)
70	Fall of Jerusalem	
73	Fall of Masada	
79	Titus emperor	
81	Domitian emperor	
85–95		Luke-Acts, Gospel of Matthew, Revelation, Ephesians, Pastorals, James
96	Nerva emperor	
98–117	Trajan emperor	
c. 100		Johannine literature
c. 112		1 Peter
c. 115+		Jude, 2 Peter

Contents

CONTENTS

Part I

Chapter I

Mark, Luke and Matthew

IF modern philosophers neglect Plato and Aristotle, the student of the New Testament cannot neglect Jesus. Attempts to annihilate him have been perpetrated with less success by those who wish him not to have existed than by others, who take his existence for granted. The latter too often make him an unintelligible, unreal and ridiculous figure swathed in impracticable garments in stained-glass windows. Jesus himself remains necessary to history. It is the fashion to regard Christianity as dead and not to be lamented, but it is impossible to explain history without admitting that it existed once. It is equally impossible to explain Christianity without Jesus.

Sociologists may delight in showing that a certain class arose within the Roman Empire at a certain date, whose movement succeeded in the end in overthrowing that empire. For them that may be sufficient account of the rise of Christianity. It is insufficient for the early Christians themselves. It is perhaps a revolutionary proposal, but it may be relevant to examine what they themselves said about the origin of their own movement. To do this we must read the New Testament; at once an emotional block occurs, for then we shall be liable to the verdict of the lady in the novel about a fellow-passenger on a cruise who was studying the Gospel according to Matthew: 'Then he is either a clergyman or mad.' Neither of these alternatives is attractive, and we may therefore urge other motives. In this book let us choose that of curiosity: why do the New Testament authors mention so much about Jesus and report so little of his actual history as a man?

There is no doubt at all of the reason for this fact; it is because they thought of him as more. Something about him made them convinced that he was a Son of God or rather the Son of God, that he was the promised Messiah, the mysterious Son of Man (i.e. not a very human person as the title seems to imply but a mysterious other-worldly being, as the history of this title makes clear) or some other more than ordinary person. For the moment we do not justify this claim, but make a point important for understanding the New Testament: those few writers who did report him (the evangelists or authors of the gospels) were themselves so much influenced by their view of Jesus's significance, that they presented a figure which could not be understood by those who did not share their language. They allowed their convictions to colour and even entirely to obscure the living person whom they were attempting to describe. There can be little doubt that the historical Jesus is all but entirely submerged beneath the admiration of his worshippers. This is, or ought to be, obvious to any reader of the Gospel according to John, but an understanding of the relations between the gospels and the way in which they were written will show that the other gospel writers also have to answer for some of our mystification.

We must then adopt a strategic approach: we cannot with any hope of success reconstruct a life of Jesus from the gospels or any one of them as they now are. The attempt has been made again and again and will continue to be made by those who, like G. B. Shaw, possess the splendid confidence of ignorance when dealing with a subject whose experts find it difficult.[1] We must in fact learn something about the gospels, and then see what can be said about the historical Jesus whom the evangelists by their very enthusiasm for revealing him have concealed.

Even an inattentive reader will see at once that the Fourth Gospel (the title reflects its difference from the others and the reluctance of scholars to attribute it to John the Apostle, as a strong tradition does) differs from the other three, and that Matthew, Mark and Luke have much in common. These three are called the synoptic gospels for this latter reason—they are written from the same 'point of view'.

These synoptic gospels themselves present a problem: they have indeed much in common, and yet each has its own characteristics, together with its own peculiar material. What then is the relation between them? Did they all copy a body of

[1] In his preface to *Androcles and the Lion* Shaw presumed that Matthew was the earliest gospel.

tradition, perhaps an original 'gospel' now lost, not all of them preserving the same bits, though necessarily overlapping to a large extent? Did they to any degree copy one another? If this last question is on the right track, we may expect to find one or more copied by the other two, for it is unlikely that they all sat down together and looked over one another's shoulders, like naughty boys in an examination.

The classical solution to the problem is that Mark is the earliest gospel, used by Matthew and Luke who had also another document (no longer extant as an independent document) probably unknown to Mark though containing material like his; and that Matthew and Luke each had material peculiar to himself. It will be necessary to explain briefly how this solution was arrived at, why it enjoys such wide support, and finally its difficulties. These preliminaries will enable us to see clearly what problem faces us when we try to reconstruct a picture of the character and activities of the historical Jesus. The Fourth Gospel will be considered in more detail separately, although a brief preliminary word must be said about it at the outset.

The Fourth Gospel, or the Gospel according to John, was once regarded as the most reliable for the historian: the ministry of Jesus in this account lasted for three years, not the all too short one year of the synoptics. Moreover, it was apparently written by an eyewitness (John 19:35). Here we are at once confronted by a problem so often ignored by professional scholars of the New Testament: how can the claim to eye-witness evidence here and claims of this kind elsewhere be reconciled with other events recorded in the same gospel? For these latter are of such a kind that for many years men have been quite unable to accept them as history, although by a process of compartmenting their minds they may have pretended in the presence of clergy to do so. The classical answer, which proceeds from conservative belief, is that though the events would be hard to believe of anyone else, they are such as we may expect when the person in question is a supernatural being. Problems persist: for example, even if the existence — or former existence — of such a being were to be accepted as a bare possibility, the particular person portrayed in this gospel, whose utterances come near to arrogant boasting, is not one in whom a modern reader is likely to be interested, and he will reflect that if he is called on to worship the supernatural in this form, he must accept the consequences of refusing to accept the supernatural. The Fourth Gospel as a historical document was in fact dethroned by the German scholar, D. F. Strauss in his *The Life of Jesus*, first published in 1835. All the gospels, as he made clear, are rich in 'mythical' elements. If the aim is to make a clear picture of what Jesus said and did, it is not a question of selecting one gospel or set of gospels rather than another. All are, when subjected to examination, unreliable evidence for the historical Jesus, but the Fourth Gospel is more influenced by doctrinal considerations and convictions than the other three and to that extent more unreliable for history.

Let us then put the Fourth Gospel on one side for the moment. As we approach the early history of synoptic gospel criticism we need mention at this point only two scholars, of whom the first must be J. J. Griesbach, for he had the good sense to publish the synoptic gospels for the first time in parallel columns so that they could be easily compared with one another. He did this in 1774, and in 1783 published his own solution to the problem of the relation between them, believing that Mark used both Luke and Matthew. This was a sort of 'common-sense' solution, for the very brevity of Mark compared with the other two suggests that he made a shorter version from them. Perhaps there was here the survival of a sense, unacknowledged, that all the material in the gospels must be regarded as authentic and trustworthy; thus no suggestion of addition to the original gospel would be psychologically acceptable. The other veteran is J. G. Eichhorn who in 1794 suggested that Matthew and Luke had used a version of the 'original' gospel to which Mark had no access. Thus the differences between Mark on the one hand and Matthew and Luke on the other would be explained. It is far from our intention to give a full account of the history of gospel criticism, but these two examples of scholars will serve to show that there was in such men's minds the concept of an original gospel from which the others had copied. Instead of going on with the long history of this branch of learning, let us set before ourselves a modern version of the sort of synopsis made by Griesbach, and show what scholars in a more modern era have made of the facts which are then almost literally staring them in the face.[2] We will take a close look at only two passages; after that an outline of the problem and of its solution will suffice.

It at once emerges that both Matthew and Luke have material at the beginning which has no parallel either in the column devoted to Mark or in that of the other. This must be left on one side for consideration later on; we find then that all three make a start – or in the case of Matthew and Luke a restart – with the appearance on the stage of John the Baptist (Mark 1:2; Matt. 3:1; Luke 3:1). At this very point all three announce John with a quotation from Isaiah, but this is preceded in Luke by an elaborate and in some ways puzzling series of references to correlate the date with secular history. There are then obvious differences between the three evangelists at this point, but they occur within an identical framework. This framework consists of the introduction of John the Baptist by a quotation from Isaiah but it is hard to see what the precise relation of the three gospels to one another is at this particular point. The matter is more complicated when we compare in our synopsis Matt. 3:7–10 with Luke 3:7–9 a little farther on. Here the synopsis shows up the fact that Mark has no parallel passage. So far Mark looks like a defective version of a fuller gospel better represented by either Matthew or Luke. In particular there are clearly quite large portions of material which are shared by Matthew and Luke apparently quite unknown to Mark, for example, John the Baptist's preaching of repentance in Matt. 3:7–10 and Luke 3:7–9 just mentioned. It is worth while remembering these passages and looking at them carefully, if not in a synopsis, then reading them in both Matthew and Luke, noticing how very alike they are.

Now move on a little – to a page in the synopsis where Mark 1:40–45 is printed in the middle, Matt. 8:1–4 on the left, and Luke 5:12–16 on the right. If you have no synopsis, stop long enough to read these passages in the order mentioned. It will be obvious at once that the story is the same, that of the healing of a leper: this story strictly speaking ends in all three gospels

<hr>

[2] E.g. A. Huck, *Synopsis of the First Three Gospels* (Blackwell, 1949), which gives the Greek text necessary for serious study; or H. F. D. Sparks, *A Synopsis of the Gospels* (A. and C. Black, 1964), which uses the English Revised Version and gives also Johannine parallels.

with the instruction by Jesus to the cured man to observe the Mosaic regulation, but Mark and Luke add a further note about the fame of Jesus and its consequences. Here you may have noticed that Mark has slightly more detail in his account. Certainly if you have a synopsis in front of you in any language, you will see that there are small gaps in the Matthaean and Lucan columns contrasting with the denser mass of words in the Marcan column. This is very clear in the comparison with Matthew. Has Mark, then, added to the account which he derived from Matthew? On reflection this seems unlikely. One of the things which Mark would have added, in that case, would be the word at the beginning of his verse 43 to the effect that Jesus in 'dismissing' the man gave him 'a stern warning' (see the New English Bible). In fact the Greek of Mark says something much more like 'Looking angrily at him, he drove him away' and commentators are exercised in trying to make out what Mark meant by this. Whatever the correct explanation, it seems highly unlikely that Mark, if he had been copying Matthew's account, in which we have the rather remote and passionless Jesus who often appears in that gospel, would have deliberately added such a difficult clause. We can understand both Matthew and Luke toning it down or omitting it but not readily understand how Mark might come to add it.

There are several passages of this kind; indeed, this is typical of the relation between the three gospels. There is a further phenomenon observable in the comparison of Matthew with Mark: in addition to giving a shorter account than that in Mark, Matthew nevertheless sometimes adds material not to be found in either Mark or Luke, and he places it in the heart of his narrative. It now becomes a matter of finding a hypothesis which most naturally accounts for all these facts: Matthew has an account in some respects more concise yet embellished with extra material, and without the puzzling and even unflattering bits found in Mark. The most natural explanation is that Matthew used Mark as a basis, condensed him, but then added material of his own.

At this point we may introduce some slightly different evidence by counting the words which in any parallel passage are (1) common to all three, (2) common to Mark and Luke, (3) common to Mark and Matthew, (4) common to Matthew and

Luke. When this is done, the most natural explanation of what emerges is that Mark was the earliest gospel, used by Matthew and Luke. It remains in this section only to add that in all ages the question has arisen, 'Which copied the other, Matthew or Mark?' but that the other logically possible question, 'Did Luke copy Mark or Mark copy Luke?' has scarcely ever been put. This is because Matthew and Mark are very much more alike than are Luke and Mark.

We must now say something about the passages, one of which has already been specifically mentioned, in which Matthew and Luke exhibit material not found in Mark and which seems virtually the same in each of their gospels. The passage already mentioned was the preaching of John the Baptist, Matt. 3:7-10; Luke 3:7-9. This is so nearly the same that it is legitimate to ask whether it is possible that one of these evangelists copied the other. We shall see that the true account of the matter probably is that neither used the other's gospel but both used a source otherwise now lost; and the minority who do not believe this canvass with some ingenuity the notion that Luke used Matthew. It is a matter of accounting for the material common to Matthew and Luke not found in Mark, so that we must think away the passages which are common to all three and which it now seems natural to explain on the basis that Mark was used as a source by the other two. We then pay attention to the other common material; if we studied it carefully we should notice that it occurs in an entirely different order and manner in each. Matthew likes to expand his Marcan outline with passages of the common non-Marcan material, inserting the latter at perfectly appropriate places. Luke on the other hand has this material in blocks which alternate with other material.

It seems possible therefore that Matthew copied Luke, as far as this material is concerned; he could have used Luke as a quarry while he regarded Mark as the best basis and stuck to the order of Mark as far as possible. There are one or two reasons why this is unlikely, although it is not impossible. First, the order in which this non-Marcan material occurs is quite different in Matthew from that in which it is found in Luke. A great deal of it occurs in the famous so-called Sermon on the Mount, which is a collection made by the evangelist rather than a historical sermon. If Matthew composed this from material which he found in Luke, he darted about from one place to another in Luke to cull his material for the Sermon on the Mount. This would be an intelligible procedure if Matthew was arranging the Sermon in a more logical order, and something depends on how logical and orderly you think Matthew's arrangement is. So far it would be hard to say categorically that Matthew could not have copied Luke, but it is reasonable to say it is not very likely.

A closer look makes it less likely still: if Matthew used Luke he also had access to further material in the form of sayings of Jesus. The Beatitudes with which the Sermon opens may be parallel to Luke 6:20–23, but a great deal of what follows has no parallel in Luke at all. Perhaps the most important argument for the independence of Matthew compared with Luke lies in spheres outside both the Marcan and the non-Marcan material shared with Luke. Gospels distinguish themselves most sharply by their beginnings and their ends. Matthew and Luke are the only gospels to contain infancy narratives and they are vastly different from one another. Again the resurrection narratives in Matthew are full in content but peculiar to that gospel. The author did not obtain them from Luke.

If, on the other hand, Luke is considered as a possible copier of Matthew, his treatment of the non-Marcan material which they have in common was very odd; for he must have gone through Matthew with care, noted all the passages which were non-Marcan and assembled them into blocks, which he then alternated with Marcan material. He might have done this if he thought the contexts in which Matthew had used them were utterly inappropriate: but this can hardly be said.

It is for reasons like these that for many years most scholars deeply concerned with this subject have believed that the most natural hypothesis to account for all the facts is that worked out by B. H. Streeter in his *The Four Gospels: a Study in Origins* first published in 1924, when it was accepted as a summary of a great deal of work carried out both on the continent and in England, largely in Oxford, during more than a hundred years. This statement, then, is that Mark was the earliest gospel, and was used as a source by Matthew and Luke: that Matthew and Luke had another source in common, consisting mostly of sayings of Jesus, and that this accounts for the non-Marcan passages in which they resemble one another, for neither read the other. This source is called Q.[3] In addition, it is obvious that Matthew and Luke each had access to material which was not used by the other, some of which may have been, and some almost certainly *must* have been unknown to the other. The material peculiar to Matthew is called M and that peculiar to Luke is called L.

Streeter showed wisdom in expressing himself with modera-tion on all the points which he made, and was shy of being too certain about the extent and even the existence of Q, at least in written form.

This latter point and even the priority of Mark are still debated, but the main points of Streeter's solution appeal to those who are attracted by a theory which seems well able to cover all the facts. Further investigation, using the priority of Mark and the existence of Q as a joint hypothesis and testing it by the reasonableness of the results, generally persuades the investigator that both assumptions are most probably correct.

The Evangelists' Material

So far we have been thinking about the material which the gospels contain without enquiring deeply into its origins; for we have not pursued the question beyond the point where quite large blocks of material came into existence. None of the evange-lists was an eye-witness, and the material which each used he obtained from others; the next question therefore concerns its origin and authenticity.

When Streeter's book was published German scholars thought it a very good book but were astonished and a little offended that the author had ignored the important work which had been going on in Germany for some years, work which was concerned precisely with the question we are now facing; where did this material used by the evangelists come from in the first place? Much of what Matthew and Luke used came from Mark, but whence did Mark get it? Papias, bishop of Hierapolis round about 130, says that Mark got his material

---

[3] *Not* because it stands for the German *Quelle* (source) as frequently stated. The origin of the symbol is uncertain.

from Peter. There are difficulties about believing this and it will be discussed later. For the moment we shall try to determine something about the origin of the material by looking at it directly ourselves.

First of all, it is clear to an attentive reader that the gospel is made up of units which are rather loosely strung together. Look again at the gospel of Mark. After the first eight verses he says, 'And it happened in those days that Jesus came from Nazareth': which days exactly? How long after John the Baptist's pronouncement given in verses 7 and 8? Again, how much time elapsed between verses 13 and 14 in this same first chapter? Look through the gospel very quickly, and you will see very many points where a new event is recorded without anything like a clue as to the time supposed to intervene between the last and the next one. This fact alone invites us to divide up the units and to imagine that they may well have originally been separate. This is all the more probable when we remember that we have already seen how little regard Matthew and Luke pay to Mark's order, if it suits their plan to alter it.

This division of units is even more inviting in many parts of the Old Testament. For many years scholars had been accustomed to making such divisions there; for the material in the Old Testament could often be divided according to its category, folk-tale, legend, liturgical recital, myth, and so on. Such stories revealed a form or forms which marked them off for what they were. At this stage the material was not written down, but was publicly told or recited. Perhaps the clearest examples come from the sphere of liturgy. In the Old Testament ancient hymns and laments like Ex. 15:21; Hos. 6:1–3; 14: 2–3 show the same sort of form as 'The Song of the Three Children' in the additions to Daniel found in the Apocrypha. Again, the exploits of Judas Maccabaeus in the second century B.C. are related according to the models of the stories of the prowess of Saul and David. We may follow this clue a little further: discard for a moment any devotional and sentimental prejudices and look at the hymn we call the Magnificat which comes from Luke 1:46–55 and is used between the first and second lesson at Evensong. Only the opening words are really appropriate for the circumstances; as the hymn proceeds, not only does it reveal clear echoes of the Song of Hannah (I Sam. 2:1–10) but echoes also of some battle in which Israel (not Mary or any individual) has been signally helped by divine intervention. Many suspect that it was a song of triumph composed to celebrate some victory of the Maccabees. Luke has inserted it into his narrative, and like a dramatist 'given' it to Mary.

This method of study is called form-criticism;[4] if applied to Mark, many of the gospel units can be divided off from the rest and put into categories by their form. Two good examples of such categories are Pronouncement-stories and Miracle-stories.

In the first the form is usually as follows: Jesus or his disciples are occupied in an activity (often Jesus is teaching, but he and the disciples may be eating with sinners, or not fasting, or doing something which excites the attention of other religious people), someone approaches and asks a question; a brief dialogue may ensue, but in any case the end is swiftly introduced and takes the form of a saying by Jesus which is memorable (in the literal and metaphorical senses). An example of this type of unit is to be found in the Rich Young Man (Mark 10:17–22 and pars.) or in the famous saying about Tribute to Caesar (Mark 12:13–17 and pars.).

Miracle-stories might not seem at first sight to be examples of a particular form but this is claimed for them too. The patient is brought, something is said to show how ill he is, Jesus speaks a healing word, the patient is healed, the crowd marvel or 'wonder'; the German name for this kind of story is *Wunder-geschichte*, i.e. Miracle-story, but the syllables 'Wunder' are appropriate because it reminds us of the emotion which the incident is designed to arouse in the reader. Bultmann, one of the greatest apostles of form-criticism, would say that many such stories arose on Hellenistic soil and not in Palestine itself, being manufactured to allow Christians to compete with their neighbours who extolled the prowess of the gods or demi-gods whom they

---

[4] Its best-known advocates are Dibelius and Bultmann. V. Taylor provided in 1935 a classical statement in English under the title of *The Formation of the Gospel Tradition*. Introductions to the New Testament always contain an account of it.

worshipped, and whose saga contained stories of healing and the like.

So far it must appear that the form-critics must be highly sceptical. They are, but not quite in the way which might be expected; they do not state outright that all stories about Jesus were invented, but they do ask, 'In what life-situation (German, *Sitz-im-Leben*) did this story arise?' They would agree that often the question would be more appropriate if changed to this: 'In what life-situation would this story most naturally be repeated and therefore remembered?'—thus admitting readily that some stories may indeed go back to Jesus himself, but insisting that in that case we cannot know what the original situation was. Again, the life-situation *may* have been sufficient to have created, not merely preserved the story; for this situation is the life of the early Church, often on Hellenistic soil and faced with all the problems of evangelism in this strange society.

We can illustrate this briefly if we remark that the word 'Lord' was more useful as a way of giving honour to Jesus in that wider world than 'Messiah' or its Greek equivalent 'Christos', for the pagan society to which Christians wished to commend Jesus often called the objects of their heathen worship by the title, 'Lord'. If Jesus was addressed in his lifetime as 'Lord', probably all that was meant was 'sir', but it is clear that the risen Jesus was given the title in a sense which made him a divine being. This must therefore have been begun in a pagan environment, for on Palestinian soil it would be blasphemy. In a way only roughly parallel, form-critics would see signs of a pagan 'life-situation' in various units of sayings or incidents: thus for example the healing of Jairus's daughter in Mark 5:21-43 (and pars.) contains in verse 41 a formula used by miracle-workers, the *rhēsis barbarike* or utterance in a foreign tongue which has a sort of magical power in stories of pagan heroes. This example illustrates the issue between form-critics and others who sometimes wonder if their explanations are too extravagant. For the words here are in Aramaic, the language which Jesus spoke, and they are very natural: 'Get up, little girl!' Yet the form-critic is not being perverse; Mark wrote for a Greek-speaking public who knew nothing of Aramaic (many of all sorts of education in Rome spoke Greek quite naturally at this time) so for them it would be a strange-sounding formula. Then again, we might argue, Mark does translate the words for his readers. It is a nice point: is this memory of an actual incident or is it a story made up to capture the admiration of the audience?

Other categories used by form-critics in the New Testament sphere are Sayings and Legends. Sayings include the parables and in them we have a rich mine of sayings which can be shown to have a likely original situation in the life of Jesus himself. The so-called Lost Sheep parable begins with just the sort of appeal which we may imagine Jesus making to the Pharisees and others who criticised his free way of associating with sinners; 'What man among you . . . ?' But it is clear that the evangelists make an extended use of it in their shifting the emphasis from the behaviour of the shepherd to the sheep. Much work has been done along this line and needs to be taken seriously: we can often see a natural situation in which Jesus himself may have uttered a parable or used one of the famous sayings, and we need not think that all are inventions of the later Church. At the same time, we cannot be sure that any of the sayings or parables were first used in the situations given them in the gospels.

The category Legends gives an obvious handle to opponents of form-critics; to say a story is a legend is to judge not its form, but its content. To us such a word immediately implies that the material designated by it is unhistorical. To this criticism the form-critics reply that no such complaint would be made if the material being discussed were from the Old Testament or from pagan folklore. Many would probably be glad to agree with them on the subject of the story of the Coin in the Fish's Mouth (Matt. 17:24–27), incidentally noticing that this story suits a time later than the life of Jesus better than during his lifetime. Perhaps a great number would agree with them that the stories of and associated with the Virgin Birth are quite rightly categorised as legend; but how many would relegate the stories of the appearances of the risen Jesus to this category without reservation or modification? Indeed, when it is extended to include the baptism stories perhaps some would wish to argue that the account in Mark 1:9–11 can be read as a private vision of Jesus, and therefore credible, even if the form which the same story takes in other gospels makes it doubtful indeed. Matthew for instance has almost certainly added the dialogue with the Baptist for obvious doctrinal reasons.

This general account of form-criticism shows how criticism moves sometimes from the finished product to the elements contained in it. There is another way yet of looking at the gospels: this is to examine the way in which each individual evangelist has used his material and consciously or unconsciously used it to make a doctrinal point for which it was not originally intended. The difference between the story of the baptism of Jesus in Mark and in John will illustrate this sharply. In the latter the emphasis lies upon the witness of John to the descent of the spirit on Jesus and the baptism is not mentioned, while in the former, as we have seen, it is possible to regard the incident as a private inaugural vision for Jesus at his initiation by John into his own public ministry. In between come Matthew and Luke, each with their own preoccupations, Matthew feeling it necessary to explain why Jesus was baptised by John, showing that this was a possible source of embarrassment in Matthew's day and therefore presumably that baptism was generally held to wash away sins rather than inaugurate a course of action; and Luke seeking to avoid giving the impression that John baptised Jesus, as though John were in some sense superior to Jesus.

The account just given of the way in which at least some material about Jesus reached written form and so was preserved for us includes as an important element the belief that this material existed in separate units of tradition, and that these units were preserved, and often invented, by the early Church in the course of its missionary, teaching and defensive work. An objection may be made at this point: why must we assume that the material has suffered so much change? Why is it impossible that vivid memories of so remarkable a person as Jesus have been kept and fostered in the early days of the Church's activity?

This is a fair question and it may well be that such memories have been well preserved and that incidents of which he was the centre have come down to us as they occurred. If this was the case, there must have been method and care to preserve them for the thirty or more years before the oldest extant gospel was written. We know that rabbis contemporary with Jesus and in the years before and after him had their teachings and interpretations of the Law remembered by pupils who devoted themselves to the task, showing great feats of memory, and for many years not relying on any written aids because they hesitated to include in what was written anything other than the Law given to Moses once for all. Other teachings were deliberately recorded in the mind and not on papyrus or parchment: it was the 'tradition' or (in the case of much which had acquired the blessing of custom) 'the oral law'. It seems reasonable to suggest, as some scholars have done with great knowledge and understanding of the Jewish methods, that the early Church adoped the same custom. Its members revered the ancient scriptures just as the Jews did, most of them indeed themselves being Jews, so may they not have preserved the teaching of Jesus in a way parallel to that of rabbis and their pupils?

There is, no doubt, some truth in this contention as far as it applies to the teaching of Jesus; the long discourse which we call the Sermon on the Mount, which is not a sermon but a collection of sayings uttered at different times, contains much which might have been remembered in this way. But there is a very important consideration which often escapes the amateur critic: Jesus was not remembered primarily because he was a rabbi who imparted a new body of teaching for which he became famous. A great deal of popular discussion proceeds on the assumption that Christianity rests on the teaching of Jesus, and the principles which he put forward. This is a great error; his intention was not to be the founder of a religion but to recall his people to the great principles which underlay and informed the Law which they acknowledged. It is true that in the course of this work of understanding and interpretation he showed remarkable intellectual power, profound moral insight, and sometimes real originality: but he did not intend to be a teacher of new things but the redeemer of a people whom he wished to restore to an old obedience. So far he might be regarded as a kind of rabbi who transcended the boundaries which they usually observed; but—and this is the point—the picture of Jesus in the gospels is of one more than a teacher. He is a healer, a healer not only of the body but (more important) of the entire person, individual and corporate, of man, woman and nation. He is the Messiah or Christ come to deliver not from the political occupying power, but from the Evil One. More than all this, he is the One from God, more than a messenger like the oldtime prophets, a representative and even more than this—he is a, or rather not even *a*, but *the* Son of God. As such his task is then not only to teach, but to have an effect, to give new power, to change by example and influence, to do to the utmost extent all those things which we acknowledge are accomplished by leaders in all ages, and which go beyond the mere teaching of doctrines.

The evangelists are trying, and with many readers brilliantly succeeding, to get all this across to us, not merely to record the teachings of one more rabbi, or even to paint with words a portrait of a great teacher. They are registering the impact of a great and immeasurable personality. Moreover, they all believed that they had a main message about him to communicate—that he was due to come again, this time as judge, and that this coming could not be long. Even the author who is sometimes regarded as having reinterpreted this element in the teaching of the early Church writes to the recipients of his letter, 'My children, this is the last hour!' (I John 2:18). It is this which explains at least in part the otherwise puzzling fact that Paul hardly ever quotes Jesus, and even with the utmost ingenuity can be shown to do no more than echo a little of the teaching found in the gospels. Often it is stated in the discussion sections of magazines or reviews of books in respected newspapers that Paul devoted his life to spreading the teachings of Jesus. This is entirely false. He devoted his life to telling as many people as he could reach in the time available that God was about to complete the consummation of the age which he had inaugurated by raising Jesus from the dead, that they ought therefore to unite themselves to this Jesus, and to await his coming. Who Jesus was mattered supremely to Paul, his teachings very little. This neglect of Jesus's teaching is not due to one reason which might be read into it: Paul was far from despising the teaching of Jesus. It was of scarcely any importance to him because he apparently had access to very little of it, and could make up for this deficiency by the guidance which the Spirit gave him and which enabled him to speak with as much authority as if he could quote the earthly Jesus himself.

Early Christians therefore had a tradition to preserve and to maintain different from the ethical and legalistic teachings of the rabbis; and it was a tradition which of its very nature meant that what Jesus had taught was of less importance than might at first sight appear: for he was himself to come again, and Christians had their minds fixed on this expectation rather than on what they must do day by day, for which latter task indeed some guidance was necessary. It is obvious that such a situation had within it the germs of its own change: with the delay in the coming of Jesus everyday life became more important and problems arose which pressed for solution, so that Christianity became less a hope for the future and more a life for today. It then became necessary to answer such problems and to answer them with authority. We shall see how writings in the New Testament other than the gospels illustrate this changing situation; but perhaps we can now already see that the situation must be a changing one, and so must account for much of the gospel material, or at least for the way or ways in which the evangelists have used it.

The Gospel of Mark

It has become clear that Mark offers us a very important book; it is the earliest extant gospel and thought of so highly by Matthew and Luke as to be extensively used by them. It therefore seems natural to ask how far it gives us an authentic portrait of Jesus.

Answers to this question have varied from the confidence of those who thought that in this gospel we have a portrait by an eye-witness to those who believe it contains almost no historical material whatever. These are not random judgments but the result of the ways in which the gospel is approached critically. It is perhaps easiest to explain the view of those who hoped that in Mark we have an authentic report of what actually occurred. The search for the historical Jesus has proceeded side by side with criticism of the gospels which provide the material for that search. When it seemed satisfactorily settled that Mark was the most basic document of those we possess, it seemed natural to regard its story as the least adorned, the least altered, the most candid and primitive. We have already seen that the gospel is in some measure more primitive than the others, and this observation, that Matthew and Luke each in his own way altered the portrait of Jesus in the direction of making him more remote, more obviously a revered figure, encouraged the notion that we have but to turn to Mark to find the original unvarnished portrait. If this was natural it was hardly logical: for there was nothing to prevent the objection that there might have been further material earlier than Mark nearer to the authentic, that indeed Mark may have disguised material more primitive than that which he presents so that in his gospel we have the first extant – not necessarily the first ever – refinement of the primitive material. Again, he may have added to simple accounts of events his own reverential colouring and interpretation, or given some simple unelaborated accounts, but included in his gospel also some which are best called 'mythical'. For example, perhaps there was a storm on the lake of Galilee and Jesus showed indifference to the danger, rebuking the disciples for their cowardice, but Mark has added that he produced a calm by supernatural power; again, there is nothing incredible in the accounts of the calling of the first disciples or even the healing of Peter's mother-in-law, but there is simply nothing credible in the story of the Transfiguration.

For such stories we often have to turn to the Old Testament or to the literature of later Judaism to explain what Mark is striving to communicate. Thus many studies have been made to show the background of the Transfiguration; for some it suggests the enthronement ceremonies of ancient ritual connected with the king, for others all is centred upon Mark's claim that 'he was transfigured before them', that is, they received a special revelation of who or what Jesus really was: for the Greek word implies a change of being, and the disciples are granted a momentary glimpse of the divine being whom they knew as Jesus, perhaps had recognised as the Messiah, whereas he was himself shy of this actual title because it was misleading. Again, the story of Jesus walking on the water recalls the vocabulary used by the Greek version of the Old Testament to describe such mysterious events as God's revealing himself to Moses (Ex. 33:17–23; see also Ex. 34:29–35 for part of the background to the Transfiguration).

Many have suggested schemes upon which the gospel of Mark is constructed, and many of these are persuasive. Such works often make use of Wrede's analysis[5] by which Mark seemed to be building his presentation round the gradual revelation of the Messianic secret, revealed to Jesus himself at his baptism, to the demonised by his exorcisms, to the disciples at Caesarea Philippi, finally to the high priest and the Sanhedrin at his trial. The precise nature of this scheme, and its relation to the historical facts, indeed whether it exists at all in Mark, all these are often debated. It can scarcely be said that Mark is without any scheme, since it is clear that at least Jesus returns from his baptism (where he is called by God to begin his work) to Galilee to announce the imminence of the kingdom, and then finds himself in conflict with various beings, some demonic, some human, until he goes up to Jerusalem where the climax of the story takes place. At various points he enlightens the disciples a little further of the significance his ministry has reached.

We find therefore that while the gospel of Mark is made up of easily separable elements, units of discourse or *pericopae*, he has given his book some kind of order, either very simple and obvious, or more elaborate, and it seems absurd to say that he did not write 'in order'. This thought introduces one of the puzzles of New Testament study: the earliest piece of evidence about Mark from outside the gospel ('external evidence concerning authorship') is from Papias, bishop of Hierapolis, in Asia Minor, about 130; his writings have perished but bits of them have been preserved by being quoted by Eusebius, the Church historian of the early fourth century. In one of these fragments Papias says some things about the gospels of Matthew and Mark which are very difficult to square with what we know about them for certain ourselves.

About Mark he says:

Mark, having become Peter's interpreter, wrote down accurately, not however in order, all that he remembered of what was said and done by Christ. For he was not a hearer of the Lord, nor did he follow him, but afterwards, as I said, [he followed] Peter who adapted the teachings to his needs, but not as though making an orderly account of the Lord's oracles . . .

[5] In his book, *Das Messiasgeheimnis in den Evangelien*, 1901.

This last old-fashioned word is used in translation because the Greek phrase may intend to include sayings about, as well as sayings by the Lord.

At first sight this may seem to give an answer to the form-critics, on their own ground, to their claim that much of the material has been invented by the early Church. Here we seem to have evidence that spokesmen of the early Church did indeed adapt the material for teaching or preaching purposes, but the material was authentic, our loss being only of the order in which the teaching of Jesus was originally given. Peter himself here appears, on this view, as the source for many of the units and to guarantee their authenticity. Two difficulties immediately arise: we cannot be sure that Peter imparted any information about the events of Christ's life, for, when Papias explains the way in which Peter spoke, he mentions only 'the teachings' and we cannot be sure that these contain Christ's deeds, or whether, if they are teachings only, he means those of Peter or those of Christ handed on by him. The second difficulty has already been mentioned: there *is* some order in Mark's gospel. To these we should add that if we take a critical point of view about the mythical elements and do not believe these can actually have happened, substantial and important elements in Mark's gospel cannot have come from an eye-witness such as Peter. Papias says that he obtained this information along with some about Matthew from a 'presbyter' John's traditions, and there are a number of difficult considerations which arise when Papias's information is studied in close detail. The difficulties already outlined are sufficient to show why hesitation is often felt about accepting the information from Papias as though it solved all our questions about the composition of Mark's gospel. Thus it has more than once been urged that Papias did not really know more about the gospels than we could ourselves discover without his aid. It must be admitted that the tradition itself about Peter having Mark as an interpreter or assistant need not be rejected: it is reflected also in I Peter 5:13; even if that was not written by Peter, someone evidently knew that he and Mark had been together at Rome. If then Papias was right at least about the partnership between the two men, but if what he says about the gospel does not tally with the facts, he may have been referring to some document now lost which Mark wrote. Since there is no independent evidence of an original gospel (an 'Ur-Markus') it is unlikely that Papias is referring to that, but he has been taken by some to be referring to Q or to a similar document. If this were right we must offer some explanation of how the gospel we call that of Mark came to be ascribed to him. Unless this ascription is correct it is hard to see how it came about. There was a tendency very early in the Church to ascribe gospels and indeed other writings to apostles in order to give them authority once they had been accepted widely; thus it was far from natural to ascribe a gospel to someone who was not an apostle and who indeed is carefully designated as one who was not a disciple of Jesus but a 'follower of a follower' (as we might summarise it), unless this was correct.

It must be admitted that this argument can be almost indefinitely prolonged: in the passage quoted by Eusebius to which we have referred, Papias, who was a bishop in Asia Minor in a city which had close ties with Ephesus, tells us that he valued the spoken word more than the written (being able still to hear information about Jesus at not too great a remove from the first hearers) but also, as Eusebius interprets him, that his informants were those who had themselves been able to hear the actual apostles. It is possible therefore that he might ascribe a gospel to one who had similar authority. This however is theory and it is best to conclude that Mark wrote some at least of our gospel bearing his name; then we have still another problem: for we have to admit that Papias did not describe the gospel accurately.

Different minds will judge the situation regarding the authorship of the gospel of Mark differently. As so often in matters affecting documents of such antiquity, we can do no more than set out the facts available. In the case of other authors it may be possible to be more definite, as for example with Matthew to whom we now turn.

The Gospel of Matthew

The end of the last section may have raised hopes that there are grounds for believing that the Gospel according to Matthew was written by one whose name is listed among the disciples of Jesus. Unfortunately this is just what we cannot say; for what we can say quite definitely is that this gospel was *not* written by an actual disciple.

Matthew the disciple is mentioned in all four lists of the twelve in the New Testament. These lists occur in the three synoptic gospels and in Acts. (The Fourth Gospel has a slightly different set of names and no actual list.) There was evidently a disciple Matthew but oddly enough it is doubtful if he was the tax-gatherer who 'sat at the receipt of custom' (or 'at his seat in the custom-house' as the New English Bible says). He is so described in Matt. 9:9 but the corresponding verse in Mark (2:14) calls this person Levi; and it has been shown that Mark is most probably the earliest gospel and a source used by the author of the gospel of Matthew. Why the latter changed the name for this incident we cannot say, but it was not because he knew better than Mark.

This last statement can be made with confidence. We have seen already that Matthew seems to betray the outlook of a later age than that of Mark; some remarkable instances of this can be given: in the midst of the story of the guests who made excuses about coming to a feast (in Matthew a wedding-feast for the king's son, i.e. the Messianic Banquet to which God is inviting his people) Matthew inserts some surprising touches; read first the story in Luke 14:15–24 and then compare Matt. 22:1–14. Attention to detail will show that Matthew alone introduces a violent element into the story. Some guests maltreat the servants sent to bring them to the feast and even kill them. As a consequence the king sends his armies to kill the murderers and to burn their city. This is an incongruous element in the story, whose opening did not suggest that the hostility between the two parties was so great as to lead to such bloodthirsty exchanges. We can offer a natural explanation for this surprising addition: if we can entertain as a working hypothesis that Matthew wrote later than Mark and used his gospel as a source, such a hypothesis will easily support a theory about this incident as Matthew relates it. He wrote after the fall of Jerusalem and he reflects here the belief, which we know existed early in the Christian Church, that God had punished the Jews by sending the Romans to burn their city for having rejected the Messiah. Several considerations can be added to this one example: now and again the author reveals that he stands at some distance of time from the events which he is relating by claiming that what he has told us explains something true 'to this day'. Perhaps the most famous instance is the story about the empty tomb, with the explanation of how the resurrection occurred and how a false explanation of it was invented and 'is current in Jewish circles to this day'. See Matt. 27:55–28:15. This is again a passage to read with the help of a synopsis for it reveals how much is peculiar to Matthew in this part of the gospel story. The category includes the whole of this account of the setting of a guard on the tomb and their being bribed to tell a false story about how the tomb came to be empty. (Incidentally it reminds those who care to read the original documents how old and how well-known to the Church is the theory so often put forward by modern 'critics', 'His disciples came by night and stole the body'.)

It is perhaps unnecessary to add all the examples which might be given to show that wherever Matthew departs from Mark where he is using him as a source, he shows the outlook of a later age. This characteristic will emerge if a general account of the gospel is given.

The first thing that strikes any reader may be somewhat disconcerting. The first word in verse 2 is Abraham and it introduces a 'table of descent' (literally, a 'book of genesis') of Jesus Christ (1:1). If the author is in any way hostile to the Jews, why does he introduce this element into his gospel? For it emphasises the continuity of the Christian gospel with its Jewish origins. The answer is partly that the author is not unconditionally anti-Jewish. All we can say so far is that he is critical of the generation who rejected Jesus and believes that they provoked God's anger. Another part of the answer is that Abraham can be regarded as Paul regarded him in Rom. 4; Jewish patriarch though he was, Abraham was intended to be the father of many peoples, not only of the Jews, and to be the source of blessing to all those peoples. The inclusion of his name therefore suggests that the privilege of bearing a blessing for all peoples—a privilege which the Jews had turned into an exclusive sense of superiority—was about to be made effective, by the birth of him who would implement all the promises made to Abraham and to the fathers of old. The table of descent has another, and far more surprising feature, the inclusion of the names of four women, not usually thought worthy of mention in a genealogy unless a special point was to be made by it. Several theories have been offered to account for this, theories which take account of the facts that not only are women mentioned but that all four are women who gave birth in somewhat irregular circumstances. Thus calling the mother of Solomon 'the wife of Uriah' draws attention to David's original adultery with her, and to his wicked action by which he engineered the death of Uriah, although Solomon was not the result of the actual adulterous union, and Bath-Sheba was David's legal wife when she conceived and bore Solomon. Quite early calumnies circulated among Jews about the birth of Jesus; and one might think that the stories in Luke and Matthew that Jesus was conceived by Mary while a virgin were an answer to these stories. In that case, Matthew's inclusion of the four women in his table of descent may be a second line of defence, conveying the argument that God can work even through irregular unions. Others would suggest the greater probability that Matthew and Luke did not meet but unwittingly provoked the calumnies by their stories of the virginal conception, which arise from other causes. Research into the character of the genealogist's art as it is illustrated in the whole Bible shows that many fictitious tables were made in order to draw together different traditions or to satisfy the demands of orthodoxy concerning the descent of a person known to have held high office. Matthew's table is certainly artificial and cannot be made to fit either history or chronology; it has been suggested that its composition was due to Matthew's considerable knowledge of the Jewish use of scripture by scholars of his time: the names included in his table, not excepting those of the women, indicate his acquaintance with these theories and his claim that their demands about the right ancestry of the Messiah were fulfilled in the case of Jesus. The story of Jesus's conception by a virgin makes our problem vastly more difficult: after the care taken to derive Jesus through the male line from Abraham and to include the 'right' people in his family tree, his conception is accounted for by a miracle which does not require and is indeed inconsistent with such a table, inconsistent with Jesus having been born after conception from a man altogether. 'She was with child by the Holy Spirit' (Matt. 1:18).

This may be an oddity to us. It was not so for Matthew. The New English Bible prints the table and then the story about Mary as separate paragraphs. Rightly, for this shows the way in which the author was thinking: he offers two quite different accounts of the origin of Jesus. One we have already considered. The second makes the point that by this means prophecy is fulfilled. Neither Luke nor Matthew in fact emphasises, as subsequent tradition has done, the biological miracle. They emphasise the action of God in this event and the fulfilment of prophecy. Matthew was exercising his skill as a scriptural scholar. To explain this we must understand how entirely different is the nature of rabbinical from that of modern scholarship. Ancient rabbinical ways with the scriptures were such as to ignore completely the questions which are axiomatic for us. When we investigate the meaning of a writing we regard it as necessary to determine as far as we can the date and circumstances of the author, so that we can decide how he looked at things, and thus make allowances for his particular perspective. One reason for finding out the date is to see if our author was influenced by, or was perhaps even quoting as authority, a previous author or authoritative writing of any kind. In our day, we would not dream of interpreting the Bible historically or 'scientifically' by quotations from Shakespeare, who lived so long after the biblical authors. We might indeed quote the great poet and argue that he had well understood what the Bible at some points was trying to teach. We should never suggest that a biblical writer meant some particular interpretation because of what Shakespeare said when he took up the theme. To take an example at random, in the Fourth Gospel Jesus says to Pilate that he has come to bear witness to the truth (John 18:37). Pilate's impatient rejoinder, 'What is truth?' is famous, and leaves open what Jesus meant by truth; how then could he bear witness to it? It would be typical of rabbinic exegesis to argue without any discussion of relative date or even without any reference to Shakespeare at all, that it meant that Jesus avoided being false to his fellow-men; they would argue, 'for it says . . .' or simply 'for—*to thine own self be true . . . thou canst not then be false to any man*'. Such an argument would bewilder us. In order to understand it we should have to grasp that anyone who used it evidently thought that

Shakespeare belonged to a body of writings with the same outlook and the same authority as that which he was seeking to
illuminate. Let us suppose that to be the case. We would still
be puzzled by the appeal to someone who to us manifestly
wrote much later and might have been thinking about quite a
different matter. This would not disturb the ancient rabbi;
he would rejoin that 'there is no before or after in scripture'. It
would therefore be useless to argue with Matthew that in applying Hos. 11:1 to the story of Jesus's return with his parents
from Egypt (Matt. 2:15) he is most unfairly applying a scripture
which, though it comes from a prophet, clearly meant originally
to refer to a well-known event in the past. He would say that
he is drawing out the meaning hidden until now and that God
had revealed to him the true intent of this passage.

If we apply this to the apparent contradiction in both Matthew
and Luke of including the story of birth from a virgin along
with a table of descent such as each gives, we must note a
further fact very curious to us. Scripture was held to be capable
not only of harbouring different meanings but also capable of
harbouring contradictory meanings. A rabbi who wished to
use one meaning at one time and another at another would
not be blamed for his inconsistency but praised for his ingenuity. All the meanings of scripture must be brought out and
it was up to the exegete who was using a particular interpretation to use as many arguments as he could (quoting other
passages) to sustain the brief he was pleading at the moment.
It is not a great step from such a use of scripture and of argument to include in a gospel these, to us, clearly contradictory
ideas.

Our own historical investigations are another matter; we
must use the knowledge we have about all the influences
operative in the composition of a gospel or other writing to
determine the value of its contents from a historical point of
view. Perhaps the hardest lesson we have to learn is the rela-
tivity of historical truth for some writers of the past. Yet this
should not altogether baffle us: the traveller in Palestine may
be bewildered to be told at Hebron that the grave of Abraham
is probably in the sealed cave beneath the famous mosque, and
a few moments later by the same guide that 'That is Abraham's
tomb' as he points to a structure above ground which a little

earlier he explained as dating from the fifteenth century of our era. He may be bewildered but on reflection, if he is wise, he will see that there is here a complete difference in the way of thinking. The western traveller has learnt that 'Everything is what it is and not some other thing'. This is far from self-evident to his Arab guide who is driving the visitor insane with his inconsistencies. For us there is a difference between 'That is Abraham's tomb' and 'That is "Abraham's Tomb" ' but this difference does not exist for every mind.

All this is not intended to convey the notion that Matthew was quite happy to write palpable inconsistencies of fact; there are a number of things which all the writers in the New Testament proclaim as truth in the sense of historical fact — that Jesus was crucified and was raised from the dead, that he was the Son of God, and many others. We feel it necessary to distinguish between these claims; they are of different categories. For example, the resurrection, being unique and involving the supernatural, is for us historical in a quite different sense from the crucifixion. No such distinction would be made by first-century Jews. The manner in which the events happened or the reason for their happening may vary in different writers, or even in different writings by the same author, but their truth is never in doubt.

What has been said may help towards understanding other aspects of this gospel and indeed other writings in the New Testament which will be considered in later chapters. Thus the truth of the story of the temptation of Jesus in the wilderness will appeal to us more if we cease to ask such questions as 'Did the devil (Matthew calls him the tempter) really come and actually speak to Jesus (4:3)?' or 'What part of the temple did Jesus actually stand on in order to be tempted to test the reliability of miraculous rescue by angels?' (Your guide in Jerusalem answers this by pointing to a corner of the wall which he has just told you was erected in 1555.) Less appropriate still is to ask, 'What high mountain could show all the kingdoms of the world to anyone?' Perhaps more teachers than one have found it hard to get from normally intelligent children the answer to the question, 'How could Jesus do this?' the common-sense answer, 'in imagination'.

Matthew (as we may conveniently call the evangelist) does

not tell us where or exactly how the temptations took place, but what kind they were. He answers the modern question, 'What were the basic spiritual problems which Jesus faced at the outset and throughout his ministry?' but he answers it in his own manner, in the manner of a rabbinical exegete, like a scribe who brings out of his treasure things new (the Christian gospel) and old (Jewish *haggadah* or story to enhance and explain it). See Matt. 13:52: in the careful translation of the New English Bible 'teacher of the law' gives a much better idea than the usual 'scribe'; no doubt Matthew thought of himself as a 'teacher' from the old school who had become a 'learner' as far as the gospel was concerned.

Matthew represents Jesus as Messiah, as healer, and as teacher. In his gospel this latter aspect of Jesus is emphasised; in the famous Sermon on the Mount the evangelist has collected together a large number of Jesus's sayings unlikely indeed to have have been delivered all at one session, but which establishes Jesus as a teacher in continuity with the old while he is nevertheless manifestly and radically new; thus in 5:17–48 the appeal to scripture (the ancient wisdom) is obvious, not least in a passage beginning 'But what I tell you is this . . .' (e.g. 5:34). It is as teacher that in this gospel Jesus sends out the twelve to the people of Israel (ch. 10), as well as interpreting afresh the ancient wisdom, provides for the Church (this is the only gospel to use the word) and its rules, warns the present generation, prophesies judgment to come, and proclaims the loss of the kingdom by those who failed to act in conformity with the privilege of being its 'sons', and finally, as the risen Christ, charges his disciples with the task of teaching all their converts what he has taught them (28:20).

The aspect of Jesus as teacher is indeed emphasised by Matthew; but it is an aspect of one whose entitlement to be called Christ, Son of Man, and Son of God is taken for granted. Thus it is as Son of Man that he asks of his disciples how men at large, and then how they themselves assess him (16:13); and it is as Messiah or Christ rather than as rabbi that he systematically teaches his disciples. He is addressed as rabbi but is represented in this gospel as disliking the title, certainly for his followers, perhaps even for himself; for in 23:8 Jesus does not exactly say, as the New English Bible puts it, '. . . you must not be called "rabbi"; for you have one Rabbi'. This is a good effort to make a point, but in fact the word translated Rabbi is not that word, in the Greek; the term used here is either the usual word for teacher or else the same as the rather rare word which is translated Teacher in verse 10. (The doubt is due to a disagreement in the manuscripts.) Jesus is in Matt. 23:8 contrasting his authority as a Teacher with that of even the most authoritative teacher. His authority to teach evidently rests not on his being a sort of supreme rabbi but on being the Christ or Messiah (verse 10). He is more than the expected Messiah: having resisted the temptation to obtain through the devil 'all the kingdoms of the world' (4:8) he is given as a reward for his obedience 'full authority in heaven and on earth' (28:18).

This general survey may help us to judge what Papias says of this gospel. Eusebius tells us about this immediately after giving Papias's words about Mark: 'Such, then, is Papias's account of Mark. But the following is the statement concerning Matthew: "So then, Matthew compiled the oracles in the Hebrew dialect but everyone interpreted them as he was able".' 'The oracles' could be translated rather by 'the sayings' but the phrase might mean something like a gospel, and the 'oracles' would include material about as well as from Jesus. On the other hand what follows in Papias's statement suggests that he is in fact speaking of a collection of sayings which others could use without taking over the whole collection at once. 'In the Hebrew dialect' is an odd-sounding phrase used to mean Aramaic. Acts 22:2 uses it of Paul's address to the mob in Jerusalem, and there it must mean Aramaic. Even if here in Papias it means Hebrew, it is clear that what he says does not describe the gospel which we know as the Gospel according to St. Matthew. Too much ingenuity has been used to explain this piece of evidence from Papias; it has been suggested that Matthew was the author of Q in its original Aramaic form, and since Q appears (though in its Greek form) in the gospel, his authorship was later assumed for the whole gospel. The theory is obviously full of gaps, not least the lack of an explanation of the existence of an Aramaic Q for which there is no other evidence whatever. It seems better to make the common-sense conclusion that Papias was here not referring to our gospel at all. The curious thing is that he almost certainly knew it; and it is this fact along with his words about 'Matthew' which has misled so many into trying to reconcile what we know about *our* Matthew with what Papias says about *his*. Abandon this task and there appear two other questions: 'What did Papias call our Matthew?' and 'To what was he referring in the passage quoted by Eusebius?' We can give reasonable answers to both these questions. It is true that Papias probably knew our Matthew but he knew it simply as 'the gospel', that which circulated almost exclusively in Asia Minor in his day. Such a theory is supported by the large number of quotations from it in the fathers, and especially by Ignatius who in writing to the Smyrnaeans when on his journey to martyrdom in Rome refers to the gospel in such way as to show that he almost certainly means that which we call the gospel of Matthew. If he knew it in the first years of the second century it is probable that Papias knew it later on in the same period, and that Papias also knew it as 'the gospel'. Nor is it odd that Papias should refer to a collection of oracles in Aramaic and not to a gospel; for in the passages quoted by Eusebius he is not trying to establish a literary canon or to show how well founded are the written records about Jesus. In fact the information about early writings is set in the midst of Papias's recollections about oral tradition which he prefers to the written. Indeed he gives instances of men he knew who can be connected with the actual time of Jesus, and Mark is quoted as one of these, having been in such close contact with Peter. This is Mark's importance, and he is excused for writing a gospel rather than commended for it.

When we turn to the task of answering the second question, 'To what was Papias referring?' we get considerable help from Eusebius; after quoting the words of Papias about Matthew he goes on immediately: 'And the same writer has used testimonies drawn from the former epistle of John, and likewise that of Peter; and he has set forth, as well, another story about a woman accused falsely of many sins before the Lord, which the Gospel according to the Hebrews contains.' While it must be admitted that Eusebius does not specifically say that Papias obtained the story about the woman (which has not survived unless it be the same as that about the woman taken in adultery,

John 7:53 – 8:11) from the Gospel according to the Hebrews, this is nevertheless a very reasonable interpretation of the passage. This then may well be what Papias was referring to, not our gospel of Matthew. We shall see later that Irenaeus (c. 130–200) is probably the agent who fused together different pieces of information under the pressure of his desire to counteract criticism of orthodox Christianity and to give the scriptures the basis for their authority. He too came from Asia Minor and must have known 'the gospel', which we call that of Matthew. If he also knew Papias's words it would account for his identifying 'the gospel' and the Gospel according to the Hebrews, and saying that Matthew wrote it. He says that 'Matthew among the Hebrews in their own language (dialect) brought out a written gospel (lit. a writing of a gospel) while Peter and Paul were preaching the gospel in Rome and founding the Church.' He goes on to associate Mark with Peter, Luke with Paul, and finally actually to identify John the author of the Fourth Gospel with John the disciple of the Lord. He thus reveals clearly his desire to find the best possible authority for those four gospels which in another and very fanciful passage he insists must be according to God's plan the canonical gospels, these four, neither more nor less; for as there are four zones of the world, four winds, so there must be four gospels to be four pillars of the Church. He even thinks that they were as it were predicted by Ezekiel with his man, lion, ox and eagle in the extremely strange vision of God in Ezek. 1:10.[6]

It is impossible then to hold that the gospel was composed by an immediate follower of Jesus: it belongs to a period later than the fall of Jerusalem and probably to a Church, perhaps in Syria-Cilicia, that province of the Roman Empire which joined the Levant to Asia Minor, which claimed to be part of the true Judaism, a Church which valued the Jewish ancestry of the Christian community, believed the Law to have found its fulfilment in Jesus who was the expected Messiah, but which believed him to be far more, in that he was rightly regarded as the Son of God whose power would be demonstrated when he

---

[6] The four living creatures reappear in Rev. 4:7. Originally they belonged to Ezekiel's strange vision and were not four creatures but one. Their fanciful identification with the evangelists is but one of the odd uses to which the prophet's vision has been put.

returned in glory, power which he enjoyed now, and which he imparted to his church in the interim period before he returned.

Luke, First Church Historian

Luke wrote two volumes and at the beginning of the first explained both his reasons and his method: he wished to give his 'patron' Theophilus the real facts about which the latter had so far 'heard'; to take the reasonable interpretation of the New English Bible, Theophilus had been 'informed' about the origins of Christianity. This could mean that he had been to some extent instructed about it and Luke wanted to give him more details and more accurate information; or it can mean something different, something related to the political situation. Any reader can see, especially in Luke's second volume, the Acts of the Apostles, that the author makes out the best possible case on behalf of both Jesus and Paul. Jesus had been crucified as a criminal rebel and Paul had been arrested as a disturber of the peace: but these facts cannot be taken at their face value. They were due to the unjustifiable and fanatical hostility of the Jews; moreover, on almost every occasion the Roman governor, where he had had anything to do with the matter, had shown himself impartial, favourable to the Christians, or at the worst uninterested. Thus Luke might be making sure that Theophilus understood that neither Jesus nor Paul was a criminal, and saw the real truth of the matter.

However, Luke's two volumes are more than a political defence of the Christian Way; this phrase itself suggests that Christianity is legitimate, a proper way to practise the Judaism which was officially allowed in the Roman Empire. But Luke offers a defence of the thesis that Christianity is *the* true form of that officially accepted religion. One example of this may be given: in Luke 23: 1–25 Luke describes what happened when the Jewish authorities handed Jesus over to Pilate. The account follows in general that of Mark but in Luke 23:4 (which is Luke's alone, although there is an interesting parallel in John 18:38), Pilate expressly finds Jesus not guilty. In the following verse the accusers insist on Jesus's having caused 'disaffection among the people all through Judaea', thus giving an example of their unreasonable hostility; for they happen to mention (again only in Luke's gospel) that Jesus's activities began in Galilee and this causes Pilate to send Jesus to Herod Antipas, who was tetrarch of that district, but staying in Jerusalem at the time. When Herod sends Jesus back Pilate says that he has found nothing in Jesus 'to support your charges. No more did Herod ...' (verses 14–15). Thus the Roman governor acquits Jesus again, and this time is supported by a Jewish ruler. Pilate acquits Jesus even a third time with the sentence, 'I have not found him guilty of any capital offence. I will therefore let him off with a flogging' (verse 22). The question 'Why then was Jesus crucified?' becomes in a way more acute, but Luke has the same answer as everywhere in the New Testament tradition: the crowd demanded the death of Jesus, 'Their shouts prevailed and Pilate decided that they should have their way.' This incident, so central to the whole gospel story, needs no comment; it is worth while, however, to draw attention to the fact that its themes are those of the entire two-volume work.

In making this clear, we can anticipate a point which must be made about the structure of Acts: the last half (15.36 – the end, 28:31) is pretty well all of a piece. It is true that the passages where the first person plural is suddenly employed instead of the usual third person could be regarded as insertions; and it is true also that some stories of rather doubtful historicity can be distinguished from an otherwise straightforward account of events in one place or another to which Paul has come as a missionary. These facts do not hinder the impression of a continuous and smooth narrative, nor can the impression be missed that this part is almost wholly about Paul. If it is true that Luke wrote a defence of Christianity, it is here that we must expect to find evidence of such apologetic. In fact, nothing is easier to show; in Philippi (16:11–40) Paul and Silas are imprisoned without trial and embarrass the magistrates greatly by telling them that they have imprisoned Roman citizens and thus broken the law. Incidentally the passage illustrates nicely certain other features of Luke's writing in Acts and we may well pause over it a little. The earthquake is amazingly selective in its effect on the people of the town. It causes the apostles to be liberated and the jailor to be converted without apparently disturbing anyone else. It is small wonder that one manuscript (that known as Codex Bezae or in the *apparatus criticus* as D)[7] adds to the original text in verse 35 a brief word or two to suggest that the earthquake had impressed the magistrate. Again, how do we explain the fact that Paul, who certainly did not lack courage, left the town instead of pursuing his advantage? Luke says that the magistrates besought the apostles to leave, but was this enough to make Paul leave a town where he had scored so signal a victory and where he had made some good progress with his mission? Again, in the following chapter Luke lets us see through to the facts, does not even attempt to conceal that Paul had a less successful visit than elsewhere at Athens, no doubt because he knew there was no Church there when he wrote his history, and knew of no Letter to the Athenians. Once more, in Acts 18 the failure of the Roman proconsul Gallio to protect the Roman citizens from harassment, and innocent citizens from injury, is passed over. Luke prefers to show that what went on could not be described as a breach of the peace for 'all this left Gallio quite unconcerned' (18:17) but Gallio's failure of duty is plain to see. More remarkable still is the story in chapter 19:21–41 which describes the near riot in Ephesus in which Paul was involved. The local asiarchs (Luke has got the technical term right) dissuade Paul from entering the assembly but do not apparently attempt to restore order or to defend him. Much more serious, there is no real explanation of several other features of the story; who was Alexander and why did the Jews push him forward? What was he going to do, make a defence of or an attack on Paul? After the trouble Paul left Ephesus (20:1); again we do not know whether he was for a time in prison there. He does say in II Cor. 11:23 that he has been 'more often imprisoned' than his adversaries while at that time in his career, if we correlate it with Acts, he had been imprisoned only once—at Philippi. Yet Luke manages to give the impression that at Ephesus Paul was the victor. In his biggest task, to show that Paul is innocent after he had actually been arrested, Luke has less difficulty than with the other situations. In this connexion the enquiry made by Felix is interesting. This man is well known in Roman history as a bad governor even by the very lax standards of the Roman Empire of the time. He was procurator from 52 to 59

[7] See Chapter VIII, p. 216.

(or on another reckoning 55) but had been a military prefect in Judaea before. His brother was Pallas, a freedman and minister of the emperor Claudius and later the favourite of Nero for a time. It says more of Felix than any summary of his character could that he was recalled and put on trial for mis-government and misappropriation of funds in the time of Nero, and saved only by the intercession of Pallas. At first it may look as if the standard treatment is given by Luke to this incident; Paul makes an excellent defence, firm and spirited, and wins from Felix particular instructions that he is to receive good treatment (24:23). But there are other points made here which show another attitude of Luke; Tertullus, the hired advocate, flatters grossly a man who had already won a reputa-tion as an oppressive governor (24:2-9), and there are one or two very palpable hits: Felix does not like to be told about righteousness or self-control (verse 25) for he could make little claim to either, and indeed he hoped Paul would bribe him (verse 26). A very different situation arises when Paul appears before Festus, of whom Josephus gives a short but good report and with whom he contrasts his unsatisfactory successor Albinus. Luke does not mind recording that Festus thought Paul was mad (26:24) so long as he can also say that Festus would have set Paul at liberty if the latter had not appealed to Caesar (verse 32). If then, Luke does enter a plea on behalf of Christians by defending Paul, and if he does at times appear to stretch a point in order to make the case more favourable to Roman governors and officials, he flatters neither Paul nor his captors. Indeed, he allows Jews in Rome to say that 'all we know about this sect is that no one has a good word to say for it' (28:22). Perhaps even worse for Luke's cause is his state-ment that when these Jews had given Paul a fair and quiet hearing, 'Some were won over by his arguments; others remained sceptical' (28:24), and that this made Paul very cross with them.

Rather a lot of detail has been allowed in the discussion just conducted; there seems no doubt that Luke did made a case for Paul and thereby for Christianity partly by arguing — or letting Paul argue — that Christianity was the true fulfilment of Judaism, partly by showing with no little skill that it ought to be regarded as a religion perfectly proper for Roman citizens, and partly by demonstrating that in Paul's own day many Roman officials of high standing had protected him. We may even say that from a modern point of view he has slanted history in favour of the Christian case, but he has been frank: he has not twisted anything knowingly. For we must remember that while we are entitled to say of the earthquake in Philippi, 'That's a bit of a tall story!' Luke regarded it as history and *for him* it was a perfectly proper explanation of what happened.

It is this point which is so often missed when the character of Luke as an historian is debated; was he a 'good historian'? If this means, 'Is everything which he relates accurate history?' the answer must be 'No'. If it means, 'Did Luke conscientiously try to get everything right?' the answer must be an emphatic 'Yes'. If it means 'Did Luke succeed in getting most of it right?' the fairest answer seems to be, 'Where he had at his disposal adequate sources, he was remarkably successful; where his sources were inadequate or even, we may suspect, non-existent, he had to make deductions or guesses; then he was less successful'. The main reason for this is that in his day even a highly educated man was more credulous than befits a historian by modern standards. We can make this favourable judgment with the more confidence since it is the verdict of recent studies from an historical point of view; laws and situations sometimes changed as rapidly in the ancient world as in ours, yet Luke has some remarkably accurate details. One of these is brought out clearly by R. P. C. Hanson in his edition of Acts in the New Clarendon Bible (p.8):

(Luke) tells us that Paul encountered the high priest Ananias shortly before he met the procurator Felix (Acts 23:2, 33; 24:2, 3); that Felix was at that time married to Drusilla (24:24); that sometime afterwards ... Felix was superseded by Festus, who shortly after reaching Palestine attended to Paul's case and gave him, among other measures, a hearing before King Agrippa II, with whom the King's sister Berenice was at that time living (25:1-27). This is a very remarkable piece of synchronisation on the part of the author. ... It would have taken a very considerable amount of research for a later historian to discover that Ananias must have been contemporary with Paul at that point, that this took place in the period when Felix was married to Drusilla (who had been born in 38 and had had one husband already before Felix), and that not long afterwards Berenice (who had already had two husbands) was living for a period (a limited period) with her brother, during the procuratorship of Festus.

Many modern Roman historians would agree with the judgment which has been suggested in this chapter about Luke as an historian, that if allowance is made for the time when he lived he is a most reliable and conscientious historian, and one who knew correctly the situation governing the actual events which he is recording, and thus avoided with greater success than many of his contemporaries the fault of describing an event as if it were conditioned by the situation existing in his own time rather than by that in which the events actually took place.

Luke's knowledge of events may even lead him curiously enough sometimes to alter his source in a way which we should regard as unjustifiable. Take the example already mentioned in another connexion: where Mark reports Jesus as prophesying the setting up of 'the abomination of desolation' (13:14) Luke has instead 'when you see Jerusalem encircled by armies' (21:20). The difference here is supported by lesser differences between the two gospels in these otherwise parallel chapters; they have led a number of critics to believe that Luke used a separate source at this point, and used it to correct Mark. It seems more likely that Luke knew what had actually happened by the time he wrote, had much information about the terrible event of the destruction of Jerusalem, and recognised that Jesus had this in mind when he made his prophecies; thus Luke altered the words of Jesus, believing that Jesus must have prophesied more exactly what had in fact happened, and that when he had warned about things to come he had made the necessary distinction between the end of Jerusalem and the end of the age. A modern critic may explain the literary facts before him by saying that if either evangelist has reported the words of Jesus correctly, it is Mark; and that Luke has altered them, or preferred another source containing different words at this point, on 'theological grounds'. In other words, either Luke has altered the words to fit what has actually happened to save the reputation of Jesus as a prophet, or he has altered them to force his own interpretation of the events on his readers. To do this, he has put into the mouth of Jesus what he himself would wish to say. This is a good illustration of redaction criticism. If we are right about Luke, he respected Jesus and his sources too much for this to be the correct account of his motives. He altered Mark, indeed; but he did so because he believed firmly that what had come to pass *must* be what Jesus had prophesied. We thus give credit both to the accuracy of Luke as a historian (he reported accurately where he had no reason to change his material) and as a very devout Christian ('from the subsequent circumstances this is what Jesus must have said').

Many critics find much greater difficulties in regarding Luke as a historian. Several things trouble them, and it will suffice to give the two main reasons for their hesitation, or even for their conviction that Luke is not a historian at all but a theologian who used the form of history to convey his beliefs. One is connected with eschatology, the subject introduced already by our reference to Luke's envisaging Jerusalem encircled by armies instead of the 'abomination of desolation'. Many scholars would say that the evangelists Mark and Matthew used indeed the language of Jewish apocalyptic to convey their message, the message of the gospel, but in doing so they entirely transformed their medium, and did not intend their eschatological framework to be taken in a literal historical sense. For about two hundred years apocalyptic had taken the place of prophecy in Jewish life. It was a form of literature which claimed to reveal secrets imparted to the author by some heavenly being, sometimes secrets about the structure of the universe but always containing prophecy or revelation (which is what apocalyptic means) of what was to come. Often it was only the initiate who would get the message ('Let the reader understand' says Mark at 13:14, as it were nudging his reader's elbow). The future was depicted as a time when God would intervene to rescue his own (his 'saints' or holy ones) from the woeful time through which they were now passing. Now, according to many contemporary critics and interpreters of the New Testament the gospel was taught by Jesus in images which were either then or afterwards expressed in the terms of this medium but which were not intended to imply that their author was a teacher of the familiar apocalyptic type, but that his entirely new message *could* be conveyed in this way. To take a perhaps over-simplified example, when Jesus spoke about the kingdom he meant the eternal and timeless kingdom or sovereignty of God which he urged his hearers to take seriously: it was here and now, and should be entered here and now. His hearers recognised that he lived according to this insight but thought he meant therefore that he would return after his death to establish the Messianic kingdom in the literal manner of their original expectations. The gospel tries to correct this but uses the old language in such a way that it is similarly misunderstood. At least, it was misunderstood by Luke. His belief that God's act of redemption is identifiable with the series of acts in history which he relates in his gospel is even described as 'a catastrophic departure from the earlier faith'. Such interpreters are therefore committed to the conclusion that in making his account a historical account Luke has falsified history, for he has given a misleading description of the original gospel.

This objection to Luke springs clearly from a remarkable trust in the objectors' own interpretation of Jesus and his gospel, a trust which others may be forgiven for failing to share. Ultimately it means that the existentialist approach to the gospel is the only one which can make sense of it. We cannot tackle this subject here; but for a clear exposition of existentialism applied to Christianity see chapter five of James Richmond's book in this series, *Faith and Philosophy*. It is enough to say here that to claim such exclusive virtue for existentialism goes beyond what is reasonable.

The other difficulty which critics often have with Luke is connected with his own hero Paul. They see in Paul's own writings strong evidence of a standpoint on many matters of great importance which is totally different from, even opposed to, that of the Paul of Acts. For instance, on this very matter of eschatology, Paul certainly lived in expectation of an early end of the age and his teaching can make sense only when this is understood. In the chapter on Paul this will be considered in more detail but it is in any case clear that Paul thought always within an eschatological framework without which his whole gospel would lack the urgency which it certainly possesses. Luke extended his conception of the ages so that the final end is for him less urgent than the work of the Church before the end; this is regarded naturally enough as a great difference between the two. Closely connected is Paul's major doctrine of 'justification by faith' and the associated teaching of the redemption wrought by Christ and the atoning force of his death. Paul places even emotional emphasis on 'Christ crucified' — the death on the cross is the means designed by God for expiating the sin of man (Rom. 3:25). For Luke, on the other hand, the cross is little more than a miscarriage of justice; it is the means by which the Messiah fulfils the scripture and so qualifies to enter his glory, the throne over the universe (Luke 24:25–27). Luke attaches no doctrine at all to the actual death such as would see it as a divinely-appointed sacrifice. Along with all this goes Paul's insistence in Galatians and Romans that circumcision, the mark of a Jew and of his loyalty to the Law, is of no value to the believer; redemption is through Christ alone. Yet according to Acts 16:3 Paul actually circumcises Timothy himself. And as far as his own adherence to the Law is concerned, he shaves his head in accordance with the procedure connected with a vow (Acts 18:18). Further discussion of these points and a possible explanation of them may be best reserved for the chapter on Paul, but it must in fairness be recorded that such considerations make the notion of Luke which we have suggested quite unacceptable to many acute critics.

From our sketch of what we know about Luke and what can be deduced about him from his writings, we can conclude that he was a man of considerable ability and industry, that he thought things out for himself and combined this with a diligent search for evidence. There is another side to him which many would find even more attractive: he has preserved for use some of the most famous pieces of literature in the world, at least in Christendom. But for him we should not decorate Christmas cards with angels, cradles, mangers and shepherds, nor sing of them in carols; much more important in the long run, we should not employ 'Good Samaritan' and 'Prodigal Son' as household words. Among less important matters, we should not be so familiar with inns called the Angel nor make flippant references to 'the archangel Gabriel'. Indeed, the game of finding familiar ideas and phrases of whose biblical origin most people have not the least idea can be played for a long time by those who have read no more of the New Testament than Luke's two volumes.

Dates of Mark, Matthew and Luke-Acts

Many readers may be impatiently asking, 'But when were these various books written?' The date of Mark has already been suggested. Mark 13 suggests that some great catastrophe is imminent and the author can see clearly (and thinks his readers ought to be able to see clearly) the signs of its coming; it does not appear that it has actually happened. The events of the First Jewish Revolt (66–70) which many must have foreseen would lead to the virtual destruction of the Jewish State, would fit this situation. Some few scholars have thought that Mark 13 implies that on the political scale the feared catastrophe has already occurred and that this can be none other than the Fall of Jerusalem. The tendency therefore is to date Mark about 66–70, or perhaps even a little after 70.

Matthew used Mark and must be not only later, but considerably later if we are to take seriously the arguments which we have already urged. These were to the effect that Matthew is a comparatively late gospel, showing clear signs of ecclesiastical development and mentioning things which have survived 'to this day'. In this time the Fall of Jerusalem is an accomplished fact but more time has elapsed even since then. The gospel may be dated about 85–90, perhaps even later.

Luke-Acts poses its own problems. A hasty reader might look at the end and observe that Paul's death is not mentioned and so wish to date Acts to some date before 64 when according to a persistent though poorly documented tradition both Peter and Paul perished. The burning of Rome in 64 is associated by Roman historians quite clearly with the persecution of Christians in the city, and it is entirely feasible that both apostles were among the victims. On the other hand the gospel, unless all the arguments about the relation of Luke and Mark are quite wrong, must be much later than 64; indeed it bears within itself indications that it was written after 70 (e.g. Luke 21:20), and it is rather a curiosity of New Testament study that the gospel shows these signs of a date well after 70 although Acts, which purports to be the second volume of the same work (see its opening words) gives no hint of any date beyond about 62, when it seems that Paul arrived as a prisoner in Rome. For this and other reasons some scholars have flirted with the idea that Acts was really written before the gospel, that is before the gospel in its present form. They were aided in this speculation by the theory that Luke wrote a first draft of his gospel which was called by these scholars 'Proto-Luke', consisting largely of sayings (Q+L), and that into this framework Mark was subsequently fitted. Thus by 'the first part of my work' (Acts 1:1) Luke meant not the gospel as we have it but 'Proto-Luke'.

The difficulties in such a theory are obvious, not least for those who do not believe in Proto-Luke. One question is, 'How was it that the first sentence of Acts was not altered to make clear that the "first part" meant an earlier edition of the gospel?' This would be specially necessary if the theory were true because according to it Acts would have been for some time, though perhaps not 'the first part', itself 'the earlier' of the two writings (which the Greek may be held to imply). Nor is there any hint in the gospel that in its present form it was written subsequently to Acts. It is true that the first paragraph of Acts reads very awkwardly and there has been a great deal of discussion about the points at which different sources may have been strung together, and so to account for the inconsistent syntax: no doubt there is a problem here, but this is amply accounted for by the fact that on any theory Luke and Acts are manifestly two volumes of one book, but the two were split up when it became customary to put all four gospels together; this separation of the two halves of the work accounts for the untidiness of the opening of Acts, since someone seems to have disturbed the original by making an attempt to pick up the threads from the end of the gospel (perhaps from Acts 1:3 onwards) as if reminding a reader who put down the gospel some time ago. Again, it may well be that the end of the gospel did not contain any account of the ascension at first, but was 'rounded off' with this when the two volumes were separated. While all this may be true, it serves rather to emphasise that the writings of Luke were originally one continuous whole; and this means that originally the impression of the date at which both Luke and Acts were completed would be that given by the latest date implied by the whole work, and the contrast in this matter between the two halves would not be so striking.

The fact that Paul is brought to Rome and no account is given of his death remains remarkable, but is susceptible of explanation; Luke was certainly among other things writing a defence of Christianity, as we saw in the section devoted to Luke-Acts. He had to show that neither Jesus nor Paul was really a criminal. In the case of Jesus he must relate the crucifixion because he had a great deal to tell about the subsequent events. He could therefore only show that though put to death as a criminal Jesus was really innocent. Let us suppose Paul was already dead when Luke wrote and this was well-known to his readers. In this case all he need do was to make as sure as possible that his readers knew the case for Paul. There was no need and some considerable disadvantage in ending his account with the statement that Paul was after all eventually put to death as a criminal. Add to this that very probably Luke did not know (any more than anyone else) exactly how Paul had died, and it becomes natural for him to end his account where he did.

We have seen that Luke 21:20 suggests fairly clearly a date after 70. A quite early tradition dating from perhaps 180 and enshrined in an ancient gospel prologue found in one of the manuscripts of his gospel represents Luke as an ascetic who wrote Luke-Acts in a retired old age, in Greece. To assign an exact date to this literary activity is notoriously hard but most would place it around 85, and there seems nothing which makes this impossible although some scholars have pleaded for a much later date on the ground that the theological outlook revealed by Luke is like that of the early Apologists and would place his activity in the middle of the second century. We may leave it at about 85 and reflect that it is reasonable to date Luke more or less at the same time as Matthew, in order to appease those who try to make Matthew as early as possible.

The *tradition* about Luke is different in some important respects. First of all there are the 'we-passages' in Acts (16:10–17, 20:5–15; 21:1–17; 27:1–28:16) in which the author suddenly breaks into the first person plural. This implies that for part of this long section of Acts devoted mostly to Paul the author was an actual companion of the apostle. Secondly, there are references in Paul's letters to his companions; Luke is mentioned as one of them in Col. 4:14 and Philem. 24, and in 2 Tim. 4:11 Paul says 'I have no one with me but Luke.' Paul was a prisoner at Rome when he wrote the last quotation, so that these facts put together suggest that Luke alone was a companion of Paul long enough to be qualified to write the account of him in Acts. The external evidence of the Gospel Prologue has been mentioned above; a fragment of the canon (list of books regarded as authoritative in the Church) known as the Muratorian Fragment of the Canon which dates from the second century also mentions Luke as the author of the gospel and Acts, and Irenaeus begins the long list of Fathers who preserve this tradition. It may be true, but we must notice that Irenaeus may have deduced Lucan authorship from the internal evidence in the way just explained to be possible — by claiming that Luke was the only companion of Paul qualified to write all the material about Paul found in Acts. If he did, it is he and not a tradition which he inherited which assigned the authorship of these two volumes to Luke; and we shall see that it may well be Irenaeus who is at the root of the long but suspect tradition that John the apostle wrote the Fourth Gospel.

Chapter II

The Historical Jesus

I F Jesus is presented by the gospels as the Christ of faith and their material has been used to make a theological and not a historical picture, what was he really like? The question is natural but impossible to answer. The first reason for this is applicable to everyone. If we have read a biography of some-one whom we knew or about whom we knew something, we are struck by how much of the portrait now offered was either a surprise, or perhaps even contradicted what we would have said. Further reflection may have led us to see that there is no such thing as describing a person as he or she really is. No one can do that, least of all the person himself. The best one can hope for is an impression or series of impressions which may provoke the response, 'Yes, that is just like him!' The case of Jesus may be regarded as a very extreme example of the impressionist literary portrait which provoked such a response from his followers, not so much those who had known him in his lifetime and considered whether the impression matched their memories, as of those who believed him to be the Son of God waiting in heaven for the time of his return, the super-natural being who was the centre of their worship and their hopes.

Not only does this make Jesus as the subject of descriptive writing a unique case, but it further complicates a matter already sufficiently complicated; for the intending author must ask whether he should include those elements which support the claim that in Jesus it is not simply a man who is being described but one who is God as well. If the claim is put so baldly, we must simplify it by making clear to ourselves that we have no clear idea at all as to what we mean when we say of a man that he is also God. It is in fact only in a few passages of the New Testament that Jesus is called God in anything like an unqualified sense, and his own extreme claims for himself are made only in the Fourth Gospel which we have already argued — and shall argue further — to be in this as in other respects unhistorical. At first it seems as if we are invited to consider the whole question of the existence of God and his being, and further then to consider what it would mean to say that Jesus is man and God. Fortunately this is unnecessary; for apart from the Fourth Gospel the New Testament does not deal in philosophical terms but is content to say that Jesus is the Son of God, or to give him some other title which can be explained on historical lines. It may seem odd that such a title should carry anything less than the uncompromising meaning which it appears to carry; but in fact both the king and the corporate body of Israel in the Old Testament, and the ideal righteous man in the book of Wisdom are called Son of God. Moreover, a common name for those supernatural beings we usually call angels is 'sons of God'. This latter fact does not help us directly with regard to Jesus but it illustrates the Hebrew custom of using the term 'son of . . .' to indicate a close relation between persons which is not necessarily either physical or metaphysical, as when an apprentice prophet is called a 'son of a prophet' or a 'son of the prophets', or a member of the human race is called a 'son of man', or a peaceful person a 'son of peace'. Perhaps the commonest instance in the Bible is the phrase 'Children of Israel' which in modern English is most naturally translated 'Israelites'. Thus to say of someone that he is 'son of God' is an extreme case of a very common linguistic usage. In English as in most languages, including Greek, the expression is given a further emphasis and significance when it becomes '*the* Son of God' thus clearly implying the Messiah or someone to whom the title has by custom been, albeit cautiously, given. It does however remain true that when an evangelist described Jesus in this way he clearly meant something more than could be explained entirely by historical antecedents; by giving him other titles also he makes clear that he cannot adequately express what he wishes to convey in terms hitherto familiar, and that when he uses the title 'the Son of God' he means the one who *really* deserves this title. It remains true also that he does not intend any metaphysical theory by it.

Although it is well to bear in mind that we mistakenly read into the title which associates Jesus so closely with God all the later Greek theology of the Trinity and the incarnation, we cannot escape the fact that such use does make Jesus uniquely one sent by God for his own divine purpose. The fact provides us with one rather startling possibility as a starting-point for our discussion of what Jesus was really like. This is that Jesus was and is what the New Testament in the aggregate makes him out to be, the divine-human being who appeared on the stage of history to offer the only effective sacrifice for man's sin, to found and by his Spirit to perpetuate a Church for the extension through time of the effectiveness of this sacrifice and for the articulation and dissemination of all the metaphysical and practical teaching which results from this event, so that eventually all men, understanding and accepting its significance, are saved from the eternal destruction which their sin otherwise entails.

Belief which accepted all this would be that of some kind of orthodoxy, and many who held it would imagine that their salvation depended on believing all the details which are thus set out and many more which derive from them. But it is possible to believe *in* the unique significance of Jesus without committing oneself into belief *that* any one of the items demanded by conservative Christianity is true or founded upon historical fact. Such an outlook would demand no belief about any particular historical facts except one, the fact that Jesus lived and died.[1] This is very close to modern existentialist restatement of Christianity; for this approach the one *historical* fact necessary is just this, that Jesus lived and died. For the rest it responds, not with intellectual assent but with the whole self—existentially—to the Word preached on the basis of the cross by the Church throughout the ages. This word of the Church constitutes the significance of the event. Existentialists would indeed restate the clause about 'effective sacrifice' by 'demythologising' it, but this is accidental, arising from the fact that most articulate existentialists are also radical critics of the gospel material. They do not demythologise in order afterwards to reclothe the gospel in existentialist dress, but

---

[1] It will be argued later (pp. 70 ff.) and in Chapter IX that a further conviction is in fact logically necessary—that the character of the historical Jesus corresponds to his character as proclaimed; but this is not part of the usual existential interpretation.

insist that the gospel is itself existential and requires that kind of response. Indeed the existentialist would not deplore simple preaching of the gospel by uncritical evangelists, but would label as faithless on their part or on the part of anyone else the attempt to support faith with historical proof. Faith which looks for such support is not faith in the New Testament sense.

Although it is then unnecessary to their point of view, existentialist Christians are usually extremely sceptical about the historical events of the gospels, and their scepticism derives from two causes; one is that such details are not part of the gospel itself. Thus Paul wrote to the Corinthians, 'I resolved that while I was with you I would think of nothing but Jesus Christ – Christ nailed to the cross' (I Cor. 2:2), and at no time does he show interest in any details of Christ's life on earth. Such a consideration would not necessarily make a man sceptical about any added details, but where they create historical problems by discrepancies between the gospels, the attitude which relegates the historical question to a secondary place is or may become close to scepticism properly defined ('doubt in absence of conclusive evidence'); the second cause leads more obviously and directly to scepticism. This is the frank facing of the fact that the gospels recount events which modern scientific man simply cannot accept as historically true, because he lives in a totally different world of totally different causes and effects. It is a commonplace that he does not 'believe in' miracles, demons or angels, but the real point is that he does not ascribe events to, and explain them by recourse to miraculous powers, demons or angels.

In this chapter we are really concerned only with the second point, the belief or disbelief in so many features of the first-century world; and we are concerned with this not as a logical difficulty, but as a historical problem (although no doubt these aspects cannot be for long separated in any adequate discussion). This brings us to the second possibility in the way of interpreting the events described by the gospels and in particular those which build up a picture of Jesus and his deeds: on this view, the events of the gospels are by and large true but in the form in which they are related to us have passed through the minds of first-century man who did believe in miracles, demons and angels. Such 'supernatural' concepts are used by him soberly as causes which explain some of the most important events which he relates. Modern man would have reported, perhaps seen the events quite differently. An enormous amount of gospel criticism has resulted from this approach: it was the way, broadly speaking, of the great liberal schools of the nineteenth and early twentieth centuries; but it had appeared before and it will appear again. At its worst it produces explanations much more incredible than the events which they are designed to render credible (a medicine chest carried by Essene attendants enabled Jesus to heal the sick, and was so well concealed that his cures appeared miraculous), at its best quite plausible (the miraculous feedings originally a fellowship meal at which the well-provided were by the personality of Jesus persuaded to share with the destitute). A fatal criticism is that the story never contains in itself more than the barest outline with very few details, and the latter are always such as to heighten the miraculous character of the story. Where this is less true than in other instances, the fatal objection remains that the story is told as a miracle-story and would not have been told at all by the evangelist if he had not thought it a story of a miracle. Moreover, almost all of the miracle-stories told about Jesus must have begun, before they came into the knowledge of the evangelist, as miracle-stories. What would be the point of stories of healing or of Jesus walking on the water if they had not contained the element of miracle?

The subject of miracle has introduced itself and it will be well to discuss it a little further, especially as it will illustrate the three different points of view which have been briefly outlined about the historicity of the gospels. For the first outlook, that of orthodoxy, it is possible and perhaps customary to say that since Jesus was the Son of God, it is foolish to set limits to what he might have done. Two main answers should be made to such a broad claim; one is a logical one and must be stated here in terms much shorter than the seriousness of the matter deserves. This is that to be Son of God, in the sense of wielding power which comes directly from the Being who sustains the universe, means to hold that power and to wield it as the God of the universe, and therefore not in ways which contradict the laws of that universe. It may well be objected that to state what are and what are not laws of that universe is arbitrary: there may be circumstances in which other laws hitherto unknown operate and thereby suspend the natural laws hitherto known. Thus Jesus might have been enabled to walk on the water because some divine law hitherto unknown operated to allow him to suspend those which would normally cause him to sink. Such an argument would open up another: is the God who allows his laws to be suspended a credible God? With this question many would want to put another; would such a God be in the last resort a moral being?

As students of the New Testament, we may decline to try to answer these questions, so long as we admit their importance and the force of the objections at which they hint; for we are only describing the problems and not trying to solve them, although where solutions are possible it is our duty to indicate at least broadly in what direction they might be found. Now, if the objections which we have so briefly described can be brought against the orthodox view, we ought to add another which is indeed in the realm of logic but lies much more certainly within the sphere of New Testament studies. If we use the argument that Jesus was the Son of God and therefore he could perform any miracles he wished, we must ask how in that case we arrive at the conclusion that he was or is the Son of God. Clearly not because he performed miracles. Such an argument may be legitimate if we begin at that end, but in that case we must establish quite independently of any claim about Jesus's divine status that he did perform the miracles ascribed to him. The Fourth Gospel takes that view and makes Nicodemus say, 'No one could perform these signs of yours unless God were with him.' Again, at the end of the long section often called the Book of Signs, that is at 12:37 the author says 'In spite of the many signs which Jesus had performed in their presence they would not believe in him ...' and puts their unbelief down to God himself having hardened their hearts (since, presumably, no ordinary explanation would suffice). This argument cannot convince us since we only read of the miracles and did not witness them, and are entitled to question them without being accused of stubbornness, for they contradict all the facts of nature as we have observed them.

To use the argument therefore that the Son of God could do anything, we must show that Jesus is rightly regarded as Son of God without recourse to the evidence of the miracles. We begin to see the force of the modern critic who perceives clearly that faith is prior to belief in miracles, or in any of the other facts which the evangelists claim to be historical. Indeed, there is a radical difference between what often passes for faith, and which is in reality a gulping effort to include in what is normally believed a number of things which being a Christian seems to require, and the faith which the evangelists report was often demanded by Jesus of those whom he was about to heal. This was obviously not a great effort to believe a normally incredible fact (as the White Queen advised, 'Draw a long breath and shut your eyes') but to trust in him as the person in whom such powers resided as would heal them; such faith is not separable from believing a fact about Jesus, which was that he was the promised Messiah and therefore could demand such thoroughgoing trust, but is another facet of the necessary attitude, a facet best described as trust or faith or belief *in* a person as distinct (but not ultimately separable) from belief *about* him.

How can such a faith arise in a person? The modern critic claims, surely correctly, that this cannot arise from intellectual assent to a number of historical facts ('belief about'), and does in fact arise from hearing the gospel preached and giving one's trust to God in Christ as a result. It is here that the real crux arises: why is such assent given? To give the right answer to this somewhat mysterious question, we must turn our attention to the facts as they occur in actual life. We then find that the gospel is preached often in the simplest and most old-fashioned forms, though sometimes in other and novel forms perhaps more suited to the self-understanding of modern man, and that, however presented, it sometimes receives assent and above all (the acid test) obedience. Some power is then at work. What is this? In New Testament terms it is the 'power of the resurrection' or the 'power of him who raised Christ from the dead'. It should be carefully noted that this description does not raise the question as to what the resurrection is but uses the term resurrection as a convenient summary of that phenomenon which energised the disciples when in human terms they were at the end of their hopes and resources, and began the task of spreading the Church, the 'body of Christ'. Many who would not regard themselves as believers in miracles are willing to call this phenomenon the one unavoidable miracle, an event for which they can find no ready explanation in the terms of human history. It does not require belief in a particular historical event or series of events, but it involves most assuredly belief in God's activity in history, an activity most emphatically not confined to a particular time, but belonging to 'now'.

Those whom we are calling modern critics, and thinking of those influenced significantly in greater or less degree by Bultmann, would then go on to say that the resurrection stories in the New Testament (not only those of the gospels but also those summarised in Paul's abbreviated account in I Cor. 15:3–8) cannot be credited as historical facts, let alone used as a foundation to support the great edifice of the Christian faith. They would say further that the stories told about Jesus which excite the wonder of the more credulous reader do not cause but derive from this belief in him as the unseen power which is otherwise called the power of God shown in the resurrection. In other words, this belief in the resurrection (to use the convenient shorthand term) has determined the miracle-stories in the gospels. Both these and the stories of the resurrection appearances are unhistorical and serve to illustrate and to reinforce in their original audiences faith in Jesus as the conqueror of sin and death which would otherwise have held captive the disciples of all ages, disciples who have in fact been enabled to claim the power of God to live what the New Testament would call 'eternal life' or simply 'life'. The term is often used in a way which the context shows means God's life, not the life of corruptible nature; the modern existentialist calls it 'an authentic existence'.

It should not go unremarked that such critics are much nearer the orthodox than they are to the liberals so far as belief in Jesus as the locus of the power of God is concerned. By contrast liberals try to find out 'what actually happened', that is, after allowance has been made for the refraction of the events through the prism of unsophisticated first-century minds. On the sum of what they think is left they build a picture of the 'historical' Jesus — Jesus as he really was. There are as many such pictures as scholars who compose them, but by far the most remarkable of them in modern times has been that of Schweitzer. He claimed that Jesus was thoroughly apocalyptic in his thought and believed that God had sent him to proclaim the imminent kingdom to Israel, that he discovered by degrees that his proclamation of the fact was not enough, that God required more of him and that this more was the offering of his own life. Jesus therefore, after the disappointment of his hope that the kingdom would come before his disciples had completed the mission journey on which he sent them (Matt. 10:23) went up to Jerusalem to provoke 'the priests' to put him to death. He really believed that God would intervene at the last moment to save him and to inaugurate the kingdom, and died a dis-illusioned man with a cry of despair on his lips. If orthodoxy based on belief in a number of historical facts is vulnerable to criticism and a man's whole faith might burn up before the flame-thrower of natural scepticism, no less is true of all liberal reconstructions of the 'historical Jesus', certainly including that of Schweitzer. For a long time this great structure was held by critics to have put a decisive end to all liberal inter-pretations of the gospels, for these were associated for many years with accounts which left on one side as manifestly un-authentic all apocalyptic utterances of Jesus and reduced the credible mass of his sayings to those which a reasonable modern educated man could accept; but Schweitzer was the last of the liberals rather than the first of a new school, for his fundamental attitude is the same as theirs, namely that it is possible to find out from the given and in themselves incredible facts what actually happened, and to do this by means of modern critical method. Schweitzer in fact has put on record his conviction that German critical scholarship was equipped for this task. He seems to have been unaware that this was to credit the modern critic with divinely given ability to judge which of the facts presented in the gospel story were true, i.e. which were the divinely given facts. All liberal critics are liable to this criti-cism unless they are avowed unbelievers and therefore do not think any of the facts were divinely given, or, to speak more accurately, that there was or is any divinely given fact.

In his attitude to belief therefore, the modern existentialist demythologiser is close to the orthodox, but since the orthodox in practice include many who do not believe all the facts narrated in the gospels, the liberals are closer to the orthodox in their attitude to history and to the narrative of the gospels.

If this is the situation, it must seem that we can never reconstruct the character of the real Jesus in any degree whatever. For example, it is as easy to show that Schweitzer's reconstruction is vulnerable to criticism as it was for Schweitzer to criticise all previous attempts.

This negative conclusion seems to satisfy a large number of contemporary scholars, but others feel uneasy both with this negative result and with some of the arguments which led to it; for it is hard to avoid a sense of the fundamental improbability that the Jesus of history was entirely different in character from the Jesus who was preached by the Church. In technical language this is a matter of the difference between the Jesus of history and the Jesus of the *kerygma*. The latter term means 'that which is proclaimed' and has been specially widely used in New Testament studies since C. H. Dodd drew attention in his book *The Apostolic Preaching and its Developments* to the recurrence of a formula which was incorporated into many statements of the gospel in the New Testament and which he thought probably represented the actual core of what was proclaimed as the gospel, even that this core was sometimes proclaimed by itself. It would run something like this: 'As prophesied, Jesus, a man marked out by God through the signs which God enabled him to do, was delivered up and crucified; God raised him from the dead, whereof we are witnesses. God has appointed him to be judge. Repent, believe the gospel, be baptised!' Those who shrink from accepting a complete severance between the Jesus who was active in Galilee and Judaea and the Jesus of the *kerygma* point out that there is a reference here to the impression which Jesus made on his contemporaries, and that this was at least in part through the miracles which he did. Let us leave out of account the miracles for the moment; it would be common ground between believer and unbeliever, because of the inescapable facts of history, that Jesus possessed in large measure a quality of leadership which it is the present fashion (borrowing curiously in an age of unbelief a very technical New Testament term) to call charismatic. He had a compelling power. More than that, he possessed it in such degree that people often felt that their encounter with him was decisive for their lives. They must decide for or against him or at least to 'believe in him' or to reject him. The decisiveness of encounter with Jesus meant for believers an encounter with God; it was so unmistakably their whole being which was called upon to decide that it was felt to be a decision before God, and for eternity. Such was the experience of the woman in Luke 7:36–50, who was so affected by knowing that Jesus was in Capernaum and by her compulsive going to meet him, uninvited though she was, that she could not control the flood of her tears or her gesture of utter repentance (verses 38 and 44). Such too in a different way was the experience of the Rich Young Man who hoped apparently to be dismissed with the assurance that there was no more he need do (Mark 10:17–22 and pars.). It hardly needs to be added that such was the experience of some of the disciples whose apparently abrupt decision is so well-known (Mark 1:16–20 pars.). If it is agreed that the general impression of the evidence, admitting that some details may be unhistorical, is that Jesus was a man of the kind to provoke in his contemporaries just such momentous decisions, it must be conceded that if we use the religious language of his time he is rightly said to have been a 'man marked out by God', and we may be tempted to include among the 'signs' these instances of immediate influence on lives through personal encounter. Again, we may be excused if we put forward boldly the instances to which we have referred as examples of authentic recollection of the historical Jesus of Nazareth.

We return to the question of miracles in connexion with this search for the historical Jesus. It must be firmly stated at once that it was not the universal custom in the Judaean world to attribute miracles of healing or of other kinds to great figures. Such miracles as are accredited to famous rabbis are very sparing in number and modest in character; of John the Baptist it was specifically part of the tradition to say that he 'wrought no sign' (John 10:41 – the Greek is rather more terse and emphatic than the New English Bible translation). Moreover in the case of Jesus his ability to heal, at least, is an indispensable part of any reconstruction of his personality; nor is the fact in itself incredible. For there have been many in all ages who have possessed this gift, even if we rule out merely temporary cures attributable to the passing influence of suggestion. The reluctance of Jesus to have his healing powers bruited abroad combined with his defence of them as divinely bestowed, when obliged to defend them, must also count as ringing true. This does not make the truth of the matter certain but it gives us the possibility to make a reasonable reconstruction of his situation. This is that he discovered that he possessed these powers—both of influencing lives decisively and of healing the physically and mentally sick, and that he concluded, as a good Jew, that they were the gift of God for him to use for his nation. It would be far from unreasonable for him to deduce from this that he was the Messiah or the Son of Man or the promised Servant, at the same time insisting on his own interpretation of these titles, made to fit a situation in which he saw what must be the fate of a leader determined to employ unusual powers never for his own advancement but for his nation's deepest needs, as he saw them.

Two important principles have been employed here, one of which is typical of the methods of the post-Bultmann scholars who are embarked on a new quest for the historical Jesus. Schweitzer's famous book was called in its English version *The Quest of the Historical Jesus* and the new questers agree that all the reconstructions contained in that book, including that of Schweitzer himself, are far too ambitious and so doomed to failure. The material of which we dispose is, after criticism, far too sparse to afford enough for reconstructing the ministry of Jesus, let alone anything like a life. These new questers are not so sceptical as Bultmann about the possibility of producing at any rate a thumbnail sketch such as we have attempted; in order to do this they employ the principle of continuity. There must be, they plausibly argue, some continuity between the historical Jesus and the *kerygma*.[2]

The other principle which we have invoked would be less popular with such investigators. They have inherited from the old questers—the liberals of all ages—something of the latter's

[2] J. M. Robinson has written a standard book in English entitled *The New Quest of the Historical Jesus* (S.C.M. Press, 1967); for a more popular and readable book and an example of a new quester's outlook see G. Bornkamm, *Jesus of Nazareth* (Hodder and Stoughton, 1960).

confidence in the results of gospel criticism. Theological colouring must be that of the evangelists, reflecting the Churches for which they wrote, and cannot be attributed to Jesus himself. In the above fragmentary and very partial reconstruction it has been hinted that the historical Jesus may well have entertained theories about his own relation to God which were expressed in the terms which the evangelists have used and which they have represented as coming from Jesus himself. The principle employed was therefore that the general drift of the synoptics is reliable in this regard; as soon as this is stated it is essential to make clear that the word 'general' is important. It is necessary to be as vague as, for example, to say that Jesus defined his own position in relation to the concept Son of Man: for the synoptic witness on such a point is not uniform. In Mark he only occasionally identifies himself with the Son of Man and in Q apparently always speaks of the Son of Man as other than himself; while in Matthew it is clear that he is consciously Son of Man from the outset of his ministry.

We venture to put forward these general considerations tentatively, noting that while contemporary critics insist that we cannot rightly do more than this, in their own reconstructions they are sometimes in practice much bolder and rely on the results of their own critical investigations, although certainly making them sound much more tentative than those of the old liberal reconstructors. To the extent that investigation by the various methods of gospel criticism available is an indispensable preliminary to even these tentative and partial reconstructions, they connect obviously with the old liberals and have in fact provoked the question, 'What is new about the new quest?' One very proper answer to this question is that the greater modesty with which results are put forward and the insistent admission that all possibility of total reconstruction has gone for ever are the main features which distinguish the new from the old.

While therefore some features of the Marcan outline, followed by the other synoptics with some additions and a number of minor modifications, remain impossible to accept as historical (the Transfiguration and the Walking on the Water, for example) the main drift may be accepted. This can apply not only to the little we can say about the character and personality of Jesus but also to the events. If Mark is according to the tradition specifically not indebted to Peter for the order of his gospel but only for material, for the order he must be reproducing a tradition preserved in the Church. It goes without saying that this account must be full of gaps and that our trust in it cannot extend to believing that a particular series of incidents followed one another in the manner suggested by Mark, or that any particular saying arose out of the exact situation given in Mark's gospel. It is the sequence, ministry in the north, journey to Jerusalem, challenge to the authorities there and final catastrophe that may be trusted; no more, particularly not the apparent limitation of the ministry to one year.

We have already seen that some elements in the synoptics, some found only in Luke and Matthew such as the birth narratives and the detailed resurrection appearances, may be regarded either as legendary or as arising from events which, if properly so called, are inner and private rather than the public events (i.e. in principle verifiable by anyone) which they are represented as being.

It seems therefore that criticism must lead to the conclusion that the Jesus of history is not essentially different from the Christ of faith. We are bound to accept Schweitzer's claim that 'He comes to us as One unknown' but perhaps Schweitzer had not noticed how near he was to orthodoxy in saying 'He comes to us', for this phrase bears witness to what orthodoxy would call the divine initiative; following Jesus was for Schweitzer, in spite of his extremely negative and even depressing conclusions, a matter of obedience to one who had summoned him with authority. The response to the *kerygma* was without question for Schweitzer, as for many others free from the suspicion of orthodoxy, a response in equal measure to the Jesus of history and to the Christ of faith. Many modern critics plead for a restatement in intelligible terms of the claims of the New Testament; their case is a strong one and their motives admirable. It is perhaps not always appreciated that, critics though they may be, they are far from despising the terms in which Jesus is described in the gospels. These terms are not now immediately intelligible but when we have understood them a little we can appreciate the fact that the evangelists are themselves responding, but in language and thought-forms now out of date, in the same way as the contemporary convert to the gospel. The experience may take many forms, but it will always include intellectual assent to the claims of Jesus, even if in some popular forms of expression he is denoted simply by this his name leaving its content undefined. He has become for many a synonym for the highest both in demand and assistance, and for a great number the way in which his paramount status is expressed is a matter of secondary importance, perhaps even of indifference. For them historical details do not matter and this brings them very close to the attitude of many contemporary critics. Nevertheless it is unnecessary to despair of knowing from historical sources something of what he was as a historical person; we have suggested that the gospels are strongly influenced by theological considerations in such a way as to employ some non-historical material but that there is a quantity of evidence which enables us to see the connexion between the Jesus of history and the Christ of faith.

Part II

Chapter III

Paul and his Letters

The Conversion

JESUS was probably crucified in A.D. 29 or 30. Very soon after his crucifixion some of his followers proclaimed that he had been raised by God from the dead and on the basis of this conviction regarded him as the Messiah. Probably many of them, though not all, had believed even before his death that he was the Messiah, interpreting this in a way different from that in which Jesus himself had done. Whatever the extent of their disappointment and temporary disillusion at the crucifixion, they were now convinced of the truth of this claim and were occupied in showing how it could be reconciled with what the scriptures were popularly supposed to have said about him; a dead Messiah was certainly for the vast majority, probably for all, a contradiction in terms. It was a 'stumbling-block' in the way of any Jew accepting such a claim. The resurrection changed the situation completely; Jesus rejected by God could not be the Messiah, but Jesus raised from the dead was evidently one chosen for singular favour by God and must be the Messiah after all, indeed this and a great deal more.

We can see already the beginnings of Christian 'theology', that is the great system of evidence and argument needed to substantiate what Christians believe about Jesus. How be convinced of the truth of the apparently fantastic claim that a man who had died on a cross had been raised from the dead by God after three days in a tomb, how show that this very fact or these very facts of his death and resurrection meant that he was the Person to accept and follow as the key to God and the universe? In Jewish terms, how render at all acceptable the claim that he was the Messiah? To do this last was obviously the most difficult before an audience whose most influential members were the very people who had encompassed his death and thus thought they were rid of a dangerous and divisive impostor.

One of the sturdiest and even most fanatical of these early Jewish opponents was Paul. It was natural enough; he was as far as we know never 'ordained' as a rabbi but he can be regarded as a scholar in the line well known and well respected in Judaism which begins with Hillel (c. 20 B.C.). By 'line' is meant a line of spiritual descent in which a spiritual son, i.e. pupil, was often an actual son. Those descended from Hillel, a great teacher of the form of Judaism which began with Pharisaism and is not yet ended, were both descendants in the natural sense and his pupils. He had a son Simeon and the latter's son was Gamaliel I, at whose feet Paul sat, according to Acts 22:3. We ought not therefore to be surprised if we find Paul arguing in a rabbinic way in some passages of his letters. For the moment we are concerned with his early opposition; he gives us few details about it but what he does say is quite consistent with the story in Acts according to which he witnessed the death of the Hellenist Christian Jew Stephen, one of the leaders of a group who existed side by side with the apostles in Jerusalem in the years immediately following the crucifixion of Jesus, and who is regarded as the first Christian martyr.

Paul does not mention Stephen but makes quite clear that he persecuted 'the church of God' (I Cor. 15:9), by which he may mean the community at Jerusalem which he came to regard as the true heir to the 'congregation of God', or the true Israel. If he did think in this way he soon came to regard all local congregations as part of the organic Church universal, or as he would describe it, the Body of Christ. If we follow the story in Acts we find that it was on a journey for the purpose of more persecution, a journey to Damascus, that Paul suffered the catastrophic change in his life known as his conversion. He nowhere describes it in his letters, but refers to its inner character in the most decisive way. Thus in Gal. 1:13–17 he writes:

You have heard what my manner of life was when I was still a practising Jew: how savagely I persecuted the church of God, and tried to destroy it; and how in the practice of our national religion I was outstripping many of my Jewish contemporaries in my boundless devotion to the traditions of my ancestors. But then in his good pleasure God, who had set me apart from birth and called me through his grace, chose to reveal his Son to me and through me, in order that I might proclaim him among the Gentiles.

(It is perhaps as well to notice that the last word might be better translated 'Nations'.) He goes on 'When that happened, without consulting any human being, without going up to Jerusalem to see those who were apostles before me, I went off at once to Arabia, and afterwards returned to Damascus.' Paul evidently regarded this experience as that which made him an apostle no less than the original followers of Jesus. The Lord had called them in his earthly days, and the same Lord had called him in a manner not at all essentially different; in I Cor. 9:1 he says, 'Am I not an apostle? Did I not see Jesus our Lord?' This seeing of Jesus is evidently for Paul the last of the appearances of the risen Jesus: 'In the end he appeared even to me. It was like an abnormal birth; I had persecuted the Church of God and am therefore inferior to all other apostles — indeed not fit to be called an apostle' (I Cor. 15:8-9, New English Bible).

In his own writings Paul does not give any further description of the event; the story in Acts (or rather stories, for it is told three times with variations in inessential details, Acts 9:1-18; 22:3-21; 26:9-20) is far less an account of Paul's inner conversion than a dramatic account of a divine intervention to save his own people from persecution by arresting a would-be persecutor and making him submit to the divine will. The Acts story is at no point inconsistent with Paul's own much more reticent narrative but describes both event and result from the point of view of the history of the Church (Acts 9:1-31; note the force of verse 31).

This event, destined to have immeasurable results for the history of the western world, seems to have occurred about A.D. 32-35. Much has been written and preached about the importance of Paul's going into Arabia; it is very doubtful whether Paul spent his time there in retreat and meditation. The country to the south of Damascus is part of Nabataean Arabia and Damascus was itself at the time of Paul's visit in the possession of the king of that extensive territory. Thus Paul may have visited it to preach the gospel there, even if he devoted some time to prayer and meditation. This would explain the hostility to Paul of the king's officer representing his fellow-Jews in Damascus, a hostility which made it necessary for Paul to escape by night from the city when he returned there from 'Arabia' (2 Cor. 11:32 f.).

Paul and Jerusalem

In the rest of the first chapter of Galatians, extensively quoted already, Paul says that after three years he went up to Jerusalem to see (almost 'to interview') Peter (here given his Aramaic name Cephas); the only other apostle he saw then was James the brother of Jesus. His visit was a very short one and he returned to the province Syria-Cilicia (Gal. 1:21), administered as one joint province 38 B.C.—A.D. 72. The time which he spent here was either eleven or fourteen years (it depends whether the number of years mentioned in Gal. 2:1 is to be reckoned from the conversion or from the last matter mentioned, i.e. the visit to Jerusalem of Gal. 1:18). It was a natural region for him to visit: he had been born in Tarsus of Cilicia and there was a strong body of Christians at Antioch, at this time and for some years past the capital of Syria. Luke's statement that Paul went to Tarsus first (Acts 9:30) and was brought by Barnabas to Antioch to help in the work there (Acts 11:25 f.) exactly fits this situation.

The point now reached is a crux for interpreters of New Testament history. According to Paul in Gal. 2:1 after this long period he went up again to Jerusalem, this time with Barnabas and Titus, and the visit was clearly an occasion for some discussion, perhaps of division for a time, but ending in a cordial agreement to divide the world among them for missionary work—'we should go to the Gentiles while they went to the Jews' (Gal. 2:9). The difficulty, which need not be fully discussed here and will be only indicated, arises when the attempt is made to fit this account with Acts. At first it seems as if this must be the same visit as is described in Acts 15 where, according to Luke, the momentous decision was taken to admit Gentiles to the Church without demanding circumcision or adherence to the Law except in a few matters. This chapter has its own internal difficulties, such as the unexplained presence of Peter who when last heard of was a fugitive for his life (Acts 12:17); but this is not the main issue. In Acts 15 the decision was taken at a council occasioned by the winning of so many Gentiles by Paul and Barnabas during their work in parts of Asia Minor beyond and exclusive of Cilicia, work described vividly in some of the most interesting chapters in Acts, 13–14. The visit of Paul and Barnabas for this purpose, which seems so like that of Gal. 2:1 ff., was only the *second* paid by Paul to Jerusalem since his conversion, if we follow Paul, and he mentions only these two; but that of Acts 15 is the *third*, for the second is a visit mentioned in Acts 11:30.

No attempt will be made here to unravel this difficulty but it is well to point out that if Paul and his companions had all this time been working in Syria-Cilicia, this fits the way in which the letter sent out after the council of Acts 15 is addressed to Christians in Antioch, Syria and Cilicia (see verse 23); but it does not fit Luke's making the occasion of the council the journeys of chapters 13 and 14 in Cyprus, Pamphylia, Pisidia and Lycaonia. In New Testament studies an important result arises from dissatisfaction with this and kindred difficulties met in comparing these two passages, one in Paul and the other in Acts; this is the attempt, often repeated, to make a radical reconstruction of Paul's life based only on his own letters, and to leave Acts as hopelessly inaccurate. Such a solution cannot appeal to those who see in Acts remarkable evidence of careful history, and who are prepared to believe that where Luke seems to be untrustworthy it is in details, perhaps including dates; and that his trouble is not inaccuracy due to stupidity or carelessness but inaccuracy due to insufficient information. Too sweeping a reconstruction ought therefore to be avoided, but one must sympathise with those who think Paul may in the eleven or fourteen years have included the famous visit to southern Asia Minor related in Acts 13–14. Thus the council of Acts 15 legislated for a problem which arose in Antioch but was probably held *before* Paul and Barnabas evangelised those parts of southern Asia Minor. This does not dispose of all the difficulties, but it is a possible theory and not so drastic as, for example, the solution which suggests that Paul during the years between his visits to Jerusalem mentioned in Galatians worked not only in southern Asia Minor but elsewhere in that part of the world, including a stay in Ephesus.

The question as to when the letter to the Galatians was written is connected with the council in Acts 15. Those—and they are many—who think that the story in Acts can be correlated with Paul by saying that Gal. 2:1 is the same visit as Acts 15 must explain why Paul does not use the decision of the council as a decisive argument in his letter, which is concerned with precisely this question of the necessity or otherwise of circumcision. If on the other hand Paul wrote the letter before the council, this explains why he does not mention it, and his two visits will correlate with Acts 9:26–30 and 11:30. This is perhaps the majority view. The difficulty now is that the visit of Acts 11:30 does not look at all like that of Gal. 2:1 in some important respects. Acts 11:30 is a visit in which Paul and Barnabas (Titus is never mentioned in Acts) go to Jerusalem to take some alms and no other matter is mentioned; Gal. 2:1 f. suggests something of a prolonged and hard debate, not perhaps specifically on circumcision, but about Paul's gospel, whether it was authentic or not.

Another thorny question relates to the addressees of Galatians. It seems natural to regard the people whom Paul and Barnabas evangelised in southern Asia Minor as the recipients, for some of them can be regarded as southern Galatians. If however Paul was being constitutionally correct he must regard Galatia as the Roman province of that name in the north. Luke nowhere relates a visit to this district, which indeed lies well away from any route which Paul is reported to have taken in Acts, but Acts 16:6 and 18:23 are sometimes held to refer to such a visit, the towns which Paul would have visited then being Ancyra, Pessinus and Tavium.

The minority view adopted here is that Galatians may have been written quite late in Paul's career, and if it is addressed to the citizens of these northern towns it must have been. The point at which it was written can be regarded as fairly certain when we study it in relation to other writings of Paul; for our present purpose we shall disregard the possibility of close connexion with the council in Acts 15, of whose edict in any case Paul seems to have taken little notice, for he uses it neither to confute the judaising Galatians nor members of the

Corinthian Church who were over-scrupulous about diet, and he wrote to the latter for certain after it is supposed to have taken place.

Galatians is in fact a sort of first draft of the even more famous Romans and in vocabulary and ideas connects also with the Corinthian letters. These belong to the period when Paul was based on Ephesus and from there visited Macedonia and Corinth. Some of the letters were written at Ephesus, one (Romans) at Corinth, one perhaps in Macedonia. Galatians may well have been written in Ephesus or Macedonia, or even in Corinth just before he wrote Romans. This judgment is based on the belief that a man does not use the same ideas in quite the same way as Paul uses those common to Galatians and Romans unless he has been working on the subject recently when he writes the second version of his thoughts. Those who argue that when a teacher turns to a particular subject he may return to a treatise which he composed a longish time ago, so that its likeness to another is no indication of its date, seem to the present writer to reveal that they have never written or attempted a serious treatise. Nor is it a matter of a particular subject; it is in a sense the whole subject of Paul's fundamental belief and the highly individual way in which he has presented it. It seems impossible to believe that Paul would have used the argument arising from the relation of Christ to Abraham in a way which makes Romans clearer if we read Galatians first, if he had not written them in the order implied, and close to one another.

It was necessary to clear this matter out of the way before proceeding to a further account of Paul's life; it will have become clear that we do not dispose of the necessary material to present a full biography or anything like it. We must be content with an outline which shows to some extent how the letters which he wrote fit into his experience.

Paul and the Christian Mission

It can be said with certainty that Paul moved on from Syria-Cilicia, where most of the time was spent in Antioch, to Asia Minor. Antioch was in fact the centre from which the Christian mission first operated. This is clear from Acts in spite of Luke's theological conviction that everything must be regarded as issuing from Jerusalem as the centre. Antioch was itself apparently evangelised by the refugees from the persecution of Stephen and the other 'Hellenists' (Acts 11:19 f. and 13:1) and subsequently became the centre from which such famous missionaries as Paul and Barnabas set out (Acts 13:3). These two evangelised the southern part of Asia Minor; whether they then visited Jerusalem to settle a dispute about the gospel or went on to other parts of Asia Minor depends on the solution of the problem already outlined, and for this solution we do not possess enough facts. At some point Paul and Barnabas parted company, according to Acts just after the council in Jerusalem which had settled the circumcision controversy in their favour. Their dispute was about taking Mark with them on further journeys for Paul would not take him owing to his defection during the earlier journey (Acts 15:36–39). Paul set out once more from Antioch, this time with Silas and a little later with a young man named Timothy whom he came to trust above all others for his faithfulness in the work of the gospel, son of a Greek father and a Jewish mother and a native of Lystra, one of the two cities of Lycaonia visited by Paul and Barnabas in the earlier journey. Paul illustrated his conviction that the Law was still valid for a Jew by circumcising Timothy; he illustrated thereby also that anyone born of a Jewish mother was in the eyes of Jews a member of that race (Acts 16:1–3).

The present journey led the little company into Europe, for they crossed from Troas in Mysia via the island of Samothrace to Neapolis in Macedonia. Their first real stay was in Philippi, a city for which Neapolis was the harbour town. Philippi had been made a colony (that is, properly speaking, a city for discharged veteran soldiers) for previous supporters of Mark Antony by Augustus, and though Luke regards it as an important city the reason for the stay of Paul, Silas and Timothy was probably that it was 'the first inland town of Europe at which they arrived where there was a Jewish settlement, although that at Philippi was not apparently very large; for it was Paul's custom, though he had made an agreement to be the evangelist for the Gentiles, to start always with Jews. This means that the Gentiles (or 'nations', i.e. 'other nations') is a geographical term in this connexion. Paul was a missionary to the areas where the population and culture were non-Jewish, but he was at liberty to begin with the Jewish colony in any place in that sphere. In many places this approach led at once to trouble and the Jews represented to the local magistrates that Paul was causing a breach of the peace by disturbing their religion, or they simply made a disturbance aimed at his life. In Philippi there was trouble but it was occasioned by non-Jews; as a consequence Paul and Silas were imprisoned (Acts 16:12–40). In a way which seems odd to us but which is typical of Acts, Timothy fades out of Luke's story, but as we shall see, he was certainly still one of the party. Paul and Silas were released after one night in the cells, successfully pleading their Roman citizenship, and proceeded on their journey. The story in Acts does not easily allow us to envisage how Paul and his companions managed to build an enduring Church in Philippi but we shall see that they must have done so either at this time or later at a time which is not chronicled, for Paul seems to have written to them when in prison, possibly at Ephesus, if not certainly in Rome near the end of his life. Thessalonica was their next place of significant stay, and here events followed just that pattern described above as usual in Paul's adventurous travels. Some success with Jews led to violent expulsion. A move to the neighbouring town of Beroea by Paul and Silas (whatever happened to Timothy?) saw a repetition of the pattern and Paul being forced to leave secretly. At this point Luke answers our question about Timothy by blandly telling us that when Paul left by sea Silas and Timothy remained at Beroea. (Why? In their preaching did they manage not to annoy the Jews as Paul did? Or for this part of the journey were they silent and did they act as the manual workers who made the journey possible?) In what follows we draw on evidence from Paul for it seems clear that Luke has abbreviated the story.

Paul went on to Athens where he was joined by Silas and Timothy; it may well be that they came with some questions for Paul to clarify what he had taught in Macedonia. At any rate he sent them back to Thessalonica, and himself in the meantime went on to Corinth, where they presently rejoined him. In Athens Paul was evidently unsuccessful, whatever we make of the historicity of his famous speech on the Areopagus. The *mise-en-scène* of this occasion (Acts 17:16–34) is one of the most plausible in the whole history. Any visitor to Athens today can see exactly where Paul may have talked to the Athenians over lunch sandwiches, within full sight of the Acropolis towering over them, the Acropolis which bears out so well his observation of the Athenians' interest in religion but which he tantalisingly never mentions. Perhaps he did not climb up to the Acropolis because that would seem like a pagan pilgrimage? His strolling in the Agora or market-place was natural enough: like Socrates he wanted to talk to people and make them see the truth.

There were Jews in Athens and Paul debated with them as well as with the public; there were Jews also in Corinth, in some ways a more important city. If Athens was a Greek Jerusalem, Corinth was an ancient Tel Aviv, a port and commercial centre. There every kind of person and every kind of religious thought was to be found. One kind was the mystery religion of the Greek world whose essential idea was that initiates into a particular mystery, a ceremony by which they were held to share the experience of the god or hero of the cult, profited henceforward from the god's protection by a mystical union with him. The superficial resemblance to Christianity is obvious, for it too had its initiation ceremony in baptism and its cultic meeting in the eucharist. Later we shall see the possible extent of the relevance of all this for Paul and his dealings with the Corinthians; for the moment we must pause at this point, at which Paul has, after his unsuccessful stay in Athens, been rejoined by Silas and Timothy after arriving in Corinth. This pause allows us to introduce the letter which we can take to be the earliest in the Pauline correspondence; it is known as the First Epistle to the Thessalonians, or 1 Thessalonians.

1 Thessalonians

This letter and its companion 2 Thessalonians fill in for us something of the gap in our knowledge about what Paul had been preaching all this time. It is best to rely on his own evidence where we have it, thus making full allowance for Luke being compelled, to a certain extent at least, to make up some of Paul's speeches or sermons for him because he did not know exactly what Paul had said. We can then use some material in Acts to supplement Paul's own evidence, and to give a general picture of the way in which Paul probably conducted his missionary campaign.

People who have not studied the matter, if asked what they imagined Paul preached and taught, would probably reply, 'The teachings of Jesus.' We have seen already that this is a mistake of great magnitude and importance. Paul taught rather something *about* Jesus, that Jesus was the person sent by God to be Messiah and Lord, and what this implied for mankind, especially for Paul and his contemporaries. If we look therefore at Acts 13:13 f. we can see a picture of what Paul would have done and said *in a Jewish synagogue*; he begins with the patriarchs! If momentarily nonplussed and disappointed we soon see the point. Rapidly he sketches the history and shows that Jesus is the promised one from God and claims that the judgment of God is near and that forgiveness of sins is through Jesus. This was always the main part of Paul's *kerygma*; but when he had a mixed audience which included pagans, many of whom liked to listen to those who expounded Judaism although only a few actually embraced it, he must add something else. He had to make sure that they accepted the one God in whom Jews believed. Monotheism attracted many intelligent people in the ancient world, but it was often a philosophical monotheism and not belief in the God who had directed the history of a chosen race. Paul had therefore to get this accepted, and it was a vital condition; for if Jesus was the person by whom God was about to end the age with a great act of judgment, then that God was not the God of the philosophers but the God of Abraham, Isaac and Jacob, this Jesus being the culmination of the long history of the chosen people whose relevance to the whole world was now plain and inescapable.

In 1 Thessalonians the authors show that they emphasised these two main points when they proclaimed the gospel to the men of Thessalonica. The authors? Yes, for this was a letter with joint authorship, and quotations will show at once the truth of the statements just made about what these early Christian missionaries proclaimed and taught. It begins, 'From Paul, Silvanus [Silas] and Timothy to the congregation of Thessalonians who belong to God the Father and the Lord Jesus Christ.' A little later the recipients are praised for their acceptance and perseverance in the gospel:

... you have become a model for all believers in Macedonia and in Achaia. From Thessalonica the word of the Lord rang out; and not in Macedonia and Achaia alone, but everywhere your faith in God has reached men's ears. No words of ours are needed, for they themselves spread the news of our visit to you and its effect: how you turned from idols, to be servants of the living and true God, and to wait expectantly for the appearance from heaven of his Son Jesus, whom he raised from the dead, Jesus our deliverer from the terrors of judgment to come' (1:7–10).

This was the gospel in its fullness—an insistence on forsaking pagan idols and a claim about God and the action he was taking in Christ. In the previous paragraph it was emphasised that Paul's real message was about this action and what this implied for himself and his contemporaries. This 'contemporary' note is of sovereign importance; Paul's *kerygma*, and evidently that of Silas and Timothy too, was *eschatological*, in other words, it dealt with the *eschata*, Greek for 'last things', and the 'last things' were imminent. Everything they taught must be understood within this framework or we misunderstand them completely.

It is with this in mind that the missionaries exhort the Thessalonians to live lives of pure morality, and go on to warn them against the idleness which belief in the impending end of the age might induce (4:11 f.). The letter then deals with something which seems to have been troubling the new Christians in Macedonia. If to be a Christian meant 'to wait ... for the appearance from heaven of ... Jesus' what was to be the fate of those who had accepted the gospel but died before this happened? The answer may seem somewhat startling; at first it seems as if a very profound doctrine is going to be expounded, one of which we shall hear more, the oneness of the believer with Christ in death and in new life: 'We believe that Jesus died and rose again; and so it will be for those who died as Christians; God will bring them to life with Jesus' (4:14). Justification for this translation of the last phrase is not quite clear, but the phrase seems to allow room for a doctrine of the oneness with Christ which will mean the new life of the believer. However, the Greek means much more probably, 'God will bring them in company with Jesus', for the following verses show that the writers think God will himself appear at the end of the age, with all the accompanying portents of an archangel's voice and a trumpet-call (ideas borrowed from the portents of Sinai at the end of Ex. 19). This rather surprising passage is introduced with the assurance that 'we who are left alive until the Lord comes shall not forestall those who have died', thus answering the question which had vexed the Thessalonians. If they ventured still to ask 'When?' — a question which became acute in the later New Testament period — the authors are not very helpful: 'About dates and times, my friends, we need not write to you, for you know perfectly well that the Day of the Lord comes like a thief in the night' (5:1 f.).

2 Thessalonians

This letter raises some problems, which need a little airing. The first is that some of the wording suggests that the three missionaries have been parted from their friends and converts for quite a long time. It is impossible to find a passage which makes it necessary to think so, but the general impression on the reader may amount to this. The second is that there is a strange passage, 2:1–12, which introduces into the eschatological teaching apparently actual contemporary historical figures, a feature unlike any of Paul's writing elsewhere.

These are not fatal objections to believing that this letter was written soon after the first to the same addressees, and we may try to make sense of it by bringing out its main message which indeed seems to lie in precisely that strange eschatological passage. Again it is Paul, Silvanus and Timothy who write, and it is reasonable to think they were still in Corinth together and therefore able together to deal with the difficulties of the Thessalonians. In view of the more developed doctrines of Paul's later letters which he wrote in association with Sosthenes (1 Corinthians) and Timothy (2 Corinthians) or entirely on his own (Galatians and Romans), perhaps Silas influenced the present letter towards a much more naive expression of eschatology than Paul would have allowed when writing independently. Certainly 'our Lord Jesus Christ is revealed from heaven with his mighty angels in blazing fire' still describes the Christian expectation (1:7). We shall see later however that this theory about the influence of Silas is far from certain.

At the end of the above description of the first letter it was hinted that the poor Thessalonians might be dissatisfied with the answer they received about the coming of Jesus in judgment and rescue. It is not easy to say how the letter was delivered, but it might have reached these people in the north quite quickly by sea, and their answer showing their undiminished anxiety might have been sent soon after they received it. The missionaries' answer to this renewed request for comfort is contained in 2:1–12 and while the plural of the first person is used a little more often than in the New English Bible translation, the singular creeps in here and perhaps suggests that Paul is revealing his greater caution in eschatological teaching than his colleagues, for in verse 5 and 6 he says perhaps a little impatiently, 'You cannot but remember that I told you this while I was still with you; you must now be aware of the restraining hand which ensures that he shall be revealed only at the proper time.' The one being restrained who is to be later revealed is the instigator apparently of the final rebellion, 'the man doomed to perdition'; 'he is the Enemy' (verses 3 and 4). It must be admitted that Paul nowhere else introduces this figure who is in opposition to God, and whose description inevitably suggests that he may be identified with the Antichrist of the First and Second Letters of John (where alone in the New Testament the word is used). The Johannine letters encourage the belief that the notion of Antichrist was a general one and did not refer to a particular personage but rather to an evil world principle, which could accordingly be illustrated by a number of people who can be called 'antichrists' (1 John 2:18). Paul does not use the term but seems rather to be thinking of an actual man contemporary with himself; is this consistent with his thought elsewhere?

To answer this question is not altogether easy and we can only urge some arguments which make it possible to answer positively: for instance, Paul did think of himself and the other apostles as *dramatis personae* on a stage whose drama was produced by God himself. This is shown by the unexpected passage, 1 Cor. 4:9: 'For it seems to me God has made us apostles the most abject of mankind. We are like men condemned to death in the arena, a spectacle to the whole universe — angels as well as men.' 'Men condemned to death' describes those gladiators who are reserved to the last in the cruel spectacle of the gladiatorial shows; they had to fight to the death since they were in any case condemned to it. Here the emphasis must fall, since Paul is certainly not complaining of the fact that he must die, on two aspects of such a performance. One is its urgency, and the other is that it comes last on the playbill of the world's drama. Hence Paul, at least when he wrote 1 Corinthians, believed that he and the other apostles had a part to play in God's plan and that it was the last scene in the cosmic drama. It is hard for us to imagine that any human being would think that his own work was of such paramount importance in the divine plan but it is manifest that Paul did think this and could not be blamed for thinking it; had he not been expressly called by the risen Lord to travel through the known world to tell all men everywhere that they must repent because the judgment was imminent? (See again Acts 17:30 f. which represents accurately Paul's message even if Luke made up this speech.)

For these reasons it is sometimes thought that the evil force which seems here in 2 Thessalonians to be identified with a particular person was in reality in Paul's mind the same sort of evil principle which was widely expected to show itself and mislead many men just before the final dénouement of the appearance of the Messiah. Such a principle is a feature of all statements of the eschatological hope (e.g. Mark 13:5 f. and pars. where the times of woe are the main subject dealt with, and these times are to be followed by the final deliverance in Mark 13:27; so too 1 Peter 4:12 f. and 5:8-10) and is even more the main subject in the book of Revelation. The restraining force on this theory would be the gospel as it is preached, for 'before the end the gospel must be proclaimed to all nations' (Mark 13:10). This is held to be the real meaning of the white horse and his rider in the vision of Rev. 19:11-16, where indeed in verse 13 the rider is given the name, 'Word of God'. Thus in verse 8 of 2 Thess. 2 the destruction of the 'wicked man' by 'the lord Jesus' 'with the breath of his mouth' means the annihilation of opposition by the Word of God, i.e. by the gospel spread by the apostles and others. It is one form of this theory to say that the restrainer in this passage is Paul himself.[1]

Ingenious as this is, and parallel as it sounds to other passages which do make sense of it and set it in a wider and intelligible context, the feeling remains that there does seem to be reference to actual historical personages here; consequently it is sometimes suggested that we must find a political situation which will make sense of these designedly cryptic sentences. Thus the threat of Caius Caligula, emperor A.D. 37–41, foiled by his death, to place his statue in the temple area of Jerusalem might well have aroused once again in Jewish breasts the horror which they had felt when they suffered the 'abomination of desolation' at the hands of Antiochus Epiphanes in 168 B.C. (1 Macc. 1:54; Dan. 11:31, etc.). 2 Thessalonians can hardly be correlated with the threat by Caligula since it would demand an impossibly early date for the writing of this letter, namely 41 or even earlier. If we seek a time when this threat may have been revived it could be in the time of Nero, 54–68, but this is too late. Some reprieve for a theory connected with Nero might be sought in a version of it which claimed that Nero was feared as the coming oppressor and Claudius, emperor 41–54, was the restrainer. This demands too much prescience on the part of those who feared the great catastrophe, for Nero's terroristic characteristics did not manifest themselves until he had been reigning five years and cannot therefore have caused anticipatory alarm while his uncle was still on the throne.

Probably we must settle for some theory like that first explained unless we are ready to give credence to more radical views that 2 Thessalonians does not really fit Paul's life at all and must be relegated to the limbo of letters composed after his death. No doubt there were such letters which were written as though with his authority, as we shall see in the chapter on the Pastoral Letters, but there are other features which fit the situation usually ascribed to 2 Thessalonians very well. One of these is the renewed injunction, this time with more insistence, not to be idle in the face of the expected end of the age. 'The man who will not work shall not eat' say the authors (3:10) and finally Paul at the end authenticates the letter as

---

[1] See J. Munck, *Paul and the Salvation of Mankind* (S.C.M. Press, 1959), pp. 36 f.

if there might otherwise be some question about his agreeing with every part of it (3:17 f.).

Paul and his companions in Corinth

Paul was, for a short time at any rate, alone in Corinth, Silas and Timothy being still expected from Macedonia. He appears to have arrived there just after the edict of Claudius that all Jews were to leave Rome. Suetonius, Claudius's biographer, rather implies that Claudius made this decree in 41 when he became emperor, but it is probable that this is a false inference and that a later historian, Orosius, is right in assigning this decree to 49; this date would make Pauline chronology easier, not to say possible. Paul associated himself with a Jewish married couple, Aquila and Priscilla, who had been expelled from Rome through this decree. It is clear from other evidence that they accepted the gospel and became his fellow-workers, though the original reason for this joining forces was that they were of the same trade (Acts 18:3). Paul evidently needed to recoup his finances. 'Then Silas and Timothy came down from Macedonia, and Paul devoted himself entirely to preaching' — which suggests that Silas and Timothy took over the bread-winning. If this was often their task it would explain why they had not offended the Jews in Macedonia as much as Paul, who did most of the preaching. He was certainly very active in preaching at Corinth, as his own letters bear witness, though not very good at it, and better at writing (2 Cor. 10:10). Again he started with Jews but was rebuffed by them, and so took over a house next door belonging to one of the Gentile adherents to the synagogue, and perhaps converted among others an official of the synagogue named Sosthenes. The work continued for eighteen months until the next major disturbance caused by hostile Jews. Luke seems to date this event by the arrival of a proconsul named Gallio, but it is not clear whether the date is quite so exact. Gallio we know to have become proconsul of Achaia almost certainly about 51–52, so we have a rough means of dating Paul's first visit to Corinth and can take it that he arrived there about 49 or 50, fitting in with the date of Aquila and Priscilla's arrival there. All this is covered by Acts 18:1–17.

Luke shows the vagueness of his dating often enough;

it is illustrated by the words in Acts 18:18, 'Paul stayed on for some time' and then left. He may have called at Ephesus as Luke says he did, though we cannot be sure; Aquila and Priscilla, now his companions, seem certainly to have stayed at Ephesus where they were joined by an Alexandrian Jew named Apollos who himself subsequently crossed to Corinth and worked there. Paul went on to 'Syria', landed at Caesarea, perhaps visited Jerusalem, certainly went on to Antioch, the base from which he had set out. Now Luke makes a chronological account of the events impossible. 'While Apollos was at Corinth, Paul travelled through the inland regions till he came to Ephesus' (Acts 19:1). Such vagueness is tantalising to the modern historian, and the more so when we find that Paul in his letters to the Corinthians gives evidence of making three visits to Corinth whereas Luke in Acts narrates only two. This brings us to two major letters of Paul.

The Corinthian Letters: 1 Corinthians

The first visit has already been noticed. Paul successfully established a Church at Corinth but it contained within it the latent causes of division and even of hostility to Paul himself. While he was working at Ephesus factions grew up within the Corinthian Church and various matters arose which required his decision. The Corinthians wrote to him, but it may well be that he had already started a letter to them because he had heard of their divisions. How serious these were is a matter for debate. Some have thought that the Corinthians' habit of saying ' "I am Paul's man", or "I am for Apollos" ' (1 Cor. 1:12), and so on, mean that they were merely quarrelling among themselves as to who had the authority in their Church, but it was not institutionally divided; others have thought that they were threatening to break up into separate congregations. The essential need of unity is in any case a theme which is never quite out of sight throughout this earliest extant letter of Paul to the Corinthians.

Paul is at his best in this letter, being compelled by circumstances to deploy all his eloquence and argumentative ability. Although there is no doubt that he held a high doctrine of baptism which admitted a convert into close fellowship with Christ, he insists that he was not sent to baptise and indeed baptised only a few of the Corinthians personally: he was sent to proclaim the gospel of 'Christ crucified' or 'Christ nailed to the cross' (1 Cor. 1:23) which was an offence to both Jews and Greeks, to the former for the obvious reason that a crucified criminal was accursed and to claim that he was their Messiah an insult, while to the latter it had nothing to do with the intellectual 'wisdom' or philosophy which had for centuries been the method by which religious ideas were assessed and often dismissed with contempt. To them a religion based on such a person must seem 'nonsense' or 'folly'.

Paul's answer is to turn the matter the other way round. It is not a question of what a man may choose: 'You are in Christ Jesus by God's act', he reminds the Corinthians (1:30). It is the Spirit in man who accepts the gospel and judges its worth, not the intellect alone, although Paul engages to discuss at an intellectual level with those who are ready for it. The Corinthians cannot claim to be so for their quarrels show them to be mere 'infants in Christ' (3:1). Paul goes on to urge strongly the necessity for a moral life. This may seem odd to us who are used to associate religion with morality and perhaps with an over-strict morality. This is because we have inherited the Jewish notion of religion; if we were heirs, as some savants like to say, only to the Graeco-Roman civilization, we should understand better how some forms of religion lead or may lead to a life of careless morality. It is easy to understand: if a man is convinced he now belongs to and is under the care of a trustworthy saviour, well then, he is 'saved', that is, he has been guaranteed victory over those powers which threaten his destruction this side or the other side of death. He need bother no more about his conduct; he has done all he needs to do by being initiated into this new status through this new god. Something of this, caught from the pagan cults around them, seems to have infected the Corinthians, or some of them. Paul uses some sarcasm: 'All of you, no doubt, have everything you could desire. You have come into your fortune already. You have come into your kingdom — and left us out.' This is 4:8 and Paul goes on to contrast the condition of the apostles as like gladiators condemned to death in the verse (4:9) which was discussed earlier. The phraseology which Paul uses in his sarcasm is taken from language which later appears in gnosticism and some have thought that some form of this kind of religion existed already at Corinth. The essence of gnosticism, which took many forms, was that the initiate, intellectually enlightened by a particular doctrine peculiar to the sect which he joined, thus gained his salvation and needed no other.

Paul scouts such ideas with all the greater earnestness when he is obliged to say, 'I actually hear reports of sexual immorality among you, immorality such as even pagans do not tolerate'; 'And you can still be proud of yourselves!' (5:1 f.). This was a case of what would be regarded as incest, since the offender had relations with his stepmother, no doubt a much younger woman than her husband. As for fornication with a harlot, Paul lays the foundations in dealing with this for a very lofty sexual morality. A Christian does not 'own' his body: in the sense he wishes to argue here, it is the Lord's. A few sentences further on, in a different section of the letter he is going to argue that 'The wife cannot claim her body as her own; it is her husband's. Equally, the husband cannot claim his body as his own; it is his wife's' (7:4). For the moment, he answers for Christians the permissiveness of Corinthian society in this way:

> Every other sin that a man can commit is outside the body; but the fornicator sins against his own body. Do you not know that your body is a shrine of the indwelling Holy Spirit, and the Spirit is God's gift to you? You do not belong to yourselves; you were bought at a price. Then honour God in your body (6:18–20).

At the beginning of chapter 7 Paul turns to things about which the Corinthians wrote to him. Often it seems that he begins by quoting a passage from their letter as a kind of heading for the following section of his own.[2] This may well be the case here, for pagan society when it went religious was apt to be prudish. At any rate the passage begins with the words, 'it is a good thing for a man to have nothing to do with women'. Paul gives this notion partial support. He thinks the ideal is celibacy, but not on pagan grounds; the friend of Priscilla, Chloe (at whose house the Corinthian Church met, 1:11), and Phoebe (Rom.

[2] For this and other clarifying suggestions see John C. Hurd, jr., *The Origin of 1 Corinthians* (S.P.C.K., 1965).

16:1) was not a woman-hater. 7:29 and 31 show that Paul is unquestionably thinking within the eschatological framework we have already explained; 'the time we live in will not last long' . . . 'the whole frame of this world is passing away.' He would not therefore have an unmarried man marry since he will then be distracted from his true purpose of 'pleasing the Lord': 'his aim is to please his wife; and he has a divided mind' (7:33). How far Paul is from regarding marriage with contempt is clear to those who will read this chapter, a minority of those accustomed to discuss authoritatively what Paul thought about marriage. In the context it becomes clear that his famous 'Better be married than burn with vain desire' (7:9) is addressed to would-be celibates, not uttered as a grudging permission to the unmarried. Again, the notion that Paul was a prude is dispelled at once when his down-to-earth remarks about the conduct of people within marriage is read.

Chapter 8 deals with meat from the slaughterhouse where pagan idols were set up and the meat could be said to have been offered to a pagan god, as was customary. Paul's immediate answer to this seems to be a sound psychological one; such meat is allowable but not if it offends the conscience of a fellow-Christian to eat it. But it is clear that he was strongly against joining in any ceremony which implied that one had been involved in pagan worship. Later, in 10:21 he says roundly, 'You cannot partake of the Lord's table and the table of demons.'

Chapter 9 changes the subject abruptly. Evidently some had questioned Paul's authority as an apostle, on the rather unexpected ground that he did not claim expenses from his converts. Hotly insisting that such was indeed his right and that it had divine authority, Paul as hotly insists that he will not claim it; his authority is that the Lord called him and that he does discharge his duty as an apostle, which their existence as a Christian Church proves. It is in this connexion that he makes his famous claim to have been all things to all men, one of the phrases of all literature quoted most inappropriately most often; this is no admission of acting like a weathercock but of this: 'I am a free man and own no master; but I have made myself every man's servant, to win over as many as possible' (9:19). He returns to the need to live a life consonant with the new

Christian status, using an argument which reveals the Jewish scholar. No good to say one is baptised and therefore saved and can do what one likes! 'Our ancestors' (probably Paul means literal ancestors for Jews, spiritual ancestors for the former pagans) were baptised under Moses in the pillar of cloud and in the Red Sea, but that baptism did not save them from the destructive wrath of God when they gave way to the temptation to indulge in an immoral orgy and to other sins. He goes on to apply this to the eucharist or Lord's Supper, though led aside into matters like the proper dress of a woman in church which are no longer of such interest to us as they were in a society which would suspect of immorality the adherents of any religion where men and women worshipped together.

The Lord's Supper, or Eucharist

In connexion with the Lord's Supper, Paul's first concern is with the travesty which such a celebration must be if the meal is held in a disorderly fashion and especially in the midst of palpable divisions which include the rich having a good feast while poorer worshippers are in want. The scene which this suggests is more intelligible to us moderns if we consider that the eucharist must have looked to the Corinthians like a cult feast such as the surrounding paganism had made familiar. It was at first a commemoration of fellowship by means of a common meal (an *agape* or love-feast) in which fellowship was enjoyed also with the spiritually present Christ who had initiated such meals in his earthly days. The accounts of miraculous feedings of multitudes in the gospels are such gatherings, whatever else they may be claimed to be as well. So also are the meetings for 'breaking bread' (Acts 2:42, 46) in the early Church which Luke mentions. It may be that a commemoration of the death of Jesus was part of such meals from the beginning, and it is hard to imagine that such commemoration would be long in establishing itself; whatever the truth of this, Paul included a most unmistakable reference to the sacrificial death of Christ. This may have been intended by the inclusion of the use of wine symbolising Christ's shed blood, for wine is not mentioned in the Acts passages any more than in the accounts of the miraculous feedings in the gospels. For Paul the cup means the blood which seals the new covenant made through the death of Christ, but the whole eucharist is a memorial of Christ's death: 'For every time you eat this bread and drink the cup, you proclaim the death of the Lord, until he comes' (11:26). It has been thought that Paul himself introduced this sacrificial note into the eucharist. Whether he did or not, his idea of what the eucharist is included this element and enabled him to rebuke and to appeal to the Corinthians on two grounds. The first was the obvious and straightforward appeal to the need for harmony and true fellowship — how else can the common meal be a fellowship meal? The other ground is clear from what Paul says after verse 26 quoted above: 'It follows that anyone who eats the bread or drinks the cup of the Lord unworthily will be guilty of desecrating the body and blood of the Lord' (11:27). This raises the question of what is meant by identifying the body and blood of Christ with the bread and cup. It is unnecessary to go into all the different interpretations which have been put on these words; it is clear that Paul regards Christ as the supreme guest, indeed the host at this meal, and it is clear from other passages in this and other writings that for Paul the corporate body of Christians is the Body of Christ. An improper celebration of the meal therefore insults both host and fellow-guests. The bread and wine are therefore the Body and Blood of Christ in two ways: they stand for the whole fellowship (the bread is 'a means of sharing in the body of Christ', 10:16) and they stand for Christ. 'Stand for' falls far short of the degree of identity of symbol and reality intended, but we will not attempt to offer more than this outline which may suggest something of the sense in which for Paul the bread 'is' the Body of Christ and the wine 'is' his Blood.

It is natural here to compare the accounts of the institution of the eucharist in the synoptic gospels, Mark 14: 22–25; Luke 22:15–20; Matt. 26:26–29. It will be seen at once that critical questions arise. The gospels were written after Paul's letters: if we are sceptical about any of the history which they are alleged to contain we may doubt the historicity of these accounts of the institution. Luke's seems like that of Paul, and Mark, with Matthew following him, seems to represent an independent line of tradition. There can be no questioning the substantial agreement between them. Paul claims to have received his information about the origin of the eucharist 'from the Lord', and this must in any case imply a very early tradition not of his invention in essentials. Such an early tradition could therefore go back to 'Jesus, on the night of his arrest' (1 Cor. 11:23), but even if it does not it must represent a relatively early practice of the Church.

If the tradition derives from Jesus himself, according to the synoptics the meal which enshrined what we now call the eucharist (or communion or mass) was a Passover celebration, and Jesus gave, in customary Jewish fashion, an interpretation of its significance, but in this case one which involved a new way of looking at the Passover as still a festival of deliverance, but, because Christ was himself the eternal Passover Lamb, the Lamb of God, this deliverance was from the power of evil, not a national deliverance from slavery. Thus the Fourth Gospel, which does not narrate the institution of the eucharist, nevertheless makes Jesus unmistakably *the* Passover Lamb at the crucifixion.

Christians celebrated the eucharist at Passover for a long time; it became for them a new festival, Easter. But from the first they did not confine its celebration to Passover, but made it weekly on the first day of the week, or Sunday, the resurrection day (Sunday has nothing to do with the Sabbath, a Jewish festival falling on Saturday). We have seen that whether Passover elements were included or not, a meal enshrined the more solemn moments which are described in the passages which have been designated the accounts of the institution of the eucharist. (In Paul the passage to set alongside the synoptic acounts is 1 Cor. 11:23–26.)[3]

Gifts of the Spirit and Resurrection

Let us return now to the situation which Paul had to face; this meal was disorderly and Paul rebuked the Corinthians for it. It may well be that some of the words which he wrote in this connexion (for example, 'If you are hungry, eat at home, so that in meeting together you may not fall under judgment', 11:34) were instrumental in dividing the eucharist proper from the surrounding *agape* and contributing to the solemnity with which it is approached by Christians today.

[3] For a full discussion of the origins of the eucharist see J. Jeremias, *The Eucharistic Words of Jesus* (S.C.M. Press, 1966).

Chapters 12–14 constitute a treatise on their own. They were apparently written to answer some questions from the Corinthians about spiritual gifts. The book of Acts gives ample evidence for the phenomenon in the early church of *glossolalia*, speaking ecstatically (for instance, 2:1 f.) and for this being regarded as the most evident sign of the reception of the Spirit by the person affected (Acts 10:44–46). It seems that the Corinthians thought of this particular manifestation as an infallible sign and a gift of the Spirit pre-eminently one to be proud of. Paul takes the opportunity provided by their question or questions, whatever they were, to elaborate his doctrine of the Spirit and his gifts, and this leads him in its turn to say something about his doctrine of the Body of Christ, of the ministry and of the character of the chief virtue of Christians. The way in which the treatise, an integral part of the letter as a whole, hangs together even when considered by itself, makes the more astonishing the theories of those who try to detach the famous thirteenth chapter from this context and to argue that it is not or was not originally Pauline. A summary of the argument may make this clear: at the opening the New English Bible is misleading for it gives the impression that the heading under which Paul is now to work is 'Gifts of the Spirit' but 'gifts' in this connexion is usually the Greek word *charismata*, and the word here is *pneumatika*, 'spiritual matters' (if there were such a word, 'spiritualics', on the analogy of phonetics, electronics and so on). It is true that much of what follows is about *charismata*, or gifts of the Spirit, but there is some important teaching on the actual subject of the Spirit. The first point, emphasised strongly, is that there is only one Spirit given by God to Christians (12:4–11). There is evidence elsewhere (1 John 4:1–3) that Christians were tempted to believe in what they regarded uncritically as a spiritual revelation even if it prompted, perhaps in some ecstatic utterance, a blasphemy against Jesus himself, probably in order to exalt the authority of the spirit who is supposed to be making the revelation. As in 1 John, so here the test of the divine authority of the spirit who may speak to a Christian is the attitude of that spirit to Jesus. There is then only one Spirit, and he is the giver of all the gifts which the Church enjoys. Paul now emphasises that these gifts are not confined to the outwardly impressive ecstatic utterance over-valued by some, but included faith, prophecy and gifts of healing (12:10 f.).

The stress on unity of God's action through the Spirit arises from the very variety of his gifts, and this leads Paul to stress the unity of the Church, each of whose members receives a different gift, and he makes this point by comparing the Church to a body, having strikingly begun by identifying this body with Christ (12:12). The unity then is caused by the Spirit acting in a manifold way in one Body which is one with Christ, and it is even the Spirit which brings about the existence of this Body: 'For indeed we were all brought into one body by baptism, in the one Spirit, whether we are Jews or Greeks, whether slaves or free men, and that one Holy Spirit was poured out for all of us to drink' (12:13) (the last unexpected metaphor probably because Paul is thinking of the rock, which he identifies with the pre-existent Christ, from which the 'ancestors' drank in the wilderness, 10:3 f.).

After arguing that the Body, though made up of individuals, suffers or flourishes together, Paul proceeds to add to the gifts given to the Church by the Spirit, apostles, prophets and teachers, and mentions again those gifts already listed. He emphasises the difference between the gifts which each has received and then goes on to write about those which are necessary for every member of the Body. 'The higher gifts are those you should aim at. And now I will show you the best way of all.' This is the last verse of the chapter, 12:31, and Paul then follows without a break in sense with the famous chapter 13 on love. In the first two verses he makes plain that he may have all the gifts which he has been describing as gifts of the Spirit indeed, 'I may speak in tongues . . . I may have the gift of prophecy . . . I may have faith . . . but if I have no love, I am nothing' (13:1 f.).

With complete consistency and relevance, indeed departing from his subject far less than he does sometimes elsewhere, for here he never wavers from it, after the famous passage in praise of love he proceeds, 'Put love first; but there are other gifts of the Spirit at which you should aim also . . .' (14:1). Love, then, is the greatest gift of the Spirit; naturally so, since without it the Body, in practice, does not cohere—people are not united by believing the same doctrines but by love—and it is therefore the one indispensable gift. Chapter 14 discusses the other gifts of the Spirit at which Christians should aim; they are prophecy and ecstatic utterance. Paul clearly prefers the former and argues its superiority though claiming to possess both himself. Since both are practised in assembly when the Church is gathered for worship this chapter contains also advice on its orderly conduct, interesting very largely for the picture of the somewhat bizarre and noisy picture of early Christian worship in Corinth which it suggests.

Near the beginning of the letter Paul seemed to equate the gospel with 'Christ crucified' but we knew already that this could not express the whole even of its essence without a reference to the resurrection; and the reader looking at this letter for the first time might be wondering if there is to be any expansion in order to correct this too brief summary of the gospel. It seems that Paul, after considering all the difficulties which beset his Corinthian converts and therefore himself, thought it was necessary to restate this very point with authority, especially as there seem to have been some among them who said there was no resurrection of the dead (15:12). The fifteenth chapter therefore deals with this matter. It is unlikely that those who said there was no resurrection meant that they rejected Christ's resurrection since if they had done so they would not have become Christians at all and Paul would not have been dealing with them in the context of a letter to the Corinthian Church. It is the general resurrection which they are denying, in this respect like the Sadducees in contrast to the Pharisees.

Paul begins with a repetition of what he says he had passed on to the Corinthians by word of mouth when he proclaimed the gospel to them. He 'handed on to them the facts which had been imparted to' him (15:3). This was evidently the tradition of the Church which existed while he was still its persecutor. It is very striking, for it consists in obvious argument that Christ really was raised from the dead because he appeared to so many people. The list does not tally exactly with those narrated in the gospels; there is for example no record elsewhere of an appearance 'to over five hundred of our brothers at once' (15:6) and the attempt to equate this with the phenomenon usually inaccurately described as 'Pentecost' (because it happened at the time of that festival) in Acts 2:1 f. is either dishonest or merely foolish, for the good reason that that was not an appearance of Christ. Paul adds his own experience to the list which he had received from the Church and closes this paragraph with, 'This is what we all proclaim, and this is what you believed' (15:11).

It is important to understand how the argument proceeds; the point is often missed that Paul regarded Christ's resurrection as the first instance of the *general* resurrection in which he believed as a Pharisee long before he became a Christian (he calls Christ 'the firstfruits of the harvest of the dead' in verse 20). 'If there be no resurrection, then Christ was not raised', he says (15:13). Here is a further clarification of Paul's eschatological framework. He thought that the events which Christ's resurrection had set in train were in fact the general resurrection of the righteous and such an interpretation of them carried with it an expectation of early completion of this series of events. In 15:24-28 he gives us clearly the sequence: Christ is raised first (that had happened), then Christ returns and those who belong to Christ are to be raised then. This is the beginning of the Messianic Kingdom during which God puts all enemies of the reigning Messiah 'under his feet'. The Kingdom thus perfected is then to be handed over to God the Father, 'and thus God will be all in all' (15:28). The long argument about the feasibility of resurrection based on the 'death' of seeds and the raising of the subsequent plants and similar phenomena in nature is of little importance to us compared with, first, the necessity to see that the eschatological framework in which Paul understands the events of his own experience are what they are, namely, previously held Pharisaic belief; and compared also with the importance of understanding that this is the form in which the substructure of Christian belief still persists to this day. Nor is it possible for us to say that Paul had advanced in the least, for all his elaboration, upon the primitive eschatology of 1 Thessalonians: 'we shall not all die, but we shall all be changed in a flash, in the twinkling of an eye, at the last trumpet-call. For the trumpet will sound ...' (15:52 f.).

In spite of all this primitive thought (as it must seem to us) Paul had made advances in the understanding of Christianity which were destined to assist immeasurably its survival when these fervent eschatological hopes were not realised and caused the difficulties expressed in, for example, 2 Peter 3:4, 'Where now is the promise of his coming?' (although there the Christian author rebukes those who ask such questions). His teaching about the Spirit and his relation to the Body of Christ, the Church, his profound understanding of the power of the gospel over against the attractiveness of more 'philosophical' doctrines, his equally profound understanding of what is of paramount importance in the daily life of a Christian, his careful statements about the reality of the presence of Christ at the eucharist and the connexion between loyalty to the Lord and loyalty to brother Christians are but a few of the theoretical-cum-practical examples of his genius.

Two points remain in this First Letter to the Corinthians with which we must deal; one is that the letter was written in company with Sosthenes, a name which we met in Corinth, but there the bearer of it was not a Christian but the director of a Jewish synagogue. There is no record of the conversion of the Corinthian Sosthenes but it may be the same man who had followed Paul on subsequent travels and now was with him in Ephesus where Paul had received news of the defects in the Corinthian Church. There seems to have been little influence on the actual letter from Sosthenes, for no material is introduced into it which is not consistent with what is found where Paul is either co-author with others than Sosthenes or sole author. Again, in 1 Corinthians Paul uses the first person singular throughout and is at times much occupied with his own position as an apostle. In this letter then we are beginning to see Pauline theology develop.

The other matter is the last chapter, 16. It is mainly concerned with future arrangements and reference to it is therefore best left until the next section.

2 Corinthians

Paul certainly endured some great trouble in Ephesus. In its account of his stay there, Acts 19:8 f. gives much the same impression and raises much the same sort of questions as Acts 16:12–40 does in its account of Paul and Silas in Philippi. The decisive trouble arises through materialistic motives; someone's livelihood is affected, they falsely accuse the apostles and the latter get into trouble with the authorities—who find they are mistaken; the end is a moral victory for Paul and his companions, but they have to leave the town. In Philippi Paul and Silas are actually imprisoned, in Ephesus, Paul is threatened with trouble, even death, but is not imprisoned. Yet Paul's description of the trouble in Ephesus exceeds in earnestness and sorrow by far what he says of that in Philippi. In 1 Cor. 15:32 he makes a not altogether clear reference to having 'fought wild beasts at Ephesus' and 2 Corinthians opens with a most sombre passage about his distress which contains the words, 'we should like you to know . . . how serious was the trouble that came upon us in the province of Asia.' Incidentally the 'we' is natural; in this letter Timothy is co-author. According to this opening passage Paul evidently had to reckon with the possibility of death; he writes, 'this was meant to teach us not to place reliance on ourselves, but on God who raises the dead' (1:8, 9), thus foreshadowing an important part of his teaching on 'life' and 'death'. In 2 Corinthians Paul constantly deals with the status of his enemies in comparison with his own; in 6:5 he speaks of having been 'in prisons' and in 11:23 says he has been 'more often imprisoned'. As far as it is possible to trace out the story by correlating Acts with hints in the letters, Paul had been imprisoned only once at this point. Perhaps then, though Acts is silent on the point, he was imprisoned in Ephesus; if so, we may be able to assign to that period some of the other letters with which we shall have to deal presently, instead of assigning them to the last part of Paul's life when he was a prisoner in Rome. However, it must not be forgotten that there is no other evidence for an imprisonment in Ephesus; it remains a hypothesis, though one into which a number of facts fit rather well. We shall return to this matter briefly later on.

We cannot be sure what happened in Ephesus; 2 Corinthians is concerned with trouble not there but in Corinth. It is to some sort of reconstruction of the events which led to its composition and that of other letters that we must now turn, with the warning that it is impossible to arrive at a wholly satisfactory conclusion. It may well be useful to remark at the very beginning that it is widely held that 2 Corinthians is not a letter but a number of pieces of letters which were put together subsequently; it is almost as widely held that 1 Corinthians can be described in much the same way, but since there is no need to use such a hypothesis in order to explain that letter this point was left on one side when describing it.

It is different with 2 Corinthians; here some reference has to be made to the possibility that it is composite, since this theory is bound up with any attempt to explain its place in Paul's life. We have to begin with a glance at Paul's activities in connexion with Corinth, and to do so must return to 1 Cor. 16. The first four verses are about a collection, and this will occupy us briefly again; here we notice that Paul expects that he may accompany members of various Churches which he has founded when they take a sum of money which they have collected for the Church in Jerusalem, and that this may well be the explanation of the list of companions in Acts 20:4. He goes on to say, 'I shall come to Corinth after passing through Macedonia' (repeating the order of his first journey into Europe). Paul thought he might stay the winter with them. It may be that he is referring to the same projected visit, but with a change of plan when he says in 2 Cor. 1:16 f., 'I meant to visit you on my way to Macedonia, and after leaving Macedonia, to return to you, and you would then send me on my way to Judaea. That was my intention; did I lightly change my mind?' In what way did he change his mind? It seems at first as if the answer is clear: he never made any of this projected journey, for in 2 Cor. 1:23 he says so: 'I did not after all come to Corinth.' But the translation is inexact; the Greek which the translators of the New English Bible used (and they had a choice of text here) can be translated, 'I did not yet come . . .' or 'I did not come again . . .'. If the latter is what Paul meant, he may have been saying that he did not make the second call on the Corinthians on his return from Macedonia, implying that he did make the first call on his way to Macedonia as planned. If that is the case it explains why he did not make the second call, for in 1:23 he says 'it was out of consideration for you'. Why leave them to themselves out of consideration for them? Because he had had a fierce dispute with them on the first call.

The fierce dispute is in itself not in doubt; there are frequent references to a quarrel, and to its being made up, throughout 2 Corinthians. This will become clear to anyone who reads for example from 1:23 to 2:11, which is too long to quote here in full. One verse will suffice and will make a further point which it is essential to understand; this is 2:4, 'That letter I sent you came out of great distress and anxiety; how many tears I shed as I wrote it!' Paul had then sent a letter before this one, a letter which is usually called the 'Severe Letter'. It was clearly a letter which Paul had sent after a quarrel, and 2 Corinthians shows that it had had its effect and Paul had learnt with satisfaction of the Corinthians' penitence and eagerness to be reconciled. The Severe Letter cannot be identified with the relatively mild 1 Corinthians; it is probably lost but quite a large number of scholars think that it is represented at least in part by 2 Cor. 10-13, mostly for the reason that after writing chapters 1–7 in a conciliatory and affectionate vein, and then eloquently and tactfully appealing for a good response to his collection scheme in chapters 8–9, in chapter 10 Paul suddenly starts again on the offenders among the Corinthians as if there had been no reconciliation.

It seems certain not only that there had been a Severe Letter (this is undisputed) but also that when Paul wrote 2 Cor. 10–13 he was about to visit them for the third time (e.g. 13:1, 'This will be my third visit to you'). The second visit was that on which the quarrel took place: the third may well have been that mentioned briefly in Acts 20: 1-2, where 'Greece' means Corinth. If however 2 Cor. 10–13 is part of the Severe Letter this visit narrated in Acts 20 would be his fourth, the third having been some time before. In order to avoid this conclusion the advocates of the '10–13 is part of the Severe Letter' theory say that 2 Cor. 12:14 and 13:1 mean that Paul was only threatening another visit but did not pay it, and that was when he acted 'out of consideration' for them, as he says in 2 Cor. 1:23. This reference is part of a letter written after chapters 10–13, for they are on this theory part of the Severe Letter to which Paul himself refers when he writes what is now 2 Cor. 1–9.

Enough has been said to show not only some of the problems, but also that a general outline of what took place can be offered. Apparently, Paul made a second visit to Corinth unrecorded in Acts; on this occasion there was a violent dispute and Paul returned to Ephesus and wrote the Severe Letter. He sent Titus afterwards to find out if it had had the desired effect. It may be that he was still so worried about the outcome that he set out himself in order to meet Titus coming back with reassuring news. Not finding him at Troas (2:12) he crossed again into Europe and met him in Macedonia; Titus was able to assure Paul that the Corinthians had capitulated (7:5 f.). To unravel the evidence in order to decide where Timothy had been all this time would be unnecessary labour; he probably was the bearer of 1 Corinthians; he had now rejoined Paul and is the co-author of 2 Corinthians.

What had the trouble been about? 2 Cor. 2:5–11 shows that an individual had offended Paul, but 7:12 shows that it was the disloyalty of the Corinthians in not restraining the offender which had chiefly vexed him. On the other hand, in chapter 10–13 the trouble is clearly caused by a number of people, claiming authority for themselves and attacking that of Paul. There are several references to them also in the earlier part of the letter, e.g. in 3:1 and 5:12. Indeed it is a weakness of the theory that chapters 10–13 represent the Severe Letter that in those chapters Paul nowhere makes a complaint against the individual offender who had been the cause of the main quarrel. Those who attacked Paul's authority claimed to have letters of credit from some authority, presumably Jerusalem, and that they were true Israelites. It seems that they belonged to a section of the Church which considered it necessary to be a Jew as a foundation for being a Christian. The majority of such people would be actual Jews by race who had lived alongside members of other nations long enough to be permanently horrified at their moral laxity and at the ritual uncleanness which they would impart to Jewish neighbours. The latter feeling was a consequence of adherence to the Law of Moses as strictly interpreted by contemporary leaders, and the former conviction was partly due to looking at life through the eyes of a person brought up in a totally different thought-world. Indeed it was possible, as Paul makes clear in Romans, for a Jew to be a hypocrite about his moral superiority to other nations. But there was enough truth in it to make the insistence on observing the Law a strong point for which, at least in some quarters, Jews would be admired. Thus when converts were made by those whom we should call Christian missionaries, many of the missionaries' friends regarded such converts as chiefly converts to Judaism.

It is probable that the consequent move to 'judaise' wherever Christian groups formed was widely prevalent. In addition to such communities actual Jews who had been converted would often be intellectual converts, faithful Jews who were persuaded by Paul and other missionaries that Jesus was the Messiah, but who regarded it as unfaithfulness to depart from their strict obedience to the Law. It is a tribute to the triumph of Pauline Christianity that we know relatively little about these Jewish Christians, although their literature is represented in the New Testament by the Gospel of Matthew, the Letters to the Hebrews, of James, Peter and Jude, and by the book of Revelation.

The ubiquity of those who were of this habit of mind and observance should preserve us from thinking that when they appear in the story of Paul they must be members of the Church which was in their eyes their stronghold, that is the Church of Jerusalem. That Church contained in its leader James and in its most famous apostle Peter two Jewish Christians who were far from being opposed, as far as our evidence goes, to Paul, although equally clearly not agreeing with him in every particular.

Let us therefore leave on one side not only the surprising theory sometimes put forward that the opponents of Paul who thought themselves true Israelites and as such the only true Christians were the twelve at Jerusalem, but also the feeling that we must identify them at all, beyond saying that they were Jewish Christians zealous for the Law and believing that Jesus was the Messiah. As we shall see presently, they gave immense trouble to Paul also in Galatia. It is in the process of defending not only himself but his gospel against these opponents that Paul develops some important theology in this letter. His basic standpoint is summarised by a statement which is a natural sequel to his doctrine in 1 Corinthians about the Spirit. Paul believed that the bestowal of the Spirit was one of the signs of the new age being inaugurated through those events which included the General Resurrection, which had begun with the resurrection of Christ. The coming of the Spirit, albeit not yet in full measure, meant the beginning of a new age and a new order. Moreover it was vital for a man to belong to this new order, the dominance of the ancient Law having now been ended. The statement which summarises this position against the background we have described is made in 2 Cor. 3:6, '... the written law condemns to death, but the Spirit gives life.' Paul in this passage does not say, but seems to imply, that the old covenant itself can be read now with new eyes and understood to mean the same as the new covenant. Certainly later on he is to argue that the gospel was known in some form to the patriarchs.

Because Paul is entrusted with the glorious gospel of God himself, he is strengthened against his opponents: 'For the same God who said, "Out of darkness let light shine", has caused his light to shine within us, to give the light of revelation —the revelation of the glory of God in the face of Jesus Christ' (4:6). It is thus inseparable from assertions about his own persistence through suffering and hindrance from opponents that Paul introduces in this letter his doctrinal convictions. 4:16–5:10, a rather obscure passage apparently about the manner of the resurrection for believers, begins with 'No wonder we do not lose heart'—for the reasons he has just given about sharing the glory of God. He goes on to apply what he can say truly of himself to all believers: 'our troubles are slight and short-lived; and their outcome an eternal glory which outweighs them far' (4:17). The passage which follows is not easy to understand, nor is it easy to be sure that the right interpretation is directing any particular translation, but it seems that Paul here ventures upon another way of thinking about the attainment of immortality; there is no sign that he has thought of abandoning the eschatological framework, and 5:10, which speaks of the coming judgment by Christ, along with subsequent writings, makes clear that he has not done so; but unknowingly he now teaches something from the depth of his own spiritual life which helps to liberate Christianity from the shackles of so literal an eschatology.

He changes the metaphor of various kinds of organism and their seeds and structure which he used in 1 Cor. 15 and says:

we yearn to have our heavenly habitation put on over this one—in the hope that, being thus clothed, we shall not find ourselves naked ... we are oppressed because we do not want to have the old body stripped off. Rather our desire is to have the new body put on over it, so that our mortal part may be absorbed into life immortal. God himself has shaped us for this very end; and as a pledge of it he has given us the spirit.' (5:2–5).

The New English Bible here quoted is rather freer than usual and conceals, as it must, difficult choices in interpretation, but it represents the general meaning for certain. There are the seeds here of a form of Christianity which will pay more attention to the way of discipleship now than to the hope of a great cosmic and human change in an unspecified — or too confidently specified — future. In this connexion the possible translations of 5:17 are relevant; literally, '. . . if anyone is in Christ, a new creation! Old things have passed away; look, new things have come into being!' Thus the New English Bible places in the margin what is perhaps the nearer to the original — 'When anyone is united to Christ he is a new creature; his old life is over; a new life has already begun' and in the text, 'When anyone is united to Christ, there is a new world; the old order has gone, and a new order has already begun.'

The great change in the cosmic situation as it affects the status of man before God has in Paul's belief been brought about mysteriously by the death of Christ on the cross. In 2 Cor. 5:21 he throws out a hint of one form of the doctrine of atonement which this implies: God has accepted Christ as a sin-offering on behalf of mankind. Elsewhere Paul has used the language of redemption (buying back from slavery), as in 1 Cor. 1:30 where Christ is described in the Greek by the use of a number of abstract nouns, one of which is 'redemption'. His use of different metaphors for this belief shows clearly that he does not wish to make any one particular idea of this work of Christ part of his gospel; it is the cross which is the gospel, not a doctrine about it.

The rest of the letter (assuming for our present purpose that it is one letter) is full of exhortation, argument against opponents and appeals (in chapters 8 and 9 one for money for the poor in Jerusalem), and this means that there is a great deal of personal material. This is best drawn upon when a point in Paul's life and relations with others comes up for consideration, but it is well to make here once again a point which, for all its personal context, perhaps transcends in importance everything else which Paul teaches. This is the place of suffering and weakness in the life of a Christian, exemplified in the experience of Paul.

We have seen already that there is ample evidence in Paul's writings for great suffering which he endured at Ephesus; but the reader of Acts can hardly confine the tale to that city. Great and almost final as was the ordeal which Paul suffered in Ephesus, his whole mission seems to have been fraught with much trouble, hardship and danger. In a remarkable passage which we should not have had but for the anger to which the opponents of his gospel had provoked him Paul claims that these trials make him more than all others a servant of Christ. He lists them in 2 Cor. 11:21–27, but the very length of this list is apt to conceal the very important religious point which Paul is making here. In verse 30 he says, 'If boasting there must be, I will boast of the things that show up my weakness.' Towards the end of the letter he writes about the power of Christ in Christians and adds, 'True, he died on the cross in weakness, but he lives by the power of God; and we who share his weakness shall by the power of God live with him in your service'. This is the explanation of Paul's previous paradox in 12:10, '. . . when I am weak, then I am strong.'

Galatians

The trouble in Ephesus was left on one side when Paul wrote his letters to the Corinthians and he showed in them the great distress to which the situation in Corinth had brought him. This makes us forget for a moment what happened in Ephesus; but Paul did not forget it, and there was even yet more trouble: the judaisers whom we saw to be at work in Corinth had followed Paul round his Galatian Churches and it was there especially that they caused much trouble through their opposition to his gospel and its message of freedom, freedom from domination of the Law for all converts, and freedom from its very prescriptions for all Gentile converts.

Paul's opponents seem to have told the Galatians that he usually preached a different gospel from that which they had received from them, a gospel which included the necessity of circumcision (had Paul perhaps invited such a distortion of the truth by his circumcising Timothy?) and that he had preached to them an easier form of it which did not require circumcision, in order to make it more popular. In order to rebut this accusation Paul uses the same basic arguments as in the Corinthian correspondence, that his apostleship was through a call from the risen Christ, that he preaches a gospel neither of his own invention nor man-made but God-given, that he had been a persecutor of the Church and that his call emphasises its divine nature in its negation of his previous conduct and therefore the completely transcendent character of the authority for his apostleship. In Galatians Paul spells out the facts and we need not repeat them here, for they were described in the section about Paul's early work (pp. 80-1). It is the theological consequence of these claims that now concerns us.

This theology in Galatians is a matter largely of the Law as a system to live by and its replacement by the gospel. In his statements about it Paul is a little incoherent, through his anger at his opponents and their injustice, as well as because he believes they will undermine his work and therefore the status of his converts before God. His teaching can perhaps be put like this; the Law was a means of bringing men to the point where they accept Christ and salvation by union with him. It is impossible to say how Paul means that the Law did this. Was it by controlling men and preparing them morally and spiritually for the climax of God's revelation? Or was it by setting them a task of moral obedience which was so hard that they were driven to despair of their own ability to succeed in it; and in this despair Christ came and rescued them? In 3:24 he says that 'the law was a kind of tutor . . .' — and how should the rest of the sentence be translated? The New English Bible shows us the dilemma. Was the tutor merely 'in charge of us' (guarding but not teaching) or was he there 'to conduct us to Christ'? Paul often seems to suggest that the Law does conduct men to Christ but he is inconsistent about how; perhaps by bringing them to the point where they see their need, perhaps by teaching the same gospel of Christ but in a hidden way now only revealed, perhaps in other ways. The difficulty about the role of the Law appears in the paradoxical statement, clearly expressing something for which Paul has not quite found the right words and echoing not a little the truth he had so painfully learnt about suffering with and in Christ:

For through the law I died to law—to live for God. I have been crucified with Christ: the life I now live is not my life, but the life which Christ lives in me; and my present bodily life is lived by faith in the Son of God, who loved me and gave himself up for me. I will not nullify the grace of God; if righteousness comes by law, then Christ died for nothing (2:19-21).

Righteousness was and is popularly taken to mean the quality of correct action, or the quality of a life which exhibits always the correct action. The Jew has no difficulty about answering the question, 'What is the correct action?' for the Law prescribes it for every detail of life; yet many thinkers had already questioned whether a man could possibly be righteous *before God*. The book of Job, whose story is about human suffering, is also about the question whether Job, described as 'righteous' at the beginning of the story, could possibly plead this fact if, as he earnestly desires, he could appear in some heavenly court and state his case. No man, it is insisted, is righteous before God. Paul not only knew this but gives us in different places unsparing descriptions of how he came to see this with the clarity of despair. Now, to be righteous has two different aspects: one is that impossible for man, of being actually 'in the right', innocent of all offence. The other is of being 'right with God', regarded by him as innocent, in one place at least expressed as not being at enmity with God (though Paul never thinks of the hostility as being God's even if God shows his 'wrath'). It is Paul's great message that the latter, the status of man before God, does not depend after all on the former, his own righteousness. This righteousness is bestowed by the grace of God, that is the free gift of God. The gift as a gift did not cost man anything; but it cost God his Son. For this reason Paul sometimes expresses the atonement, or reconciliation between man and God as due to the sacrifice of Christ, and as the price he paid for men.

Such a sacrifice could hardly be of avail, even if the metaphor is acceptable at all (as it must fail to be to most modern men) unless it can be shown that the believer in it is somehow so connected with the sacrifice that he reaps its benefits. Hence there is some pretext for a Corinthian, for example, seeing the

Christian gospel as a form of mystery: the god has suffered and brought salvation for his adherents. Why bother any more about a life of morality? (Probably some Corinthians had never bothered over much.)

It could be said that for Paul no account of the matter is satisfactory unless the form of the 'adherence' is morally acceptable. It must mean a change, and a most profound change in the actual quality of life in the adherent. In his own case, as we have seen, it meant such close unity with the Person who had performed the act of redemption, atonement, sacrifice (Paul is not wedded to any particular expression) that he could describe it as a death and a new life. But the relation between Christ and Christian can be expressed in less dramatic terms; it is a matter of self-committal to the Redeemer, a unity of will and purpose and a readiness to suffer with him, as he had, as in a sense he still does through his unity with his followers. Hence it is a life 'in Christ', a typically Pauline phrase.

In Galatians Paul uses the term faith to describe this relation of the believer to God through Christ. He had adumbrated such a use in the Corinthian correspondence but now he draws out its meaning and emphasises its character as never before. This is the chief subject of chapter 3, and the way he handles it reveals the Jewish scholar, both here and in 4:21 f. It was a commonplace that Abraham was accounted a 'righteous man' before God. It was debated whether this was because he kept the Law even before it had been given or because he 'believed God'. Certainly he had *believed* God, but did not his virtue lie in *doing* what he did as a result of that belief? We shall find echoes of this point of view in the letter of James, but in the meantime we note simply that Paul in Galatians insists upon two things; one is that Abraham 'put his faith in God, and that faith was counted to him as righteousness' (3:6). The other thing is that it is a fulfilment of the promise made to Abraham that 'In you all nations shall find blessing' that 'it is the men of faith who share the blessing with faithful Abraham' (3:8 f.). Paul sums up this section of his argument with the words, 'For through faith you are all sons of God in union with Christ Jesus. Baptised into union with him, you have all put on Christ as a garment' (3:26 f.).

The status of sons is of the greatest importance to Paul. Sons are free but slaves must obey the Law, and here Paul

enters on a curious argument contrasting Abraham's sons,
'one by his slave and the other by his free-born wife' (4:22).
'And you, my brothers, like Isaac, are children of God's
promise' (4:28). As such, Christians must not share their
inheritance with those who are under the Law. This they will
do if they accept circumcision for 'every man who receives
circumcision is under obligation to keep the entire law' (5:3).
To this Paul adds the doctrine of the Spirit which he has
already taught in the Corinthian letters. The sons of God are
led by the Spirit but this is far from being the equivalent of
lawlessness, because 'the harvest of the Spirit is love, joy,
peace, patience, kindness, goodness, fidelity, gentleness, and
self-control. There is no law dealing with such things as these'
(5:22 f.). The Christian is urged then to abandon the Law not in
order to be free and led by his own spirit, as though free to do
'as the spirit leads' (which means 'as his own inclination leads').
It is the Spirit of God who is to lead him as the source of life
and the director of its course (5:25). The life according to the
Spirit is the same as the life of faith, and an alternative way of
describing the Christian life to saying that it is free and according to the Spirit is to say, as Paul does, with an echo of I Cor.
13, that 'the only thing that counts is faith active in love' (5:6).

The literary activity which has been summarised in these
last sections dealing with the Corinthian and Galatian letters
occupied Paul while he was at Ephesus, except that 2 Corinthians may have been written in Macedonia when he finally
left Ephesus in order to find Titus, to meet Timothy again, and
to discover from Titus how the Corinthians had responded to
his appeals. 2 Corinthians shows that they had responded with
affection and obedience; Paul wrote it to make clear his acceptance of their regret, and we can assume that Paul in due course
visited Corinth again as is narrated in Acts 20:2. The next verse
says that he spent three months there before leaving. These
three months produced his greatest work, the Letter to the
Romans, but before we consider it, two tasks await us. The first
is to try to determine as nearly as possible how to date the time
he was in Ephesus and endured so much trouble and wrote so
much out of the anguish of his heart; the second is related to it:
to weigh the possibility that this period included also some
letters manifestly written from prison.

Paul at Ephesus: Chronology

The last date mentioned was that of Gallio's arrival in Corinth which was probably 51–52. After the incident which occurred during Gallio's proconsulship and is therefore not datable exactly 'Paul stayed on for some time' (the Greek says 'many days', Acts 18:18) and then went on the journey which took him by way of Ephesus to 'Syria', i.e. to Caesarea, perhaps Jerusalem, and so to Antioch where again Paul spent 'some time' (a literal translation of the phrase in 18:23); he then travelled by land to Ephesus (19:1) — a laborious and slow journey of which Acts gives absolutely no details.

The date of Paul's arrival in Ephesus is therefore a matter of guesswork based on these all too vague references to time and events. It can hardly be dated before the end of 53 and it would be better if we could say about 54 or 55. He stayed in Ephesus two and a quarter years if we may trust Acts 19:8, 10, but 20:31 shows how imprecise such notices of duration are by making Paul refer to it as three years, which we should have thought far more likely from the impression we get of all that happened during the time he was either staying there or based on the city, leaving it for journeys to Corinth (and for all we know many other places) and returning. Indeed all this activity makes it hard to think when he can have had time to spend some of it in prison in Ephesus.

If we add the three months at Corinth we cannot make Paul's departure from Corinth and eventual arrival at Jerusalem (21:15) earlier than the summer or autumn of 58. This presents a famous problem. Paul became the prisoner of Felix, who was recalled to Rome to answer charges of misgovernment and was saved by the intervention of his brother Pallas, a freedman and favourite of Nero. Acts 24:27 says that 'when two years had passed, Felix was succeeded by Porcius Festus. Wishing to curry favour with the Jews, Felix left Paul in custody.' All this is very intelligible but it is probable that the two years should be understood as two years of the procuratorship of Felix and not Paul's imprisonment under him. In this way we can just about make a plan which means that Paul was his prisoner only a short time, and not for the whole of two years, which would much increase our difficulties. They are bad enough, for there are considerations which make our provisional dating impossible if we accept their force; Pallas, who saved Felix from the wrath of Nero, appears to have fallen from favour in 55 and so the very latest date for the handing over by Felix to Festus described in Acts 24:27 would be 55 also. Festus died in 61 and, as little is said by Josephus about his procuratorship, his accession has been dated 59, which would of course be the date on this basis for the handing over from Felix to Festus.

The later date alone gives any possibility of a reasonable Pauline chronology, and it must be accepted as nearer the truth than the earlier date. The puzzle about Felix and Pallas may be resolved if Pallas came back into favour in or before 59 and so was able to plead for Felix when the latter was re-called, or if Pallas's action was a guess on the part of our authorities (Josephus and Tacitus) or simply that the date suggested by Josephus is unreliable, as many of his dates are. We have now looked briefly at the dates possible for the events of Paul's life after he left Ephesus and Corinth, and have in this way brought him as far as his last visit to Jerusalem where he was arrested, the beginning of the imprisonment which was pro-bably ended only by his death. Later on we shall return briefly to the question of further dates for this latter end of his life, but must now go back for a short time to Ephesus.

Hard as it is to work out a chronology for Paul it seems that his stay in Ephesus — or perhaps the time when he was based on the city — must have occupied all or most of the years 54–58. This period must include also the visit to Corinth via Macedonia and the stay in Corinth for three months before Paul finally set out for Jerusalem. It is difficult indeed to find time for an imprisonment of Paul during this period, but the same is true of much else, including the second visit to Corinth implied so clearly by the Corinthian correspondence and entirely omitted in Acts. Any claim therefore that Paul may have written some letter or letters from an Ephesian prison must be made with diffidence but cannot be ruled out.

Colossians and Philemon

These two letters have perhaps the best claim, if any has a claim at all, to have been written in Ephesus. The latter was the capital and the largest city of the Roman province of Asia, the chief market centre of Asia Minor and the proud possessor of a huge temple to Artemis guarding an image supposed to have fallen from heaven. Inland from Ephesus were three towns in the valley of the river Lycus, forming a triangle, Laodicea, Hierapolis and Colossae. At all four places the Christian Church was established in New Testament times and persisted through subsequent centuries. In Paul's time the three in the triangle enjoyed close civic associations with one another and with Ephesus itself. Paul did not himself visit Colossae but it had been evangelised by one of his companions named Epaphras (Col. 1:7 and 4:12; Philem. 23) and the occasion of Paul's letter is the rise of some false teaching which threatened to remove Christ from his paramount position in the hierarchy of creation. If this matter is represented, as often in the past, in the language of theology later than Paul, it is stated in this form: that heresy was being preached to the Colossian Church; such terminology makes it much easier to argue, still in the the same vocabulary, that therefore some time must have elapsed between the evangelisation of Colossae and the writing of the letter. 'Heresies' are thought of as complete systems of belief which take time to develop.

Such a view entirely falsifies the picture; the basic culture of Colossae was Phrygian, but there were a number of Jews there, and the inhabitants must have been used to a mixture of religious ideas and cults, pagan and Jewish, and no doubt syncretistic as well. They may even have been familiar with a number of different schools of thought in Judaism, and one well-established theory is that those who were now altering the doctrine in which Christ alone was the way to God were— or had been—Essenes. This theory was put forward when our knowledge of the Essenes depended on notices in ancient authors and we possessed, as far as we knew, no literature which came from them; this makes it the more interesting and indeed the more impressive now that the Dead Sea Scrolls provide us, in the opinion of many scholars, with first-hand information about Essenes from Essenes.[4]

The theory may well be correct, but whether the new teachers of the converts were Essenes or not, they were in all probability

[4] J. B. Lightfoot argued this case and wrote an essay on the Essenes, which is still useful, in his edition of Colossians and Philemon, published by Macmillan and Co. first in 1875.

some Jewish sect. The situation in which the Church there had been formed was not simply one in which a number of naïve pagans were introduced for the first time to a true gospel but one in which a religious public, in part at least highly sophisticated, had accepted Epaphras's gospel as the most attractive and persuasive form of the kind of religion to which they had already been drawn. The sect which now attempted to persuade them to accept further doctrines may well have provided many of the converts, but now urged that salvation depended not only upon acceptance of Jesus as Messiah and Lord, but on various practices, and on holding the beliefs associated with them, which they had already followed when they were converted. These practices and beliefs included the observance of strict dietary laws and of a strict calendar. This would indeed be consistent with their holders being Essenes, but falls short of proving it.

Essenes believed also in angels, as did the new Colossian teachers; it may be rejoined that this was true also of Pharisees, but it was more characteristic of the Essenes to believe in a hierarchy of angels with different allotted functions in the creation. Whatever the provenance of this belief, it is interesting to find it part of the Colossian 'heresy' that angels seem to have been inserted into the scheme by which the believer attained to fellowship with God. The answer to this challenge provided by the letter to the Colossians may be put clearly by quoting one or two extracts; whereas the new teaching claimed that many spiritual treasures were to be had through these angelic agencies, 'God's secret . . . is Christ himself; in him lie hidden all God's treasures of wisdom and knowledge' (2:3). 'Therefore, since Jesus was delivered to you as Christ and Lord, live your lives in union with him' (2:6). 'The solid reality is Christ's. You are not to be disqualified by the decision of people who go in for self-mortification and angel-worship, and try to enter into some vision of their own' (2:18).

It is sometimes argued that there is evidence, in such passages as are briefly quoted above, for the presence among the Colossian Christians of gnostic teachers. The usual view about gnosticism has been that it constituted a heresy or series of heresies which arose after the orthodox line of thought had established itself in the Church, so that gnostics represented a deviation from the Church's teaching in various ways. Such a view seemed and still seems to many to be very reasonable, because our only evidence for full gnostic systems belongs to this later period in the Church's history, even though as early as 179 Irenaeus is writing his defence against gnostic heretics, and we know that gnostic systems flourished in the first decades of the second century. There is no question that in Colossae the beings we have so far called angels seem to have been regarded as of equal importance and equal divinity (if we can use such language without anachronism) with Christ, and that in their scheme he was in danger of losing his pre-eminence. It is in opposition to this conception that Col. 1:15 f. urges of God's 'dear Son' that 'He is the image of the invisible God; his is the primacy over all created things. In him everything in heaven and on earth was created, not only things visible but also the invisible orders of thrones, sovereignties, authorities, and powers: the whole universe has been created through him and for him', echoing the doctrine about Wisdom found in the book of Proverbs.

The conceptions revealed and contested here may all have come from Jewish sources and it is probably correct to identify the teaching with that of Jewish heretics; what then of the gnostic theory? The answer seems to be that Jewish belief in angels or powers, well known to be a source of later Jewish mysticism, was also one of the tributary streams which combined eventually to make up the great river of gnostic thought. Further than this we need not go, and it is more profitable for our purposes to examine briefly the positive doctrine which opposition to the importance of the powers has brought to clear expression here in Colossians. The passage quoted above goes on, 'And he exists before everything, and all things are held together in him' (1:17). Thus Christ is seen in a way analogous to that in which the Fourth Gospel conceives Christ as the incarnation of the Logos; the latter is described as 'God', but the noun is used almost adjectivally conveying more than 'divine' and yet not committing the author to a statement which would mean that the Logos exhausted the whole Being of God (p. 161). In Colossians the emphasis falls more upon the atonement and its consequences than on the 'mystery of the incarnation'. Christ 'is the head of the body, the Church' because he is 'the first to return from the dead' (1:18). It is therefore as the focal point of the *new* creation that Christ is considered here, and then, as a consequence, of the whole of creation. In this latter capacity he is described in language reminiscent, as we have seen, of the book of Proverbs; in fact, he is like, but greater than, the figure of Wisdom who according to the literature about this conception in the Old Testament and Apocrypha was with God as a kind of first assistant in his creative activity. But it is not only as the first to return from the dead (the Greek of 1:18, 'the firstborn from the dead' represents better the thought of the beginning of a new creative process) that Christ is supreme. He has conquered the powers not by his resurrection, though that was the sign of his conquest, but by his death. 'On that cross he discarded the cosmic powers and authorities like a garment; he made a public spectacle of them and led them as captives in his triumphal procession' (2:15).

A doctrine of baptism to be expressed in full in Rom. 6:1–11 makes its appearance in this letter, in connexion with the cross as a saving action: 'in baptism you were buried with him, in baptism also you were raised to life with him through your faith in the active power of God who raised him from the dead ... he has made you alive with Christ' (2:12 f.) and in 2:20, 'Did you not die with Christ?' The conception is clearly that the Christian has as it were a hidden life after he becomes a Christian by baptism into Christ. This hidden fact is to be revealed, that is, those who belong to Christ are to be revealed at his coming:

'Were you not raised to life with Christ? Then aspire to the realm above, where Christ is, seated at the right hand of God, and let your thoughts dwell on that higher realm, not on this earthly life. I repeat, you died; and now your life lies hidden with Christ in God. When Christ, who is our life, is manifested, then you too will be manifested with him in glory' (3:1–4).

The letter divides fairly easily into sections: 1:1–2:5 insists on the lordship of Christ over all other spiritual beings: 2:6–23 argues that the person baptised therefore owes no allegiance to any rules proclaimed on the authority of these other beings or their worshippers. 3:1–4, the passage just quoted, not only summarises the Christocentric doctrine but makes a ground for a further exhortation which is then extended in detail, 'Then put to death those parts of you which belong to the earth' (3:5); thus 3:1–4:6 is ethical teaching firmly based on doctrine. The last section 4:7–18 is concerned with practical matters to which we shall have to return.

For the moment we must be briefly occupied with the question of authorship. The letter claims to come from Paul and Timothy and we may expect by now that it would be full of Pauline language and thought, the colleague seeming to play always a very secondary part. In the case of this letter, the matter is complicated by the introduction of some vocabulary and ideas not before found in Paul. The most important appear in the Christological teaching and it may be argued that this is influenced by the special circumstances at Colossae; yet in forming the answer Paul, if it was he, breaks absolutely new ground with his teaching about Christ and his relation to creation. Perhaps most important, those little habits of vocabulary and expression which it seems betray the author of anything quite unwittingly are not present to the extent that they should be if on computer grounds we are to attribute this letter to Paul (the computer takes the author of Galatians as the norm for 'Paul'). If we remember that Paul himself had not apparently been to Colossae, we may well be tempted to say that he gave the gist of what he wanted to say to a lieutenant (Timothy?) who then wrote the letter — or the bulk of it — himself. The weakness of any such theory is that this would explain the different writing habits but not the important difference in doctrine. If, however, the interesting development in Christology may be explained as a development in the thought of Paul himself elicited by the false teaching in Colossae, then the theory of an assistant who was entrusted, in the manner of letter-writing in the ancient world, with the actual composition of the letter, may be acceptable.

This letter-writing convention often included the feature that the real author wrote at the end in his own hand a summary of what he had instructed his amanuensis to write. It should be observed that this was a variant on actual dictation; the latter was used apparently in Galatians, with Paul's own hand adding 6:11—end, and certainly in Romans where Tertius, the long-suffering secretary, whose inability to catch it all may account for some of the syntactical and even dialectical oddities, manages to insert his own greetings and tell us he was the scribe (Rom. 16:22). In Colossians this reconstruction will not account for all the facts, but the other practice by which the author gave only the substance to his amanuensis may do so. It is just possible therefore that Paul himself wrote Col. 4:7—end although verse 18 at the end rather implies that this verse is all he wrote.

Let us then assume the reasonableness of some theory which will ascribe effective authorship of Colossians to Paul; we have now to consider the occasion in Paul's life when he wrote it. The last section of the letter gives us much of the information on which to base our answer to this problem, but another letter of Paul also is intimately involved. Tychicus is evidently sent with the letter (4:7) and he is accompanied by Onesimus, a runaway slave whom Paul has converted and is returning temporarily to his former owner Philemon, apparently a citizen of Colossae. Then follow greetings which include the famous mention of Luke (verse 14) but, more to our present purpose, greetings from 'Aristarchus my fellow-prisoner'. (The New English Bible translation here uses the phrase, 'Christ's captive' which is not a strict translation but a paraphrase enabling those who wish to do so to understand the situation as one where the 'prisoners' mentioned are not literally prisoners but voluntarily enslaved to Christ; but the translation of verse 18 where Paul says 'Remember I am in prison' does not lend itself to such an interpretation.) Paul was then in prison and we have seen that there is a case for believing that he was imprisoned in Ephesus. The close association with Colossae, Laodicea and Hierapolis which is part of the background fits such a view admirably, and there is a further consideration of which this is true; a slave who had run away from his master in Colossae was more likely to have arrived in Ephesus than anywhere else, especially if Paul regarded it as a practical proposition to return him to his master with a request for his eventual further return to himself. We must now consider the other letter involved in this discussion.

The Letter to Philemon

Onesimus had evidently run away from his master Philemon, himself a convert of Paul and a Colossian. Paul had converted the slave also and Onesimus had become his faithful helper; at the same time as Paul sends his letter to the Colossians he sends also a brief personal letter to Philemon to say he is returning Onesimus and to ask that Philemon let him come back to be the servant of Paul himself, but now as a brother in Christ, just as he regards Philemon as being.

Here we must notice an ingenious theory about this brief personal — and altogether charming — letter which gives a live meaning to Col. 4:16 f. There Paul asks that the letter to the Colossians be read at Laodicea and 'the one from Laodicea' be read at Colossae, and asks also that Archippus be reminded to discharge the duty which Paul has placed upon him. The theory is that the letter we call Philemon was really addressed to Archippus (Philem. 1 f.) and that the request for Onesimus was made to him; moreover, that the letter we call Philemon is the letter from Laodicea, since it was intended to go via that town, to which indeed Philemon may have belonged, and not to Colossae.[5] There are a number of difficulties about this otherwise very attractive theory but it is unnecessary to detail them; there is not enough evidence to make us think that the natural interpretation of Philem. 1 f. is wrong. According to this Philemon is the person addressed, we may guess that 'Apphia our sister' is his wife and Archippus 'our comrade-in-arms' their son, and that their house was a 'house-church' (this last point being no guess — see verse 2).

It is therefore rather too speculative to identify the slave Onesimus with the future bishop of Ephesus known to Ignatius and to suggest that it may have been he who preserved Paul's letters and composed Ephesians as an introduction to the corpus. It is speculative, but we set the theory aside with regret because if true it links together a number of facts, including Ignatius's apparent wide use of such a short letter as Philemon, and indeed explains its survival.

Wherever Paul was imprisoned when he wrote these two letters he expected, or at least greatly hoped, to be released

[5] See the attractive small book by J. Knox, *Philemon among the Letters of Paul* (University of Chicago, 1935).

soon (Philem. 22). Thus Ephesus is possible, and Caesarea, otherwise suggested sometimes as the place of writing, less likely. Paul was then indeed a prisoner (Acts 23:33–26:32) and could have written letters from prison, for he seems to have been humanely treated. The theory can be elaborated to include the writing of Colossians, Philemon, the lost letter to Laodicea and even Ephesians, by any who are happy with the view that the last named was really written by Paul; on such a view the carriers of these letters made the overland journey made by Paul according to Acts 19:1 (of which we have already complained that it gives no details). This journey would pass eventually through the cities of the Lycus valley and on to Ephesus, and it must be admitted that Tychicus, the bearer of Colossians, is also the bearer of Ephesians (Eph. 6:21) if the latter is regarded as belonging to the authentic Pauline corpus. Such a view is beset with difficulties. Paul did not as far as we know entertain at Caesarea any hope of early release (had he not himself appealed to Caesar?) and Onesimus's escape thither is not as natural as to Ephesus. Finally, Acts gives us for the stay in Caesarea only a series of notices of short periods, amounting in all to only a few weeks at the most, unless we take the notice about Felix in 24:27 to mean that Paul was kept a prisoner by him for two whole years. Only with that interpretation can we accept such a theory of the provenance of Colossians and Philemon.

The conservative view has generally been that these letters, along with Philippians and Ephesians, and even with the whole of 1 and 2 Timothy and Titus, comprise the 'Captivity Epistles' and were all written from Rome during Paul's final imprisonment or imprisonments. It is possible that Colossians and Philemon do belong to this period and therefore that Onesimus did run as far as Rome. This is the view taken for Philippians, that it dates from very near the end of Paul's life and final imprisonment; but on balance we assign Colossians and Philemon to Ephesus. Picking up the threads of the story of Paul we recall that when he left Ephesus it was to travel via Macedonia to Corinth, with whose Church he was now reconciled but which he was never to see again.

Romans

While Paul was in Corinth for this final visit he intended to leave by sea in order, probably, to take the collection to Jerusalem. He then discovered a plot against his life which decided him to travel instead by land. It seems that it was while he was in Corinth but before this plot was discovered that he wrote the most famous of his letters, that to the Christians in Rome, for he says in Rom. 15:25 f., 'at the moment I am on my way to Jerusalem, on an errand to God's people there. For Macedonia and Achaia have resolved to raise a common fund for the benefit of the poor among God's people at Jerusalem.' Acts says nothing of the 'common fund' but as noticed earlier the companions mentioned at Acts 20:4 look as if they were the representatives for whom Paul had asked in 1 Cor. 16:3. The Corinthian correspondence and Galatians had prepared Paul to write a definitive thesis about his whole theology, and it seems that he wished to assert his authority as the apostle to the Gentiles by doing so and by sending a copy to Rome and, as we shall see, perhaps to other places also. The immediate occasion of a letter to Rome may only be guessed at. We do not know how the Church there was founded, and must deduce from the very lack of evidence that it grew from the arrival in Rome of unknown Christians from the east. It seems also to have included both Jews and former pagans; it has indeed often been thought that the letter is best understood if Paul was writing to the great city where more than one community existed within the Christian Church and that there may well have been quite separate Churches, or at least one Church which was composed entirely of Jewish Christians.

In our account of the letter we shall confine ourselves almost entirely to the theology contained in it, although this inevitably and very clearly implies the rival claims of Gentile and Jew within the Christian community. As the letter is comparatively long it will be necessary to abbreviate even a summary of it, and some of the more intricate arguments which do not contribute to its main flow may well be omitted from at least our first view.

The opening passages, eloquent in themselves and affording a good introduction to the study of the gospel according to Paul, can be thus passed over, because Paul himself resumes his theme clearly at 1:16, and it is there that we can begin our survey. Although the subject of the letter may be said to be righteousness, and the insistence that in its truth it is bestowed by God and cannot be acquired by man otherwise, Paul introduces his subject as 'the Gospel' (verses 2 and 16). 'It is the saving power of God for everyone who has faith' (1:16) — 'because here is revealed God's way of righting wrong' (1:17). 'Righting wrong' might be immediately misinterpreted by one brought up as a Jew, for whom this might well mean vindicating his nation to whom God had of old promised supremacy over other nations, and already granted it moral and spiritual superiority. Paul is going to take the other meaning, less obvious, that to right wrong God must remove guilt and bestow his own righteousness as a free gift. Thus freedom from guilt is a free gift and obtainable only by faith in God; it cannot be won by adherence to the Law which serves to show up sin and give a moral ideal and thus in one way to make man's task more difficult. In Christ God grants freedom from the Law in this sense, freedom from its condemnation. The Law does not bestow righteousness though it is righteous itself. Let us see in what way Paul presents the argument.

Although Paul is aware that a Jewish reader might misinterpret the conception, 'righting wrong' (here the Greek word means literally 'righteousness') he ignores this danger by painting a lurid picture of the wickedness of mankind, though he may well have been aware that the former Jews among his readers would think he was talking only of those wicked pagans. Two main points emerge; one is that Paul, true to his Jewish heritage, identifies the root cause of this immorality (which he details without squeamishness and calls by its true names, knowing nothing of the euphemism which would describe it as permissiveness) as idolatry. It is neglect of God that means moral chaos. The second point which emerges is that both Jew and Gentile are equally to blame, the Jew because his boasted superiority is a sham: mere possession of the Law and 'being a Jew' (being circumcised) is no use unless that superiority is shown in actual conduct whereas in fact the behaviour of many Jews causes the name of the God whom they worship to be blasphemed. The Gentile is equally without excuse because he does not lack a law by which to judge his conduct. Gentiles 'are their own law, for they display the effect of the law inscribed on their hearts' (2:14 f.). The often quoted 'they are a law unto themselves' is the old version of the first phrase in this passage; it is always misapplied, for it means the opposite of 'they acknowledge no law'. According to Paul, the Gentile does know what is right and what is wrong; but his neglect of God through his worship of other 'gods' plunges him in darkness (1:21).

It is no wonder that Paul finds himself at this point drawn aside from his main theme to try to face the question, 'Well, then, what is the advantage of being a Jew?' and he finds himself unable to say 'There is none', which would have perhaps been the obvious answer so far. The subject is here a red herring and we may attend to it when it recurs at chapter 9.

At 3:21 Paul begins an immensely important part of his answer to a kindred question. Instead of explaining what advantage it is to be a Jew he answers rather the question, 'If God did not give the way to righteousness by the Law, how did he give it, or how does he give it?' It is 'now, quite independently of law' that God's way of righting wrong 'has been brought to light'. (It is at first sight a little strange that the New English Bible used the revealing and helpful phrase, 'way of righting wrong' in 1:17 but here translates the same word, literally 'righteousness', by 'justice'; but it returns to 'way of righting wrong' at the beginning of verse 22. The implication is that God's justice consists in righting wrong and not in condemning.) Paul now states very clearly a summary of his whole belief:

> For all alike have sinned, and are deprived of the divine splendour, and all are justified by God's free grace alone, through his act of liberation in the person of Christ Jesus. For God designed him to be the means of expiating sin by his sacrificial death, effective through faith. God meant by this to demonstrate his justice . . . (3:23–25).

Paul's sense of need to justify his insistence that it is not through the Law, but through the faith that responds to God's free gift, that man is redeemed from guilt, makes him return to the question of the alleged superiority of the Jew again. In chapter 4 he makes good use of this necessity by facing the questions which he naturally imagines might be put to him, 'Surely you will admit that it is necessary to be a son of Abraham, a Jew, in order to be "righteous", for it is admitted by all that Abraham was regarded by God as righteous? And does not the righteousness of the Jew consist in being a true son of Abraham?' Paul faces these questions in such a way as to make the example of Abraham serve his own view.

Paul insists that it was no deed of Abraham by which the latter won his reputation, but scripture says that 'Abraham put his faith in God, and that faith was counted to him as righteousness' (4:3, quoting Gen. 15:6). Besides the main point Paul makes others: Abraham's righteousness was 'counted' to him. That is, it was the graciousness of God which allowed this status of Abraham, not what the patriarch had done. Similarly, no man *is* righteous but God by his grace may count him as such. Again, when this 'counting as righteous' was done, Abraham was uncircumcised, still not a Jew — and therefore the father of all nations, we might have expected Paul to say. In fact he uses here an argument which is given clearly and fully in Gal. 3:7-9, '. . . it is the men of faith who are Abraham's sons. And scripture, foreseeing that God would justify [i.e. 'right the wrongness of'] the Gentiles through faith, declared the Gospel to Abraham beforehand: "In you all nations shall find blessing". Thus it is the men of faith who share the blessing with faithful Abraham.' So here in Rom. 4:11, Abraham is not the father of all nations so much as 'the father of all who have faith'. A further argument is so surprising that at first it is difficult to grasp what Paul is saying; in fact it reveals, more even than those which he has used already, the essentially rabbinic character of his way of thinking things out; he claims that the faith of the Christian and that of Abraham are alike in being in 'the God who makes the dead live and summons things that are not yet in existence as if they already were' (4:17). This needs no explanation if it is a description of the believing Christian, but Paul applies it to Abraham on the ground that believing God's promise of the coming birth of Isaac involved the belief that God would bring to life again 'his own body, as good as dead (for he was about a hundred years old), and the deadness of Sarah's womb' (4:19).

The next chapter reveals Paul still using his own experience of suffering to show the great truth that God's power is shown in, or as applied to, man's weakness. He begins this chapter with an exhortation to patience under suffering but goes on to make a new use of his conviction about suffering and weakness, interpreting sinfulness as a form of weakness. 'For at the very time when we were still powerless, then Christ died for the wicked' (5:6). This 'is God's own proof of his love towards us' (5:8). What follows this majestic and gracious beginning is somewhat disappointing and obscurely expressed. What it comes to is this; through one man sin entered into the world and since then death, the consequence of sin, 'held sway from Adam to Moses' and indeed beyond this point, for 'Law intruded into this process to multiply law-breaking' (verses 14 and 20), but grace 'immeasurably exceeded' sin. Two main points are made, of which the first is the most important; Adam's sin was the occasion and means of sin and death (evidently thought of as 'powers') entering into the world. There is no doctrine here of 'original sin', for the reason why 'death pervaded the whole human race' is that 'all men have sinned' (5:12). Thus it seems that Paul would have approved of the sentiment in 2 Baruch 54:19 (latter half of first century), 'Adam is therefore not the cause, save only of his own soul, but each of us has been the Adam of his own soul.' The introduction of the malign powers, Sin and Death, was a matter of the first importance, though Paul does not enlarge upon it here. The other point he makes is that since the Law had multiplied individual transgressions and sin had spread over all mankind the effect of God's grace for good was immeasurably greater than that of Adam's for evil. It is an odd point to make since it is not obvious that this is the case and therefore the argument is a statement of faith rather than strictly speaking an argument likely to persuade men of God's gracious action.

The insistence on God's grace as alone the way to righteousness may have dire consequences for morality. We have already met the example of an adherent to a mystery religion who having secured, as he thinks, his salvation feels free to do as he pleases, perhaps partly because he has been convinced that salvation is a matter of the spirit, and therefore what the body does is no concern of his real self. In a way analogous to this the

Christian recipient of the divine grace may be tempted to say, as Paul himself frankly imagines at the beginning of the next chapter, 'Shall we persist in sin, so that there may be all the more grace?' (6:1). Paul faces this frankly but is unable to answer it logically with conviction. He recoils from the suggestion as if it were impossible for a real Christian seriously to entertain such a thought, and this is in practice probably the right way to answer it—by an appeal to loyalty which should have been aroused by the love of God for his gift of free forgiveness and by the love of Christ for having made this gift available. But it is not in logic enough to say as Paul does, 'No, no! We died to sin: how can we live in it any longer? Have you forgotten that when we were baptised into union with Christ Jesus we were baptised into his death?' (6:2 f.). In the whole passage 6:1–11 Paul enlarges on this theme and concludes with '... you must regard yourselves as dead to sin and alive to God, in union with Christ Jesus' (6:11). This is an appeal, not a statement, but it is based on previous sentences which sound like assertions of actual fact, such as, 'we were baptised into his death' or 'we died to sin'. Many might feel that it was all too easy to answer 'How can we live in it any longer?' with 'Just watch me!' The interpretation is open that by accepting baptism the new Christian committed himself to trying to live sinlessly; no doubt this is part of the truth and it might be added that the attempt would be assisted by the Holy Spirit whose leading he could welcome or refuse. So the argument could continue indefinitely, but it is impossible fully to reconcile the element in Paul which says, '*You are* free from your slavery to sin' and that which says, 'Act as free men who have given their allegiance to Christ and for whom therefore the life of sin is "unthinkable".' Paul does seem to urge a way of living which can be summed up by the imperative, 'Be what you are', but he does not resolve the logical difficulty involved.

Paul certainly tries to resolve the apparent paradox and in 6:15–7:6 explains that the new life in Christ may be compared to having exchanged an alien master for a proper master, or to being set free by death from a union by marriage with the old self for remarriage to Christ, in union with whom 'we may bear fruit for God' (7:4). Paul has now set himself another problem which indeed has been dogging him for a long time. This is to give an account of the Law which does justice to its own divine status in God's plan for his people but makes room also for the experience of its enslavement of those who try to live by it. He expresses the conviction that if there could have been life by law, it would have been by the Law of Moses, but he is overwhelmed by what had happened to him personally: 'The commandment which should have led to life proved in my experience to lead to death, because sin found its opportunity in the commandment, seduced me, and through the commandment killed me' (7:10 f.). Paul avoids the implication that the Law 'was the death of' him (7:13) by saying that 'it was sin that killed me'. In the famous passage 7:14−8:11 (the usual division which would see a natural break at 7:25 sadly interrupts the argument) he introduces another dimension into the conflict of Law versus Freedom in Christ; this is the hold which sin has upon the self. 'What I do is not what I want to do, but what I detest. But if what I do is against my will, it means that I agree with the law and hold it to be admirable. But as things are, it is no longer I who perform the action, but sin that lodges in me' (7:15−17).

Paul's feeling that sin possessed him like a living entity within him is akin to the idea of demonic possession but Paul does not mean to go as far as this in personification, real though the concept of Sin as a power was to him. He concludes that he is 'subject to God's law as a rational being' but in his 'unspiritual nature' he is 'a slave to the law of sin' (7:25). Paul has perhaps used the Jewish doctrine of the two inclinations in man here, but it is obvious that he found out the truth in that doctrine for himself by painful experience.

Paul does not reach a logically satisfactory account of the individual's struggle with evil in himself, not even an account which does justice to the total situation for a Christian; for he does not succeed in making clear to his readers or to himself whether the grace of God makes him free only from guilt or whether it liberates him also from sin. If not, he may incur further guilt even after the experience of forgiveness. This ambiguity is not resolved when he affirms, 'There is no condemnation for those who are united with Christ Jesus, because in Christ Jesus the life-giving law of the Spirit has set you free from the law of sin and death' although he introduces this as 'the conclusion of the matter' (8:1 f.). In the next two verses he makes it look as if he has been assured of the remission of guilt but not of the banishment of sin which was after all what he was trying to secure for his converts; for, assured of this freedom from sin, they would sin no more.

These next two verses are a very important turning-point in the course of Paul's thought; he returns to his doctrine of atonement here and claims that God provided his Son as a 'sacrifice for sin' and in so doing 'condemned sin to death' (New English Bible says 'passed judgment against sin'). Clearly the condemnation could not be real unless the sin so put to death by God had been located in the person who was in fact put to death. So Paul sets himself a tough christological problem: if Christ was the *locus* of sin for this purpose did he share the sinful nature of mankind? If one recoils from this thought it is hard to see how sin can have been 'put to death' in him, for if he was sinless, sin was just not there to be put to death. Paul does not impress when he says that God accomplished the atonement 'by sending his own Son in a form like that of our own sinful nature'.

The other subject which he introduces here is more promising; the picture he suggests of those for whom atonement has been made who are 'no longer under the control of our lower nature' but are 'directed by the Spirit' (8:3 f.). Here is a viable doctrine, not free from difficulties but intelligible and consistent with the experience of Paul and many other Christians. To 'live on the level of the spirit' is one way of describing the daily style of life of the man who has sensed his freedom from an old slavery to the routine which was a demonic maypole dance round the centre of himself. For Paul this freedom of the inner self is 'given', and its being given is bound up with the conviction that in the death of Christ the power or powers which held the self in thrall were overcome decisively. So vivid is such an experience that it must be described as if the Spirit is given for the first time in it, although a modern way of describing it might be that the Spirit has at last been set free within the person concerned.

The new level of life means inevitably a sense of a new relation to God. To live on this level is no longer slavery but to be in personal relation to God, to be in Pauline and New

Testament language a son of God. In 8:15–39 Paul explores some of the consequences of this situation. To begin with, this 'sonship' is not much more than a potentiality. Its full glory, like the Spirit, will be given in full only when God's purpose is complete. In this passage Paul extends his thought to include the destiny under God of the whole creation and aligns the sufferings of humanity with those of the creation, all being subject to 'the shackles of mortality'. While we are still under this bondage the Spirit assists us in 'our weakness'.

In the last verses of this chapter, 8:29–39, Paul expresses his response to this evidence of the love of God for those whom he has called into such close and mysterious fellowship with him through Christ by dwelling on the initiative of God: 'If God is on our side, who is against us?' Just before he asks this triumphant rhetorical question he has expressed his joy in an assertion, 'God knew his own before ever they were, and also ordained that they should be shaped to the likeness of his Son' (8:29). This extension of Paul's thought takes its rise therefore from the wonder he feels at the love of God who has taken the initiative in redemption. It does not rise from a deterministic philosophy. This is clear from Paul's explicit and exultant claim that none of the 'spirits or superhuman powers . . . the forces of the universe', felt by some to be malignant supernatural agencies which hovered over human destinies like grim fates, had any longer the power to 'separate us from the love of God in Christ Jesus our Lord' (8:39). Paul says therefore, admittedly in language which has unfortunately lent itself to deterministic doctrines of predestination, that the love of God shown in Christ has delivered those who belong to him and live the life of the Spirit precisely from determinism.

Such an eloquent peroration to the first eight chapters might lead the reader to expect that Paul might either stop here altogether or follow with a 'Therefore . . .' passage, proceeding with the practical consequences for daily life of such belief and conviction. There is a big 'Therefore' at the beginning of chapter 12 which would follow quite logically here, but before we reach it there are three chapters of a rather involved nature devoted to the subject, 'What then is the place of Israel in God's plan?' which has never been far from Paul's thoughts and has already found explicit expression in 3:1, where it was regarded as a red herring. Probably 9–11 are not, as some have thought, an insertion into the plan of Romans, for 12 follows as well upon them as it would at the end of 8; but they can be considered conveniently by themselves.

An important question arose for Paul in chapter 3, a question at first sight not connected with the main subject of that chapter and of 9–11. He uses the argument that Israel does not mean all Israel in the national sense, but those whom God chose from each generation; this makes him turn aside to try to justify what might seem arbitrariness and indeed unfairness in God. Such unfairness seems to be even rank injustice when Paul faces the question raised by his own conviction, supported by scripture, that the hardness of heart which moved Pharaoh's actions was God's doing. He says to Pharaoh, 'I have raised you up for this very purpose, to exhibit my power in my dealings with you, and to spread my fame over all the world' (9:17 quoting Ex. 9:16). Paul comments honestly enough, 'Thus he not only shows mercy as he chooses, but also makes men stubborn as he chooses' (9:18). This is a landslide away from the position of chapter 8 where any tendency towards predestination seemed due to Paul's sense of the love of God in choosing those who accept his gospel and his Son. Nor is the present passage made any more acceptable when Paul goes on to argue that it is not proper for man to question the ways of God.

Paul's total view is in fact much more attractive than this; he has begun by at last facing the question, 'What is the advantage of being a Jew?' and has given a good answer all the better because it lists not the advantages *to* the Jews but the advantages which have been given to the world *through* the Jews. Briefly these are: sonship, splendour of the divine presence, the covenants, the Law, the temple worship, the promises, the patriarchs and, as far as natural origin is concerned, the Messiah. He proceeds, less successfully, saying that the apparent arbitrariness which would limit the privileges is really a sign of God's mercy, for his plan was to bestow the advantages on a people formed from those who accept his Son, the new and, Paul argues, only true Israel. The argument is complicated by Paul's manful attempts to show by scriptural quotations that this was always the true understanding of God's purpose, even that the gospel was present in the ancient scriptures.

In chapter 11 Paul does come at last to an honest facing of the question as it concerns 'Israel according to the flesh', i.e. the actual nation of Israel, who may seem to have been rejected by God because the nation itself rejected the Messiah. He believes that it is God's purpose that their 'falling-off' should be a means to their acceptance! This extremely paradoxical idea is explained by the argument that the consequent grafting-in of Gentile stock into the true Israel — regarded as impossible without the falling-off of Israel — will stir unbelieving Israel into 'acceptance' through envy of others receiving an inheritance meant for them.

Paul is for modern readers not at his best here, but when he returns to the mainstream of his argument, he is not only once more readable but perhaps for many modern readers at his very best. In Chapters 13–15 he draws out the consequences of Christian belief for ethics. Details need not be given here; Paul deals with conduct within the Church, towards individuals outside, and towards the state. He is in the usual sense of the word no revolutionary; to be so would be forbidden by his being a Christian. For the Christian principle of obedience to civil authorities is derived partly from Jesus himself, and partly from the section of Pharisaic thought with which Jesus may be said to have been in agreement, though he apparently thought out his position more thoroughly than they. They accepted the necessity of obedience to authority in the political sphere, he saw it as a positive duty. Paul follows him, but to an extent which cannot be shown now to have been intended by Jesus and may not have been. To render to Caesar what belongs to him and to God what belongs to him allows room for further argument when the question is asked, 'What if the two clash?' Paul, no doubt strongly influenced by his eschatological convictions, does not apparently think they can clash; for the 'existing authorities are instituted by' God (13:1). Before this is dismissed by a generation which sees revolution as the primary virtue, it is fair to remember that Paul had far more reason than most to be a thorough and relentless rebel against authority, for he had suffered at its hands bitterly enough.

If this be remembered when we read these chapters close to the end of his letter, his temperate urging of the duty of tolerance and respecting the other man's point of view is shown up for what it is—remarkable consistency of loving in a fiery temperament which must have severely tested it.

Some slight but significant signs which cannot be detailed here suggest that very early Romans existed in at least two forms, and that only one of them was destined for Rome. One very obvious sign which can hardly be called slight gives the impression that the letter, or rather one form of it, must have been intended for the Church of Ephesus. This is the final chapter 16, containing a host of greetings which not only often suggest when studied in detail that they are intended for friends in Ephesus, but do so by their very number. It is a very feasible theory therefore that Paul recognised in his own letter a statement of value for any Church, and saw to it that it was despatched to more than one. There can be no doubt that in the later part of his ministry Ephesus was his main centre; this impression is strengthened if we can regard Colossians and Philemon as written from there to a surrounding district which had been evangelised under his direction from Ephesus. In any case it was the centre of Paul's dealings with Corinth and probably with the Galatian Churches, an experience which caused him to develop so much of the theology which he was later to put into Romans, a theological statement which has had as immeasurable an influence on western civilisation as the spread of Christianity itself.

Paul's Last Journeys

Paul hoped to visit not only Rome but afterwards also Spain (Rom 15:23 f.), perhaps because he saw in such a programme the completion of a task which meant travelling to the 'end of the earth', that is the 'western boundary' of the civilised world, practically coterminous with the Roman Empire. We have already given advance mention to his journey from Corinth to Jerusalem when discussing the possible dates for his arrival there. James received him cordially but warned him of the danger he was in, suggesting a way of putting himself in the right with Jewish Christians in the city (Acts 21:18–26), but in the event it was non-Christian Jews who caused his arrest into protective custody by a Roman officer (Acts 21:27–40). He thus became the prisoner of Felix, and then of Festus, who sent him for trial to Rome.

It has often been suggested that the author of Acts must have been not a physician but a seaman; there are various scraps of evidence for this but the most substantial is perhaps that the author of Acts gives so full and circumstantial, not to say technical account of the journey to Rome by sea, and of the famous shipwreck which landed Paul and his companions in Malta, whence they came finally to Rome (Acts 27-28). The question of the date of Paul's arrival in Rome depends upon that given for his arrival and arrest in Jerusalem; this we saw to be a major problem, but we were inclined to make it about 59 (the same year as Felix handed over to Festus, not two years before he did so, on the ground that the two years of Acts 24:27 are those of the office of Felix, not of Paul's imprisonment with him). Thus Paul left Judaea a prisoner towards the end of 59, too near the end for safe sea travel as he thought and, as it turned out, rightly. Let us suppose he arrived in Rome in 60 or 61. The two years of Acts 28:30 then brings the story near to the time of his death in the persecution following the fire in Rome in 64, according to the widely accepted tradition. It is therefore now appropriate to consider briefly the letters which he wrote as a prisoner in Rome.

Chapter IV

The Captivity Epistles

TRADITION assigns to this category Colossians and Philemon, Ephesians, Philippians and the Pastoral Epistles, that is 1 and 2 Timothy and Titus. Colossians and Philemon we have ventured to put into the period when Paul was at Ephesus, and have given some account of them. Ephesians is so widely regarded as post-Pauline that it must be reserved for treatment by itself; the Pastorals also notoriously fail to satisfy all the criteria of Pauline authorship in the judgment of many students of the New Testament. Philippians, the only letter left after this preliminary sifting, fits fairly obviously into the period when Paul was a prisoner in Rome.

Philippians

This letter contains not only clear references to Paul being a prisoner when he wrote it but also to his being in Rome. In 1:13 the word translated 'headquarters' by the New English Bible is almost certainly really a reference to the Praetorian Guard, the soldiers rather than the building or other people associated with it. These were present at Rome and only at Rome, evidence to the effect that there were similar regiments elsewhere being now interpreted otherwise. 'Those who belong to the imperial establishment' (literally, 'Caesar's household') also hardly makes sense except as a reference to the establishment in Rome (4:22). With this evidence in mind it is far from difficult to make excellent sense of the letter.

Paul shows some weariness and sadness in spite of his own cause for rejoicing (that the gospel is being taken notice of and widely and boldly preached) and his exhortation to the Philippians to rejoice in 4:4, if we follow the usual translation (but the New English Bible may well be right to translate as the expression of a wish). He wishes 'to depart and be with Christ' as far as he himself is concerned (1:23). This is not in the least evidence that Paul had abandoned his eschatology, but evidence for his having begun to entertain the possibility that the coming of the Lord might be delayed beyond the time of his own death. For in 3:20 f. he can still write about the Christian expectation of 'our deliverer to come, the Lord Jesus Christ'; and in 1:6 he has already spoken of 'the Day of Christ Jesus'. He would regard himself as awaiting the resurrection 'in Christ', consistently with the teaching he gave in 1 Thes. 4:13–18 (p. 90). Most of the letter is personal and given over to encouraging the Philippian Church to remain steadfast through the trials which he knows are theirs as well as his: '... you have been granted the privilege not only of believing in Christ but also of suffering for him. You and I are engaged in the same contest; you saw me in it once, and, as you hear, I am in it still' (1:29 f.).

The religious value of suffering as a Christian leads Paul on to a famous passage in which he states a fundamental principle of the life of a Christian, 'Let your bearing towards one another arise out of your life in Christ Jesus' (a less emphatic alternative translation does not change the meaning). In what follows Paul traces the divine coming down and returning to glory: Christ was of 'divine nature' 'from the first', 'but he made himself nothing'. He 'accepted ... death on a cross. Therefore God raised him to the heights' (2:5–11). Thus a Christological statement of great importance, saying that Christ began with a divine nature of which he divested himself in his desire to obey God, is employed rather to illustrate the necessity for humility on the part of Christians than for its own sake. For this reason and because Pauline vocabulary does not elsewhere include some terms vital to the passage, it has often been argued and is now widely accepted that this is a pre-Pauline hymn which he has quoted. Although some do not believe a word of this theory, it bears witness to its eloquence and marks it as a passage very precious for Christians.

A curious feature of the letter is that at the beginning of chapter 3 Paul bids his friends farewell and then goes on as if he has not done so; moreover he goes on with a somewhat bitter passage against judaising Christians such as he had to contend with in Corinth and Galatia. This 'circumcision' party he calls 'those who insist on mutilation', a phrase made only a little less odd for the circumciser of Timothy by his subsequent protestations in a manner reminiscent of 2 Corinthians. In 3:4–8 he lists impressively the grounds upon which he might boast of being a true Israelite himself and then says, 'I count it so much garbage, for the sake of gaining Christ and finding myself incorporate in him . . .' The abruptness is curious, but the consequent theories that Philippians is not a single letter but an amalgam of two or three may be countered by showing that there is a certain scheme and balance in the writing in its present form. In the first part Paul enjoins a certain imitation of Christ, but does not wish this to be understood in the terms in which others might interpret it, and so balances it with the exhortation towards the end of the letter 'to follow my example'. Paul does not perhaps take over much care to avoid misunderstanding, and this sentence invites criticism on the grounds that Paul thinks too highly of himself. But criticism is silenced when we remember that a little earlier he has made plain his disclaimer to 'have already achieved all this' (3:12). To follow Paul is to follow Christ in abasing himself, in accepting death in hope of resurrection. Thus we can forgive the boasting which is apparent only, and recall that Paul was writing in prison as a 'prisoner of Christ'.

The circumstances in which the letter was written may be seen in a little more detail; 2:17 shows again that Paul was *expecting* death ('if my life-blood is to crown that sacrifice which is the offering up of your faith . . .') but nevertheless *hoping* for release ('I am confident, under the Lord, that I shall myself be coming before long') (2:24). The link between Philippi and Paul was Epaphroditus, himself apparently a Philippian, but Paul has with him Timothy, who is a co-author, and he thinks he may send Timothy to Philippi soon. These circumstances will recur to our minds when we come to give some account of the Pastoral Epistles.

The Pastoral Epistles

If these letters are approached with the wish to find Pauline doctrine and Pauline characteristics in them, they cannot but give some surprise. There is no fire, little confidence, only rather formal modesty, above all no sense of 'pressing on' but a pervasive sense of consolation, not to say digging in. There is also a great difficulty attached to trying to find places for them in the outline of Paul's life. So great is this that some have supposed a release of Paul from imprisonment, further travels in the east, rearrest and final imprisonment and death. Sometimes Rom. 15:23 f. in which Paul expresses hope to go on from Rome to Spain, together with faint echoes of this hope in the Muratorian Canon, Clement of Rome and Ignatius, are used to support this rather desperate theory in spite of evidence being required by it for journeys in the east and not in the extreme west. The theory, which does not deserve detailed exposition, meets the difficulty about a place in Paul's travels for some of the references in the Pastorals by the notion that during the time of his release he wrote I Timothy and Titus; then during his second imprisonment he wrote Colossians and Philemon, Philippians and 2 Timothy.

The best way to tackle the problem of the origin of these letters is to look first at their contents and to analyse them a little. We then find that 1 Timothy and Titus have many parallels between themselves and with other epistles, both Pauline and non-Pauline. This applies to the subject-matter of ethics and of Church order and discipline. These two subjects alternate roughly with another easily recognisable subject, exhortation to sound doctrine. This latter category is prominent in 2 Timothy but not the others, the rest of the material being personal, and the tone of 2 Timothy being far more that of a personal letter than that of the other 'letters'.

The passages on ethics, dealing with the proper place and conduct of men, women, families, widows and slaves read always as though there is a much more settled life for Christians, much more institutionalised than in the period when Paul was building up the Churches from the beginning. This sense of settled existence is increased when we turn to the passages which exhort to sound doctrine; it is intensified still more when we read those on Church order. Such analysis may be summarised in this way: in 1 Timothy, exhortation to sound doctrine, 1:3–20; 4:1–16; 6:3–21; Church order, 2:1–8; 3:1–13; 5:1—6:2. This leaves very little other material, mostly of an ethical character. In 2 Timothy, exhortation to sound doctrine, 1:13–14; 2:1—3:9; 3:12–17; 4:2b–5a. The rest is personal. In Titus, exhortation to sound doctrine, 1:10–16; 2:11–15;

3:3–11; Church order, 1:5–9; 2:1–10; leaving only a negligible amount not classified.

The character of the writings is already partly revealed; let us take the sound doctrine element first. In certainly genuine Pauline letters there are elements of 'tradition' but these are small, concise and of the greatest importance, such as that which gives the material which Paul had received and already passed on orally to the Corinthians, mentioned in 1 Cor. 15:3–8. Such tradition is there made the starting-point for developing original thought, not regarded as doctrine beyond which one must not go. In the Pastorals sound doctrine is already a given deposit which is to be guarded unchanged — 'Timothy, keep safe that which has been entrusted to you' (1 Tim. 6:20) is typical. This deposit is to be preserved against speculation which seems to be rife, to come from Jewish sources and to be incipient gnosticism, weaving fantastic theories described aptly enough as 'godless myths' (1 Tim. 4:7).

There is another characteristic feature of the Pastorals connected with sound doctrine: only in them do we meet the formula, 'Trustworthy the saying —' to introduce, perhaps sometimes to conclude, a favourite piece of teaching. It occurs in 1 Tim. 1:15; 4:9; 2 Tim. 2:11; Titus 3:8; and perhaps also at 1 Tim. 3:1 where however the translators of the New English Bible have adopted a reading which means 'A popular saying —' (elsewhere their translation of the formula lacks the conciseness of the original, and here they have, 'There is a popular saying'). The word translated 'saying' here is *logos* whose special use we shall find in the Fourth Gospel. There Jesus is the incarnate *Logos* or Word, of God. In the Pastorals some traditional material, not known as scripture in the established sense, evidently contained a number of *logoi* (the Greek plural) which possessed for the believer saving power. Thus in Titus 1:9 the whole Christian tradition is called 'the trustworthy *logos*' (New English Bible here condenses the full phrase, literally 'the teaching of the true *logos*', into 'the true doctrine'). The Pastorals therefore have a high doctrine of tradition which the author seems to regard, as others in later generations have regarded scripture, as possessing in itself saving power. This would hardly have been possible for Paul, or for the author of the Fourth Gospel for whom the *Logos* primarily means Christ himself; though *Logos* also includes his teaching, even this teaching mainly concerns himself and who he is.

The Church order element is even more surprising. Paul's remarks in this sphere, in certainly genuine epistles, are directed to securing order in a fluid situation; while he commends respect for those who are natural leaders in the community he says nothing of the qualities required for a bishop, presbyter or deacon. In fact these terms are mentioned outside the Pastorals by Paul only once, when in his opening of the letter to the Philippians he addresses the 'bishops and deacons'. The word presbyter never occurs in Paul. These assertions are made on the assumption that speeches ascribed to Paul in Acts cannot be used as evidence for his vocabulary; if they could, the picture would be changed slightly but definitely with regard to presbyters, but give us only one exception for bishop. In the Pastorals on the other hand the qualifications for all three, with an implication in Titus that bishop and presbyter are synonymous, are carefully and thoroughly laid down.

The impression grows that these writings belong to a time when the Church has become more of an institution than previously, and the doctrine of the ministry has become a matter within the realm of order and discipline rather than of the doctrine of the Spirit and his gifts. This impression is strengthened when we consider the qualifications for office in the Church which are urged as essential, for these include abstention from drink and brawling as well as wanting to do the job for love not money. We have to imagine a time when not only have such abuses grown up but when the conception of a paid ministry had established itself. This must be in the sub-apostolic age; when Paul was in close contact with his Churches it is true that he had enough trouble with them, but afterwards it seems certain that they entered upon an age of real decadence. His own speech in Acts 20:18 f. to the presbyters of Ephesus, for whom he sent without revisiting Ephesus itself as he passed on his way to Jerusalem, shows that either he foresaw a decadent future or there was a tradition that he foresaw it. In either case the probability is that he would not have been represented as uttering the dire prophecies which the speech contains if his author had not known that they had been fulfilled ('I know that when I am gone, savage wolves will come in among you and will not spare the flock. Even from your own body there will be men coming forward who will distort the truth to induce the disciples to break away and follow them', Acts 20:29 f.). John 10:12 f. deals with the same subject, for the hireling is the minister who does not care for the flock and allows divisions in it, in contrast to Jesus himself who alone can maintain unity.

It seems clear that the absence of an impression of vital argument and developing doctrine and the presence of the impression that things have gone seriously wrong date these letters, or the bulk of them, to a period after the death of Paul. The author used the authority of his name and copied some of his vocabulary (without its fire) in order to arrest the decline. He has the insight to see that the ministry which has now grown up must be given honour for the sake of preserving the truth in the Church; and that this honour will be forthcoming only if its holders are men whom it is possible to respect.

The occasion for writing these tracts, as we may now call them, is therefore clear. The question of the authorship remains a mystery. If they are not Pauline, why the personal element in them? The most attractive solution of this problem seems to be that part of the letters, or at least of two of them, 2 Timothy (in which so much personal material is found) and Titus, are genuine Pauline fragments to which an author who had Paul's Churches' welfare at heart and who possessed a fragment or fragments, added to them in a manner which made the best use of the authority of Paul's name that he could. He wrote in the time after Paul's death, indeed probably as much as thirty or forty years afterwards, and did not intend to deceive anyone; but by the device of pseudonymity he conveyed what he thought Paul would have said in the situation of that later time.[1] If there is anything in this theory, we may see Paul's farewell letter to Timothy, written when the apostle saw that his own death was imminent, preserved in 2 Timothy, revealed most clearly at its end, which includes 4:6–8 and probably

[1] This theory was presented by P. N. Harrison in *The Problem of the Pastoral Epistles* (O.U.P., 1921) and slightly recast in his article, 'The Authorship of the Pastoral Epistles' in the *Expository Times*, LXVII, 3 (Dec. 1955).

4:14-18. Verses 9-13 illustrate our difficulty for they seem by contrast to envisage release and further activity as a real possibility; perhaps they belong to another fragment, part of an earlier letter. There are then details into which it would take too long to go, and we must be content to hope that we have here genuine farewell words from Paul to his close friend Timothy.

The latter was with Paul when they wrote Philippians, probably from a Roman prison. Timothy's part authorship does not seem to have been very real for it is obviously Paul who says in Phil. 2:19, 'I hope ... to send Timothy to you soon.' Perhaps he did, and so Timothy was in the east to receive the farewell note which may be disinterred from 2 Timothy. If this is correct, it is interesting to notice that in Phil. 2:17 Paul wrote, '... if my life-blood is to crown that sacrifice which is the offering up of your faith, I am glad of it ...' and uses exactly the same metaphor in 2 Tim. 4:6, '... already my life is being poured out on the altar' (in Greek the same actual words are used, the turn of phrase referring to the custom of pouring a libation to accompany a sacrifice). Thus Paul would be referring to his own death, which he saw now to be imminent and inescapable.

If the authorship provides a puzzle, so does the question of where these tracts were written. If the theory of their origin which has been outlined so briefly here has anything to commend it, since the tracts might have been sent as letters to any of the Pauline Churches, the place from which they were sent and the place where they were composed must both remain problems too hard to solve.

Ephesians

This is at first sight obviously one of the captivity letters, there being clear references to this situation in 3:1, 4:1 and 6:20; slightly deeper study immediately brings its surprises: it is not just that some manuscripts, but that with virtual certainty the earliest form of the true text omitted 'in Ephesus' in the opening address. The sentence might then mean '... to God's people contemporary with myself'. For the phrase 'those who are in Ephesus' if robbed of 'in Ephesus' and reduced to 'those who are' is like 'the existing' in 'the existing authorities' in Rom. 13:1 ('the powers that be' of the older translations). Thus the writing might be either a circular letter intended to be taken or sent round a number of Churches, or never intended for any particular Church or Churches but to be an essay or tract for all Christians. If considered as the second it may also be considered as an introduction to the Pauline corpus when all Paul's letters were collected together and seemed to require an introduction summing up the whole of Paul's gospel and teaching. How far the letter does that may be judged a little better when an account of its contents is given. For the moment we may continue with critical matters.

Paul had many friends in Ephesus which, as we have seen, was for a considerable time his main centre. Yet this letter contains no salutations to individuals at all. Again, Marcion (c. 150) knew it as the letter to the Laodiceans, but he may have been speculating from the hint in Col. 4:16. The teaching is not contrary to Paul's as known from other letters but in some of this teaching and above all in methods of expression and style it is unlike him. The vocabulary is largely Pauline, though some familiar words are rare, and others lacking altogether; moreover, there is also an extensive use of non-Pauline words and phrases. The relation to Colossians is very close indeed; Tychicus according to Col. 4:7 was the bearer of that letter and he is apparently also of Ephesians (6:21). Yet Ephesians does not develop the Christology which is characteristic of Colossians and which implied Christ's pre-existence. It uses some of the Colossians vocabulary, but oddly; for some key words common to both letters carry a different meaning or at least receive different application in each letter. This is true but not so completely as is sometimes claimed. For example, 'fullness' in Colossians is said to mean the fullness of divinity in Christ but in Ephesians it is the fullness of Christ in his body, the Church (cf. Col. 1:19 and 2:9, where N.E.B. translates by 'complete being'; with, for example, Eph. 1:23). This is a point to which we shall shortly return.

There is a most interesting and perhaps curious difference between Ephesians and previous letters of Paul; Gentiles are firmly within the Church and so far from there being controversy about the relative place of Jew and Gentile, the fact that they are united in one body is not only regarded as a sublime cause for thankfulness but is the very heart of the gospel. This is found in 2:11–3:6 with which we may contrast the tortuous arguments in Rom. 9–11 to render this idea palatable to both Jew and Gentile. Another feature which may well betray a period later than Paul is the appeal to the authority of apostles and prophets as though ancient and established founders of the Church (2:20 and 3:5). Again, with regard to the ministry we get a surprise: in 4:8–12 the chief gift of Christ to his followers consists of his ministers in the Church. The doctrine of the Church is very high, that is, it is regarded as enjoying a most honourable place in God's plan and is considered as an entity specially sanctified by Christ in such a way that the sinful individuals who compose it are almost forgotten.

No one of these features would render by itself the letter to be certainly non-Pauline. The arguments are often said to have a cumulative effect. This is largely true and there are considerations, such as style — or, better, writing habits — which suggest that Paul himself cannot have been the author. The developed view of the ministry is a borderline case: Paul could have thought in this way, but it seems more natural that someone who unconsciously extended Pauline thought will have done so. One argument seems on the other hand to be thoroughly exaggerated and even quite wrong; this relates to the key words alleged to have been used in ways quite different in Colossians and Ephesians. The suggestion is whoever wrote Colossians, it was an imitator who wrote Ephesians, one who liked the vocabulary but did not fully understand it. For the sake of example, apply this to the concept of 'fullness': if Christ possessed the 'fullness' of divinity (Colossians) is it not natural that he and he alone can fill the Church with the same divine fullness (Ephesians)? The N.E.B. translation of 1:23 is in fact not certainly a fair one, implying as it does just this point; but the logic seems to be natural enough, and the slightly different use of a technical term consistent with identity of authorship.[2]

We may now benefit from a brief outline of the letter's argument; the address, 1:1 f., is followed by a long *berakah* (or 'blessing' of God in thankfulness for something he has made or done) for the act of redemption through Christ. At the end

[2] For an up-to-date summary of work on Ephesians see J. C. Kirby, *Ephesians, Baptism and Pentecost* (S.P.C.K., 1968).

there is a reference to 'you too' having become 'incorporate in Christ and received the seal of the promised Holy Spirit'— a reminder of the addressees' baptism. 1:15–23 follows with a prayer for the full realisation of the consequences of this redemption by believers. 2:1–10 tells of the redemption of man from sin into a new relation with God and 2:11–22 of the reconciliation of Jew and Gentile in the Church, the Body of Christ.

Paul is agent and servant of this work of God (3:1–13) and 3:14–21 is a prayer for the full realisation of God's work, ending with a doxology. 4:1–16 is an appeal to maintain this unity in the Church's life, and to realise it to the full. Mingled with this are doctrinal passages showing God's work for unity: Christ fills the whole universe and his Body. 4:17–6:9 can be read as a fluent and straightforward sermon. It is an exhortation (beginning with 'Therefore . . .') to the moral life of a Christian. Abandon all pagan ways and follow the Christian way (4:17–5:2); avoid all sexual and other licence by partaking in the Christian fellowship (5:3–20). 5:21–33 suggests that the writer did not take marriage as a metaphor for the relation of Christ to his Church so much as discover the true nature of marriage from that relation. Husband-wife is like Christ-Church and part of the order of grace as well as of creation.

6:1–9 describes the duties of children, parents, slaves and masters which may be said to complete the matter of the sermon. But to it is added a very eloquent peroration—in the battle with evil use the whole of the armour which God supplies (6:10–20). Then the letter closes with the reference to Tychicus already mentioned (6:21 f.) and the final valediction (without names!), 6:23 f.

This account fails to do justice to one or two passages which must now be considered. First of all, there are those which (contrary to what is often said with great lack of understanding) reflect the eschatological background in the author's mind: Christians are 'sealed' (marked in baptism as belonging to Jesus) as a 'pledge that we shall enter upon our heritage' (1:14) and are urged to 'Use the present opportunity to the full, for these are evil days' (5:16)—no doubt regarded as those of the Messianic woes preceding the final deliverance. Again 6:13, if translated literally, refers to 'the evil day'. This means a particular day, again part of the woes, the day when persecution meets you before the final deliverance.

Secondly, there is the passage which seems to teach something about both the ascension of Christ and his descent into Hades after his death (4:7 f.). But it is probable that the meaning is not 'to the regions beneath the earth' but 'down to the very earth' (New English Bible): it has even been argued that the descent may mean, or include, the notion of Christ's coming to Christians in the eucharist. Certainly the way the passage continues suggests that the descent is thought of as after the resurrection and ascension and to be for the purpose of giving gifts to the Church, here strikingly headed by apostles, prophets, evangelists, pastors and teachers.

Thirdly, 5:14 contains a quotation, though that it was from a hymn, as the New English Bible so confidently translates (or rather inserts), is debatable. However that may be, the words 'Awake, sleeper, rise from the dead, and Christ will shine upon you' magnificently express the situation of someone just baptised and bidden to awake from the sleep of (spiritual) death into the life and light of Christ. Converts in the days of the early Church (we do not know how early in its history) were often required to wait, keeping vigil before the sunrise of Easter Day when in the context of a eucharist they were baptised. Eph. 5:14 may not have been a hymn, but may well have been spoken to those baptised on such an occasion. We may conclude by giving the references to those passages where the close relation of Christ to his Church is expressed with unique intimacy in this letter; they are 1:22; 4:15; 5:23.

Ephesians seems to be best regarded as an eloquent tract or sermon based on the idea of Christian membership of the Church loftily conceived, perhaps deriving from a baptismal sermon or indeed to be identified with one. The author draws on ideas which cannot be properly called non-Pauline, even though there is evidence that Paul did not actually write it himself. It does not seem possible that it was originally sent as a letter to the Ephesian Church, yet what can be then said about the personal touch, the mention of Tychicus? Once again we are puzzled, but must remember that the device of pseudonymity is not meant to deceive in any sense which in those days would strike anyone as reprehensible. Some follower of

Paul may well have written it, but for what immediate purpose it is too speculative to say. For example, why should a collection of Paul's letters require such an introduction?

In fact, in Ephesians Pauline theology receives something of a final rounding-off. The essence of his thought lies in his having experienced and seen as paramount for all men the initiative of God; God saw the plight of man and provided in Christ both the demonstration of evil conquered and the means, that is faith, by which to appropriate the prizes of that conquest. Paul saw the conquest as ushering in a new age whose inception was proved by the event of the resurrection, itself the beginning of the resurrection of the righteous who were destined to share the new age with Christ, who is at the same time designated as the coming saviour and judge by having been raised from the dead. The form of Paul's gospel is thus tied to his belief in the unrolling of a series of events and to his interpretation of them in the terms of his own eschatological beliefs; but his sense of God's love and of the companionship of Christ was so real that he evolved perfectly naturally features of his theology which could be independent of his eschatology, however closely they were related to it in his own mind. These features include above all the concept of the Spirit of God or of Christ as giving real life to the corporate body of the faithful and providing it with those supernatural gifts which enabled it to live the divine life on earth. Thus the idea of an ever-present Christ might have been substituted for that of the Christ to come, and some have argued, though quite falsely, that such a transformation was achieved in Ephesians. While this is untrue, Christians in the modern world, paying some kind of lip homage to eschatological hopes, in reality try to live the life of the Spirit in a 'fallen' world concerning whose ultimate redemption they must—if they are honest—be less optimistic than Paul. Such has in practice been the shift of the emphasis that the ultimate question is not whether the Lord will come again, but whether the notion of the divine initiative which Paul called grace is or may be a reality in human experience.

Part III

Chapter V

The Johannine Literature

The Gospel according to John

THE corpus of literature which consists of the Gospel according to John and the three Letters (formerly called by the old-fashioned term Epistles) of John can be considered to a large extent together; for they illuminate one another, and their style and teaching are distinctive both in the sense that they are unlike those of other writers in the New Testament, and also in the sense that they are like one another. For mistaken reasons the book of Revelation was in the past included in the category of Johannine literature; it is written by a 'John' indeed but he does not claim to be the apostle John nor to be the author of the gospel and letters. As long ago as the third century Dionysius of Alexandria (died *c.* 264) recognised both the strong affinity between the gospel and the letters and the great difference between this corpus of literature and the book of Revelation in both matter and style.

It will be best to begin with the gospel and to say something about the very vexed and difficult question of its authorship, which can never be finally settled, and indeed cannot be adequately treated without bringing into the discussion the character of the gospel itself, which is again a very complicated subject.

The evidence from within the gospel is at first sight easy to comprehend: here, as with Acts, we can start at the end, where we find a straightforward statement about the author (John 21:24); he is identified with the 'disciple whom Jesus loved'. This disciple has just figured prominently in the story of Jesus's appearance at the lakeside after his resurrection. His curious title makes him easy to identify within the gospel story, although he is nowhere given his actual name; he reclined against Jesus at the Last Supper, may well have been the disciple known to the high priest who was therefore allowed into the latter's house for the hearing after Jesus's arrest, he was present with the mother of Jesus (in this gospel never given her name) at the cross, and ran with Peter to the tomb after Mary Magdalene had reported to them that it was empty. In connexion with the presence at the cross the writer claims to be an eye-witness of what he saw when the soldier's spear pierced the side of the crucified Jesus. It is even easy at first to form a theory about the identity of this author: tradition (which must be discussed later) says that he was John the son of Zebedee; John was one of those present at the appearance by the lakeside so he could be the 'disciple whom Jesus loved'. Moreover, his close association with Peter corresponds to that of John with Peter in the early chapters of Acts. It would be possible to go further, and to recall the fact that of two disciples originally followers of John the Baptist (always called simply 'John' in this gospel) one is identified as Andrew, Peter's brother, and the other is not named (1:35 f.). It has often been claimed that this must be John son of Zebedee in view of the various facts already mentioned, and above all in view of the call of the disciples in Mark and Matthew. There the first to be called are Simon, Andrew, James, John—in that order. However, this theory does not offer a parallel in the Fourth Gospel to the call of James, and assumes—what ought not to be assumed—that the tradition followed here in this regard is the same as in the synoptics. It is impossible to read the first chapter of John and at the same time to maintain this with simplicity. Not only is there a different order in the call of the disciples but an entirely different story about it.

We touch here on something already hinted: this gospel is a composition of a quite different character from that of the other canonical gospels. This is often urged on the grounds that the Fourth Gospel implies a ministry of at least three years in contrast to the apparently single year of the synoptics. Incidentally, in the past this was a point which suggested to many critics that the Fourth Gospel was therefore historically more reliable, but no responsible critic would think of arguing in this way today; for it is now clear that all the gospels must have been written without the necessary knowledge and (except in the case of Luke) without the necessary desire to give a chronological account of the matter. The difference in character is far more obvious than this. In the Fourth Gospel the Jesus who speaks is manifestly different from the Jesus of the synoptics. In the latter he is a Jew among Jews and appeals to them on the ground of their own convictions; he makes no claims to divinity and even objects to being hailed as 'good'. In the Fourth Gospel he insists again and again on his unique authority and status. Shy of being forced to make any capital whatever out of his acts of healing in the synoptics, and reserving there the significance of any miracles for his disciples, in the Fourth Gospel he appeals to his miracles as 'works' which ought to compel belief; and the author calls them signs, manifestly meaning that they are signs which show who Jesus really is. Amidst all this the Jesus of the Fourth Gospel does not appeal to the Jews as sharers of a common tradition with him; he may appeal to the Law, but it is in order to make a point, to show how unreasonable they are. 'The Jews' are in fact in this gospel curiously enough the enemy; this ceases to be curious when we reach the conviction that the writer lives at a later time, when the Jews, as such, have become identified with those who blindly rejected the Son of God and crucified him.

Moreover, the doctrine which Jesus propounds is a doctrine which it would have been impossible for an actual human being to have declared without being himself deranged. It is almost totally about himself: he is the way, the truth, and the life: he is the light of the world, no one comes to the Father except by him, and so on. Such writing is acceptable only if it is already believed by the reader that the person who says such things is in reality being used by the author to convey what the author profoundly believes about him. Indeed the author prepares us for this manner of presentation by his famous prologue (John 1:1-18), which serves among other things to prepare the reader to hear of the teaching and the deeds not of an actual historical man but of the Logos incarnate. The Logos is the Greek term which has for so long been translated by 'Word', and some explanation must be given of it. We can in fact easily justify the use of the term 'Word', otherwise so unexpected. The gospel begins with the phrase 'In the beginning', deliberately leading us to expect a reference to the account of the creation, for Genesis begins with the same phrase.

We are not disappointed, but must understand that this author goes back behind the creation of the world for his notion of 'in the beginning'. He is thinking not only in temporal terms but in terms of the ground of being, the reality behind existence. This reality is God whom no man (in spite of Old Testament stories to the contrary) has ever seen. He can be known only when he makes himself known by his actions. One of these was to *say* 'Let there be light' and to *say* all the conceptions which thereby became realities. To get this clear, read the first few verses of Genesis; you will then see that in biblical terms it was a Word of God which made the world. It is no wonder that (for example) Ps. 33:6 says 'by the word of the Lord were the heavens made'. It is not that God just spoke. The idea is that God actualised what was in his mind, if we may for a moment speak in the anthropomorphic way which the writer of the gospel would dislike. His word then takes on a reality and power of its own, as in Isa. 55:10 f. where God insists that his word 'shall not return to me empty, but it shall accomplish that which I purpose . . .'. A link was made also with the concept of Wisdom which is most attractively and sometimes rather playfully personified in the Wisdom literature of the Old Testament and Apocrypha. The aspect of her personification which concerns us is that in which she is represented figuratively as a kind of foreman, or rather forewoman, in the building of something for which God is the architect. In Prov. 8:30 she says that when God was making the world 'I was beside him like a master workman', an idea repeated in Wis. 9:9. This last-mentioned chapter gives us a clear instance of the close inter-relation of Wisdom and Word, for in its two opening verses it speaks of God 'who hast made all things by thy word, and in thy wisdom hast fashioned man . . .'. The coalescence of these two ideas, Word of God, and Wisdom, was so balanced that it would have been no surprise to find the author of the Fourth Gospel speaking of Wisdom (in Greek, *sophia*) instead of Logos or Word as 'in the beginning'. The reason for his choice of Logos rather than Sophia is probably that he could thereby make himself at once intelligible to the Hellenistic educated world for whom in part he was writing.

Not only the unknown author of the book called the Wisdom of Solomon, from which we have just quoted, but also Philo the sophisticated Jew of Alexandria was familiar with Hellenistic thought; the Stoics, members of a widespread school of philosophy originating in Athens in the fourth century B.C., thought of God as the world reason or Logos, manifesting itself in the order of the universe. Philo had therefore no difficulty in working out a doctrine of the Logos which assimilated this idea to those of the Word and Wisdom in the Old Testament. It was one of the main ways in which he was able to commend Judaism to the Hellenistic world without disloyalty to his birth as a Jew. We cannot say immediately that the author of the Fourth Gospel thought exactly as Philo did, nor even that he knew Philo's work; but we can say that both he and Philo are illustrations of the fact that Judaism had been infused with Hellenism by the time with which we are concerned: even those who fought to maintain the purity of Jewish faith and practice could not help being influenced by Hellenistic ways of thought and life, ways which had been present in Palestine since Alexander the Great turned south from Issus in 336 B.C. after his victory over Darius the Persian. Thus the very notion of a kind of parliament or sanhedrin (itself a Greek word only slightly Hebraised) to govern the affairs of Jews under alien regimes is a Greek idea, and the scriptures had been translated into Greek since the third century B.C. (with the inevitable translation also of concepts which goes with a translation of words, as is not only admitted but even claimed by the pious translator of the apocryphal book, Ecclesiasticus). Jesus, who did not leave Palestine, travelled among the group of Greek cities in Palestine which formed the district known as the Decapolis. Again, the Maccabean rebels who had protested so violently against the Hellenistic tyranny of Antiochus Ephiphanes in 168 B.C. produced a line of rulers indistinguishable from petty Hellenistic princes and their line ran out with a queen named Salome Alexandra and her two sons, the younger of whom was called by the undeniably Greek name of Aristobulus. Their place was taken by the Herods who aspired, especially in the person of Herod the Great, to be regarded as monarchs within the Roman Empire renowned for their Hellenistic culture and patronage of the arts.

The theology of the author of the Fourth Gospel therefore need not have been derived directly from Philo in order to be influenced by Hellenism. In fact, opinion is strengthening along the line that his ways of thought are typical of the Judaism found in Palestine rather than in Alexandria, the Judaism represented by the Dead Sea Scrolls. These works are the scriptures of a strict Jewish sect which flourished from about 160 B.C. to A.D. 68, and may well have been a branch of the wide movement known as the Essenes, who are, curiously enough, never mentioned in the New Testament. Strict Jews as they were, they could not escape the influence of Hellenism even though they thought that all their doctrines and rules were rigidly opposed to it. Thus, for example, their teaching concerning the life to come, as reported by Josephus, seems to have been nearer the Greek idea of the soul as immortal than to the Jewish belief in the resurrection of the body.

It is not in this sphere of the doctrine of the life after death that we may discern an affinity with Hellenistic thought or Palestinian Jewish thought on the part of the author of the Fourth Gospel, but rather in other areas, such as in his ideas about the spirit and about the figure which he calls the Paraclete, along with his further notion of the Spirit of Truth. This last is a conception clearly the same as that found in one of the main Dead Sea Scrolls, the *Rule of the Community*, for there too, as in the Johannine literature, he is contrasted with the Spirit of Perversity or deception. The phrases occur clearly in I John 4:6 and the division of mankind into two classes, each governed by one of the two spirits, seems to have been inherited from the men of Qumran (the home of the Dead Sea Scrolls). The author of the gospel indeed deliberately identifies three concepts—the Paraclete, the Spirit of Truth, and the Holy Spirit of the early Christian Church. It is unnecessary to cite further examples here to show that the author used Judaism loyally, but in such a way as to commend it to the educated world of his day. His opening words are indeed a challenge to that world from a Christian Church based on Judaism.

We should not expect the fisherman John, son of Zebedee, to be able to assimilate and use different modes of thought in the manner of the author of the gospel. Acts 4:13 describes both John and Peter as laymen and non-experts. The passage does not mean that they were illiterate, indeed, but rather that they were not scholars. Even with this concession, it is inconceivable that a work of such subtlety of thought and betraying acquaintance with ideas from so many sources could have been written by one rightly described as non-expert.

Perhaps the most convincing argument against the Johannine authorship is that in the west, including Rome, the gospel was very slow to be accepted into the canon. We have incontrovertible evidence of this for the time of Hippolytus (c. 225). The reason was no doubt largely that it was a gospel very popular with gnostics, a fact scarcely surprising when we reflect on its high Christology, which leads it to commit such historical absurdities as narrating the falling to the ground of the soldiers who came to arrest Jesus, yet after showing this apparent conviction that he was a supernatural being, proceeding to arrest him as though he were a criminal.

What then becomes of the author's claim not only to be an eye-witness, but to be a specially privileged one? First we must notice certain further insuperable difficulties in accepting such claims: the presence of a disciple and the mother of an alleged public criminal at his crucifixion is an impossibility, and the synoptic gospels nowhere suggest that there were any followers of Jesus present. On the contrary, they had all fled. In the Fourth Gospel indeed the element of a public execution is as far as possible played down; all that is done or said has a religious significance. Again, the claim to be a specially privileged disciple in the eyes and affections of Jesus makes the absence from the synoptic gospels of such a person, or of any person who might be thus represented, so remarkable that it is impossible to reconcile his existence with that tradition.

We are forced to consider the matter from another point of view. In fact the author does not claim to be an eye-witness; the word is used in the strict sense by Luke at the opening of his gospel, but the Fourth Gospel uses and elaborates the idea of witness in general, using a different word from that for eye-witness. In his sense the scriptures are witnesses to Jesus, and even God can be so called. In the sort of sense in which he uses the word any faithful Christian can and should be a witness, in the sense that he 'confesses', that is believes and openly states and defends that belief, like the man born blind in the story in the ninth chapter of the gospel itself (see verses 24-39). Thus to be present at the eucharist is to recline in the bosom of

Jesus, to meditate upon the crucifixion is to 'see' that blood and water, that is, redemption and life, flow from him. No doubt there was a time when only the apostles, or those who knew the whole story of the historical Jesus, including his death and resurrection, could be accepted as witnesses: but as time passed, this state of affairs must change. If there are to be witnesses, and without them the continuance of the gospel and of the Church is impossible, they must be those of any generation who really believe. If they have the spirit given from God to every believer in Jesus they do not need witnesses to the history of the earthly Jesus. Thus the first letter of John says expressly, 'He who believes in the Son of God has the testimony in himself' (5:10, R.S.V.) and we should perhaps emphasise the last two words.

Some interpreters have seen in Lazarus the person who fits all the requirements for identification with the disciple whom Jesus loved, for in chapter 11 such words are certainly used of Lazarus. Once again, it seems impossible to make sense of all the evidence unless we have the candour to accept that Lazarus is himself an ideal figure. This is a problem into which it is impossible to go fully here, but it should at least be noted that the story is told in such a way that it partly prefigures the death of Jesus himself (hence the strong emotion of Jesus before he goes to the tomb, and the disciples' fear that they will be going to their death if they accompany him); and it is designed partly to answer the question whether he who is called by Christians the Resurrection and the Life can raise from the dead his followers who have by the time of his coming suffered corruption (for Lazarus is a corpse of four days, which means that life has finally left him and revival is entirely impossible). Nor does the amazing story occur anywhere else, even if Luke's ending to the parable of the Rich Man and Lazarus (16:31) is held to be a hint about it.

The author of the gospel therefore seems to have been a Christian belonging to an age later than could make him an eye-witness. There has been time for the development of a theology with its own unique characteristics, although it would be a mistake to try to date the gospel later than the end of the first century: for a fragment found in Egypt (the Rylands Papyrus) makes certain that it was known there very early in the second century. The development was rapid because, as we have seen, the materials for such a theology were already available to the author.

To characterise the gospel in a short compass is very hard. It may help if we begin from one of its own famous sayings, in 14:6. Here Jesus says 'I am the way, the truth and the life.' Perhaps a great deal of this can be intelligently interpreted by the non-expert: the way of Jesus is the way of the cross, of service and of the willingness if necessary to suffer for one's belief. Jesus is the life because to believe in him and to be united with him as the risen Lord means to share in the divine life which God gave him when he raised him from the dead. But how can a person, even such a person, be the truth? Before we try to explain this, it will be useful to notice that the saying is one of those which cause a great deal of difficulty for thoughtful Christians because they sound as if Jesus is boasting, and as if he is giving orders to all with whom he comes in contact that they must believe in him, or suffer the dire consequences. Everything in the saying, and almost everything in the gospel is directed to making clear who Jesus is. When so much of this comes from Jesus himself, it sounds to us offensive. This is very largely because we treat the gospel as we treat the synoptics, as claiming to give the words of an historical person, whereas, as we have already agreed, in the Fourth Gospel the words of Jesus are in reality the teachings of the incarnate Logos, who appears under other titles in the body of the gospel, such as that of 'the Son' or 'Son of Man'. Thus in 3:12–13 he is the person who alone can impart heavenly secrets to mankind, because he alone has been in heaven and descended thence in order to redeem mankind and at the same time to teach them the truth. Perhaps we begin to see already that the main truth which he must teach them is that he embodies truth. This must be made clearer. The Law given by God to Moses for the Israelites was regarded by them as the truth or as truth; for this was the true way of life, the way by which men could live in conformity to God's law and plan. To live thus would be to live according to the truth, which means at one and the same time truthfully, honestly and with full integrity, *and* according to the prescribed law of God. There could be no difference in the way of living for a man who lived according to what we should call his own light and conscience from that followed by a man who obeyed in every way the Law of Moses. The author of the Fourth Gospel quarrels with this conception; for him only the Law — the rules — were given by Moses, and the truth came through Jesus Christ (John 1:17). By this he meant that the true way of life as lived and visible, as embodied in a living human being, was just not there, not available in the world, until Jesus came. Such a form of truth could not be learnt as lessons in school are learnt. They could be learnt only by living. Hence Jesus is the way and the life for a Christian. Further, we must repair an omission when we referred to John 1:17: for there it is claimed not only that truth came through Jesus Christ, but also that grace came through him. Here the word means clearly what it most often means in the New Testament, divinely bestowed power which enables the Christian to live the divinely demanded quality of life which is otherwise impossible for mere man.

We can take even one further step in our explanation of the claim that Jesus is the truth; if he is the truth in the sense that he embodies a life and a way of life which is divinely given and divinely ordered, what teaching can he give other than that about himself? In these circumstances, *given that he knows this truth about himself*, he must himself be the subject of his teaching. The synoptic Christ differs in this all-important respect from him of the Fourth Gospel. The former does not know of his own divinity and must point away from himself to his heavenly Father; the latter — the Christ of the Fourth Gospel — is represented as being all the time conscious of his divine origin and destiny (see, for example, 16:28 and 17:5). Hence the truth which he teaches is the truth about himself, and because there is a true sense in which he is God (20:28), what he thus teaches is the truth of God, the truth, and he teaches it both by word, and by being and acting the truth.

It may sound curious that Jesus acts the truth. In a sense his action is a suffering. His sacrifice on the cross is the main action which reveals the truth of who he is, the Son and Redeemer whom God sent into the world. Hence he can be represented as saying, 'When you lift up (i.e. on the cross) the Son of Man, you will know that I am He' (8:28); the last three words are the formula for the divine Being, as used in the book of Isaiah.

Thus he is recognised as God because he embodies and enacts God's redemptive action.

While we can therefore understand what prompts the author to make Jesus speak as he does in his gospel, it becomes more and more impossible to believe that Jesus himself so spoke; more and more feasible that in this book we have a theological presentation in the form of a fragment of biography. Even the time divisions, as we shall see later, are artificially liturgical, proceeding from festival to festival so that the actions and discourses suit the spatial and temporal environment, until finally the Paschal Lamb is offered at Passover time.

By making cryptic references to himself the author has succeeded perfectly in his aim to make good his claim to be a witness and yet to remain anonymous. It is impossible to say now who he was, and we have to be content with the indications of what sort of man he was. This has been shown by the discussion already undertaken; it remains to explain how the authorship got attached to so unlikely a person as the fisherman, John, son of Zebedee. A great part of the explanation lies in the facts already mentioned: it was natural to look for someone who was an actual eye-witness and close to Jesus personally and who was also a close associate of Peter. From the other literature in the New Testament relevant to this issue the answer, John son of Zebedee, is natural, although really mistaken.

There is other evidence which, while by no means establishing John as the author, does explain why he came to be so in the tradition. To begin with, Papias is reported by Eusebius as having mentioned two Johns. One is mentioned along with other apostles, in the sense of those who had been immediate disciples of the Lord. The other is mentioned as an 'elder' along with a certain Aristion. Eusebius discusses what Papias had said in the passage which he has quoted from him, and is at pains to make clear that Papias himself does not claim to have known John the apostle, although Irenaeus says that Papias did. As Eusebius says, Papias knew the elder, not the apostle, named John; but both Irenaeus and Eusebius speak as if there were already a tradition that John the apostle wrote the gospel and the epistles. Eusebius, while he does a service to the truth by pointing out Irenaeus's mistake with regard to Papias and his acquaintance with John the apostle, comes too late in history to preserve any further clear evidence. However, he shakes our confidence in Irenaeus who indeed made one or two mistakes easy to spot in some of the information which he passed on. For our purpose we are concerned with what Irenaeus wrote in a letter to a friend called Florinus who had doubts about the authenticity of the early Christian traditions. Irenaeus rallies him by recalling to him how they had together in their youth listened to the elderly Polycarp who, says Irenaeus, had in his youth consorted with John and others who had seen the Lord. Irenaeus is very positive that he has made no mistake about this and mentions the well-known phenomenon that in age one remembers the remote better than the immediate past, and applies it to these memories. Against this must be set the known propensity of Irenaeus to make mistakes and his obvious unconscious motive for being sure that Polycarp had known the apostle John.

Irenaeus was a man of remarkable ability, and his life is interesting, even though we know so little about its details. He seems to have been born in Asia Minor, perhaps at Smyrna, but studied at Rome. He became bishop of Lyons after a persecution there which caused the martyr death of his predecessor Pothinus which occurred while Irenaeus was absent on an important visit to Rome. He thus formed a link between east and west, and is best known for his writings against the heretics. In these he expressed an orthodox theology and relied on the Church's traditions to counter the views of gnostics, rather than take the line of many in the east (such as Clement and Origen at Alexandria) whose way was to show that Christianity was the true gnosticism. The Church's traditions were still in an early stage, but included some scriptures which were still liable to acceptance by some and rejection by others; they included also such information as that of Papias. Irenaeus had no hesitation in bringing all these traditions together and arguing strongly for them. His enthusiasm for basing the Church's gospel on historical facts may well have made him go beyond what were really facts.

Among his traditional materials Irenaeus found the information given by Papias about the evangelists and added considerable interpretation of his own. Thus he says that Luke set out in a book the gospel preached by Paul, a judgment which makes scholars rub their eyes, and adds 'then John, the disciple of the Lord, who also reclined on his breast, himself also published the gospel, living on in Ephesus of Asia'. It begins to look as if Irenaeus must have identified two Johns known to Papias in the interests of establishing the teaching of the Church about its own teaching and authority on strong historical foundations. These foundations, however, as far as the author of the Fourth Gospel is concerned, do not appear to have existed. For if Irenaeus were right, Ephesus must have been famous in the early Church for being the home of an apostle, especially one who had written a gospel. Yet in the earliest traditions there is a strange silence about any such association of the city with so important a person. Ignatius, for example, on his way to martyrdom at Rome, writes to the Ephesians with whom he had stayed for a short time on the way; in his letter he refers eloquently to Paul and calls the members of the Church at Ephesus Paul's 'fellow-initiates' and exhorts them in effect to assemble frequently together in order to carry on the excellent traditions which they have learnt from the apostle. He makes no reference at all to John, though his own theology is very like that of the gospel. It cannot be said that it is certain that he knew it, but the point lies in this: he does not quote Paul exactly but represents his thought in general. The same is true of the Fourth Gospel but while he actually mentions Paul as one whose association with Ephesus is a matter for pride, he shows no sign of knowing that the author of the gospel had anything to do with the place, nor that an apostle John had lived on there to a great age. We conclude then that it was Irenaeus who fixed the tradition that the author was John the son of Zebedee, but that the actual author is unknown.

One of the most remarkable facts about this gospel is its ability to express itself in theological terms which appeal to the intellectual and the contemplative. It has long been thought and is still thought in many places that this trait indicates an author more familiar with Greek or the later Hellenistic thought derived from the classical Greek times; it was believed that his hostility to 'the Jews' indicated among other things a contempt for their ways of thinking. There were dissentients, but to many Christian scholars it was a shock when a Jewish scholar, Abrahams, characterised the Fourth Gospel as the most

Jewish of the four. This proved to be a real insight, for the discovery of the Dead Sea Scrolls has shown that there was a strict Jewish sect which used theological concepts derived from Jewish sources and giving the clue to the origin of some of the features in the Fourth Gospel which distinguish it so sharply from the other canonical gospels.

It is fairly easy to plot a time chart of the events in the gospel which shows that the chronology on which it is based is not historical but liturgical: events follow the pattern of the calendar and features in the narrative of them are appropriate for the feast against the background of which they take place. The crucifixion, as already remarked, associates the death of Jesus with the Passover. This is undeniable whether we regard the Last Supper as a Passover meal or not. Other examples are equally clear: 7:1 begins the narrative of events associated with the great feast of Tabernacles. Water libations and lights were a great feature of this feast; consistently from a literary point of view Jesus during this celebration calls people to come to him for the gift of living water (7:38 f.) and a little later says that he is 'the light of the world' (8:12). Such echoes represent a feature which is apparent in every part of the gospel. For example, the sectaries at Qumran, the authors and owners of the Dead Sea Scrolls, held a strange belief about the calendar. Briefly, they were convinced that God had ordained the movement of the heavenly bodies so as to indicate by the position of the sun relative to the constellations the right day according to the divine will for these feasts to be kept. Their solar calendar contrasts with the lunar calendar of orthodox Judaism. Consistently with this, their version of history was such that the main religious events which required pious celebration had all occurred first on these astronomically and religiously significant days. It would be going too far altogether to say that the author of the Fourth Gospel held the same views of history, but he seems to have shared the conviction that religious events happen on days already religiously important by divine ordinance.

Again, we may think, naturally enough on a cursory reading, that when the author equates the Holy Spirit with the Spirit of Truth and again with the Paraclete, he is teaching for the first time that it is appropriate to understand the Holy Spirit in this way, that he is unfolding the meaning of the term as he sees it, and coins these phrases in order to apply them to the Holy Spirit. We can now be sure that this is not the case. His language about the Spirit of Truth and indeed his ideas about truth already discussed briefly above are clearly derived from the store of ideas also held by the writers of the scrolls. They divide mankind into those who belong to the Spirit of Truth and those who belong to the opposite Spirit, that of perversity. They wrote in Hebrew, but the phrase in 1 John 4:6 translated in the New English Bible, 'the spirit of truth' and 'the spirit of error' are exact Greek equivalents.

Paraclete means advocate or intercessor and is largely a forensic term. As a friend (in ancient Jewish law your chief witness, for the professional advocate did not exist) argued for you in court, so did a spiritual paraclete intercede with God for you in the heavenly court, as Michael did for Israel in the tradition of apocalyptic writing. This notion is well-known in the Judaism of the period preceding and contemporary with the New Testament, and shows itself in Paul (Rom. 8:26 f.). The idea is developed in the Fourth Gospel in a thorough manner typical of the writer, but its roots lie in Palestinian Judaism as it is represented by the Scrolls and other similar writings. The contribution of the author of the gospel is therefore to see that the power of God who performed for mankind these various functions was really the same; and that the Holy Spirit, who according to the synoptics assisted the persecuted Christian in the day of trial (Mark 13:11) could be identified with those spiritual powers which had so far been called by other names.

It is not the task of this book to make a thorough appreciation of this gospel;[1] but it would be wrong not to point out some of the literary features which make it a work of genius; first and foremost is the extraordinary inter-weaving of themes which convey what the author believes. To take some examples: 'in the beginning' is obviously a main theme of the opening

[1] From the point of view of deep and sympathetic understanding the commentary by E. C. Hoskyns (ed. F. N. Davey), *The Fourth Gospel* (Faber and Faber, 1940, 2nd. ed. 1948), is probably still the best in English. C. H. Dodd, *The Interpretation of the Fourth Gospel*, (C.U.P., 1953) is also invaluable.

passage, the Prologue; it develops as the theme of the Logos, who was from the beginning, and of his entrance into the world, but the exposition introduces the themes of light and life as archetypal attributes of God as creator and redeeemer. These are woven into the pattern. Very early the theme of witness, which is to be constant throughout the later and narrative elements of the book is introduced. The actual statement of the incarnation brings with it the theme of grace and truth as brought by the 'only Son' (another theme) – and these introduce the polemic theme of the supersession of Moses. This does not exhaust the subjects woven together in the Prologue: another critic might give a different account, emphasising philosophical aspects and dwelling on the theme of the invisibility of God, and on the author's teaching about how God can be known. So interwoven are these themes that many scholars treat it as an item of critical orthodoxy to believe in the existence of a pre-Christian hymn to the Logos, arising in a philosophical-religious circle such as that of Philo, which originally contained no mention of the incarnation, the latter being the addition of the Christian author as he adapted the hymn to his special Christian purpose.

Such theories are quite unnecessary: a literary appraisal of the gospel shows that interweaving of themes is an essential aspect of the author's style; for instance, the story of Lazarus, with its mixture of drama and discourse, its extraordinary juxtaposition of deep emotion with restraint, illustrates the interweaving of themes while remaining an undeniable unity. The emotion which Jesus suffers in this story is not of the kind which can be explained by the actual situation. Commentators appear foolish in their remarks if they think, as many do, that it can be explained within such a framework. In raising the daughter of Jairus, in the story of the synoptics, it is Jesus who remains above the emotional scene, and his calmness is in character, indeed more in character for the Jesus of the Fourth Gospel than for him of the synoptics. His deep emotion, his groaning within himself in the Lazarus story, can be explained only when we realise that by a number of touches (waiting *three* days before going to Lazarus's home, the risk of death in going at all, the rock tomb and the body swathed in grave clothes, and so on) the author is showing Jesus contemplating not only Lazarus's death but also his own death and the agony which preceded it.

More remarkable still, from the point of view of complicated interweaving, is the passage in 12:20 f. which opens with the approach of the Greeks to Jesus. Many readers must have been puzzled by the fact that Jesus does not say anything to the Greeks who are introduced in so attractive a way at the outset. At first sight it is difficult to see what the words of Jesus in verses 23 and 24, with their declaration that the time has come for his own glorification, can have to do with the context. Indeed, this is one of those passages which repel the modern reader. It seems that the Jesus of this passage is absorbed in the subject of himself. We have already seen the answer to this: it is emphatically not the historical Jesus who is speaking, but the author through him. We can then see that Jesus in verses 23 and 24 is presenting a theological statement which is not an answer to the men who have come to see him, but an interpretation of the situation, which is that of the wider world of Greek civilisation come to 'see' Jesus. These Greeks may well be Greek-speaking Jews from the Diaspora, but if so, like the Jews present at Pentecost in Acts 2, they symbolically represent the world outside Judaism which awaits the enlightenment which Jesus, the fulfilment and flower of Judaism, has ready for them. There is then another scene in the mind of the author than that which appears to be set on the stage here. The message of the Greeks' arrival and request has scarcely been delivered when Jesus says something which possesses significance only in another scene, into which the original scene dissolves after the fashion of modern cinema. This other scene is that of the world, for which Christ has come to die. His dying for them in fact is the subject which he takes up in the following discourse (verses 24 and 25). In a manner which at first seems very curious, this leads straight on to Gethsemane. It is curious not because the subject does not follow perfectly logically, but because Jesus begins to speak as if he were already in Gethsemane (or 'the garden', as it is called in this gospel). In this way we can even explain the somewhat exotic feature of the thunder. This is a rather odd (to us even 'corny') way of saying that a voice from heaven has addressed Jesus. We think at once of the angel in Gethsemane according to the Lucan account

(Luke 22:43), thus hinting something in common between these two gospels, and at the same time giving the author an opportunity to contradict the impression gained from Luke that Jesus in the hour of his trial needed or indeed could profit by strengthening from an angel, a being of lower order than himself. The voice, the Jesus of this gospel claims publicly, came not for him but for his hearers: it marks a great 'crisis' or moment of judgment and decision on the part of God in the heavenly court which is constantly in session *behind the scenes*; the result of the crisis is that the 'prince of this world' will be 'cast out', that is, thrown out of heaven. By Jesus's death on the cross, Satan is defeated in his effort to accuse and gain the destruction of God's people. He will lose all his followers and the crucified victor will draw all men to himself (verse 32). The skill which the author displays elsewhere cannot avail to make these themes into a really harmonious whole from the point of view of narrative or discourse. He has made here too bold an experiment, by presenting us not only with a number of themes, but in a bewildering way a number of scenes, taking Jesus abruptly from the place where the Greeks actually came to see him to the world scene, then to the garden, then to the heavenly court where Satan continually conducts his case against mankind, and then to the crucifixion. Finally we are back to the starting-point in verse 34, but the Greeks have vanished and only the usual crowds, with their constant arguments and disbelief, are present. It would have been easier if the author had hinted in a way easy for people of all ages to follow what he was doing; but he does not, and we have to take his rather obscure hints if we are to understand him.

A perhaps unexpected result of the above interpretation follows here; to see that there is a shift to the scene of 'the garden' it is quite essential to recognise features, such as the prayer of Jesus to be saved from 'this hour' followed by the expression of willingness to serve the will of his father, and to recognise them immediately, just as a listener to a symphony must be able to recognise during the development the reintroduction of a theme, perhaps in a disguised form, if he is to get the best out of the music. This implies clearly that the author, relying upon his readers' acquaintance with the synoptic tradition, must have been completely familiar with it himself. This is the chief reason for the rejection by many scholars of the theory that the author of the Fourth Gospel is giving an alternative version of material which has affinities with the synoptic account but is independent of it. Such a theory might be said to be possible only for those who do not fully see what is the method and literary style of the author. To give one further clear example, how could John 1:32-34 have been written without familiarity with the synoptic account of the baptism, although it does not itself narrate the baptism of Jesus?

The Letters of John

The letters which almost certainly were written by the same author as that of the gospel are often studied among the epistles, in the relatively unexplored hinterland of the New Testament, a country into which only eccentric people like theologians usually enter. It is in some ways better to consider them with the gospel, for they are very like it in style, and, as we shall claim here, in teaching. In our discussion we shall be for the most part speaking of the first letter, for that alone is long enough to include any teaching of substance, but, as we shall see, the third letter has its particular importance.

The likeness in teaching between the gospel and the first letter has been disputed, for instance by Dodd,[2] a specialist in the New Testament and in this part of it in particular. He contends that the eschatology of the letter differs from that of the gospel, that there is in the letter primitive teaching on the atonement absent from the gospel, and that its doctrine of the Holy Spirit is also different. In urging the contrary we can at the same time draw out some of the main points in this teaching. First, eschatology: there is indeed primitive eschatology in the first letter; 1 John 2:18 says that it is the 'last hour' in which he and his friends are living. Here, as also in one or two other places in this letter, and once in the second letter, he uses the term Antichrist, unknown to any other book in the New Testament, though the idea appears in several. The author says that his friends have been taught to expect the rise of Antichrist, a

[2] In his commentary in The Moffatt New Testament Commentary series, *The Johannine Epistles* (Hodder and Stoughton, 1946).

figure variously interpreted in the New Testament ('man of lawlessness', 'beast from the abyss', 'abomination of desolation', and so on). He is sure that this phenomenon has now appeared in history, but it should be noted that while his belief in an actual last hour is primitive and simple, his interpretation is somewhat sophisticated: he regards very human opponents, who are not at all mysterious, and who are sinister only in the sense that they are opposed to the right teaching, as fulfilling the warning about Antichrist which he has received as part of his Christian heritage. He says that there are many antichrists in fact, and identifies them with the false teachers who seem to have belonged at first to the Church but to have led away from it and out of it a number of members, persuading them by their false doctrines (1 John 2:18 f.). There is little doubt that these teachers were gnostics who are regarded by him as both heretics (teachers of false doctrine) and schismatics (those who split the Church). It is the naïve identification of a 'last day', which Dodd (and others) regard as inconsistent with the 'transmuted' eschatology of the gospel, to quote Dodd's useful description.

The author of the gospel does try to transmute eschatology: for example, in John 14:18–24 Jesus expressly says to his disciples at a time when he is preparing them for his departure, 'I am coming to you' (i.e. again). This is a reflection of the eschatology of the synoptics according to which Jesus in his person as Son of Man will return to the world in glory to judge it: but there is a difference, carefully brought out by the question of Jude in verse 22. He asks, 'Lord, what can have happened that you mean to disclose yourself to us alone and not to the world?' This is a question which the reader familiar with the synoptic teaching can as it were paraphrase into this form: 'What change of doctrine makes it possible that Jesus will not return to judge the world but will reveal himself only to his followers?' The answer given in the following discourse amounts to this: Jesus will come and be present to those who love him. The same will be true of the Father. There is a hint that Jesus will 'come to' his disciples in the sense that the Holy Spirit will come to them (verse 26). This 'transmutes' the eschatology indeed, and Dodd is amply justified in saying so. But the author does not abandon the primitive eschatology, curious though this may seem. There are several passages which make this clear, but the easiest way to see the matter straight is to take another look at the chapter about Lazarus (John 11).

In that famous story the eschatology is of such a kind that we might be tempted to use the same phrase, and say that here also it is 'transmuted'; for Jesus describes himself as the resurrection and the life and implies that those who believe in him may die in the natural way indeed, but because of their unity with him will not die for ever. This leaves open the very obvious question, 'How then will they live again?' and the answer which is given is surprising. At first it is not given, and Martha is content to believe less in the series of events which eschatological doctrine promises than in Jesus himself who seems to wish here to replace the more primitive and naïve doctrine by such a personal trust (for the course of the argument see 11:24–27). The answer to the question which we formulated is implied later on, just as it has been given earlier, also, in 6:39, 40, 44, 54. Jesus will raise them on the last day. It is implied also in 12:48, where indeed the subject is judgment rather than the resurrection of the righteous, but where there is clearly a belief in the 'last day' with its important attendant events. The passages in chapter 6 just listed are decisive for the fact that the author retained belief in this primitive eschatology, but we can to a large extent sympathise with Bultmann[3] (who influenced Dodd) in boldly omitting these references to 'the last day' as interpolations made by someone who did not understand that this author was 'transmuting' older doctrines, and (in Bultmann's view) thus revealing himself as the first demythologiser of Christian 'myth'. But the characterisation of inconvenient passages as interpolations is 'a short way with dissenters' and too reminiscent of the Queen of Hearts in *Alice in Wonderland* with her panacea for all awkward situations: 'Off with his head!' The solution has an admirable simplicity but tends to deprive the subject of an important feature.

It seems therefore a reasonable interpretation of the facts that the author of gospel and first letter in some way combined what for us is a reinterpretation of the standard teaching of the Church with an adherence to that teaching in its simplicity. Critics may ask, 'How is such a thing even possible, let alone

[3] R. Bultmann, *Das Evangelium des Johannes* (Göttingen, 1950).

probable?' Strange as it may seem, the answer to this apparently awkward question stares us in the face. If, as we are now so much inclined to believe and to emphasise, this writer thought in Jewish modes, then he was familiar with the rabbinic standards of interpretation of scripture also exemplified by Philo; according to these standards it was right and even obligatory to interpret statements parabolically or allegorically, but not thereby to cease believing in the plain literal sense. The different levels of meaning, which often seem to us logically to exclude one another, are held together. A rule of our thinking which we cannot abandon, derived from the Greeks, and we may claim from common sense, is that 'everything is what it is and not some other thing'; this is not true for the Semitic mind (a fact which we ignore to our peril when trying to make sense of Middle East problems). Thus Paul is quite sure that the two women whom he discussed in Gal. 4:21 f. are an allegory, but it would not occur to him to doubt that the history of them was also literally true.

We must next consider the doctrine of the atonement as it appears in this literature. There seems little doubt that the earliest Christians believed what Paul records in his list of items which he received from his predecessors in the Church, 'that Christ died for our sins according to the scriptures'. This is in itself an early statement and refers to another even earlier as a brief reference to 1 Cor. 15:1 f. will show. Absolutely all scholars agree that there is no one theory in the New Testament which explains how this is true; indeed absolutely all scholars agree that the Church has never decided on any one theory of the atonement as the correct explanation of how it is true that 'Christ died for our sins', though all Christians agree that this is true in some way. The agreement on the fact and acknowledgment of the variety of ways in which it may be interpreted is expressed eloquently in the liturgy of the eucharist where God is addressed as having given 'his only Son Jesus Christ to suffer death upon the cross for our redemption; who made there (by his one oblation once offered) a full, perfect, and sufficient sacrifice, oblation, and satisfaction, for the sins of the whole world' (the words are from the 1549 Book of Common Prayer, subsequent revisions adding 'of himself' in the parenthesis after the words, 'by his one oblation' to exclude any possibility that the sacrifice of the Mass added anything to the once-for-all sacrifice of the Lord).

The first letter of John certainly has a phrase which suggests the efficacy of shed blood, on a Jewish cultic model: 1:7 teaches that sincere sharing in the common life of the light ensures that we are cleansed from sin by the blood of Jesus his Son. Again, in 2:2 Jesus is described, according to the New English Bible, as 'the remedy for the defilement of our sins'; this is a useful interpretation for modern man of the Old Testament notion of expiation, and older translations described Jesus here as the propitiation for our sins. It may well be right to use rather the term 'expiation' and to refer to the New English Bible for interpretation of this idea; but this must not obscure the fact that it is a cultic reference and that in the Old Testament model the shedding of blood is necessary for the effectiveness of a sacrifice of this kind, a principle summed up in Heb. 9:22, '... without the shedding of blood there is no forgiveness.' Now, it is further said in this letter that Jesus 'came by water and blood', a curious way of referring to his coming to assist mankind and bequeathing the twin sacraments of baptism and eucharist, the latter's significance lying in its recall of the bloody sacrifice on the cross. It is to the historical moment when the death of Christ provided this sacramental water and blood that the author of the gospel witnesses in John 19:34 f. For the gospel Jesus is the Paschal Lamb and for the epistle he is the eternal expiatory or propitiatory sacrifice: the two concepts are linked by the same vocabulary and symbolism and by the connexion with the eucharist.

The Spirit is thought of in a way similarly consistent with the doctrine of the gospel; he too is witness and is the Spirit of Truth. The gospel only once (14:26) and the letter never mentions the full phrase which must be translated 'the Holy Spirit'. The gospel has the phrase 'holy spirit' which is not necessarily the same concept, and the letter does not use even this phrase. For the letter 'the Spirit' often suffices, this and the general treatment suggesting, consistently with the gospel, that what is meant is the Spirit whom, or even which, Christ has bestowed.

The letter is concerned with those who deny that Jesus has come in the flesh (1 John 4:1–3) and complains of the gnostics who taught this idea of Christ, a Christ who was in the view of the author literally and theologically bloodless. This controversy is part of the author's situation. In place of such error he gives his own highly individual version of the truth. So too in the second letter he writes 'to the Lady chosen by God' (i.e. a Church within orthodoxy) that he is 'delighted to find that some of your children are living by the truth' (4) and warns again about the 'many deceivers' whom he again equates with a corporate Antichrist (7). Here and in the opening of 3 John the author identifies himself as 'The Elder' (or Presbyter), a fact which led to doubts about the author being the same as that of the gospel when the tradition that the latter was John son of Zebedee had established itself. The third letter in fact may provide a clue to the position of the author which enables us to understand it further; in verse 9 he writes to his friend Gaius, 'I sent a letter to the congregation, but Diotrephes, their would-be leader, will have nothing to do with us.' The translation, 'would-be leader' is not certain. The word naturally means 'who likes to be leader', that is it describes the attitude of one who is already in authority and wields it to the disadvantage of others, not one who only wishes to be at the top. If this is a clue, then the author is in a position where he depends on the goodwill, in part at least, of others in authority and is not necessarily himself in such a position. If there is any truth in this observation, it is consistent with what we know not only of the theological character of the gospel and the letters which we call Johannine, but also with the fact that the gospel was a long time finding complete recognition in the universal Church.

We have to conclude about this author that he had a highly unusual mind, able indeed to adapt the ideas and categories of others, but above all with the ability to see how the Christ of the Church to which he belonged made sense of and enlivened those categories; as such he dared to call himself a witness who had seen. On the view we have put forward such sight was that of the seer, not that of the ordinary day-to-day 'eye-witness', but it is part of his idiosyncrasy to use language which suggests this latter fact. It is possible that he was a disciple of the second or later generation who lived in Ephesus. The present writer may perhaps be forgiven for doubting this, on the ground that evidence is conspicuous by its absence, and that the author reveals more of the temper of Alexandria than Asia Minor. Finally we must acknowledge one thing with the best grace we can muster: the author took immense pains to conceal his identity, using curious periphrases to refer to it. It is probably one of the most significant facts about western Christendom that we think that only when we have pierced this disguise (and thus shown our hostility to the author's own wishes) we can understand properly what he wished to say. Perhaps a due mixture of two texts would be better for this purpose than trying to identify the 'witness' with another known person: one will be John 19:35, 'This is vouched for by an eye-witness' and the other is 1 John 5:10, 'He who believes in the Son of God has this testimony in his own heart ...'

Chapter VI

Hebrews, James, 1 and 2 Peter, Jude

A Letter to Hebrews

THE Fourth Gospel begins with a famous passage about the word of God appearing in flesh, that is in human form, as an incarnation of the eternal Word or Logos. The term is not used in Hebrews in this way but a corresponding verb is used in an opening not less impressive than that of the gospel. The idea that God 'spoke' in his creative activity was in the latter used in connexion with his word; in Hebrews it is used in connexion with his activity throughout the ages. The Word of the Lord came to the prophets causing them to be creative agents in history; but 'he spoke in fragmentary and varied fashion through the prophets. But in this the final age he has spoken to us in the Son whom he has made heir to the whole universe, and through whom he created all orders of existence' (Heb. 1:1 f.). It is clear that God's 'speaking' is not meant to be understood as oral teaching but rather is used as a metaphor for action through the Son, who has appeared at the end of the age.

At first it may seem that the author (whose identity we shall discuss later) is as concerned as the Fourth Gospel with the Person of Christ, and as exclusively. But in this work the Son is set forth as the supreme author or agent of the atonement. The first two chapters argue that this Son was not an angel but fulfilled the idea in Ps. 8:5 that one who was (representative) Man was made temporarily 'lower than the angels' but raised above all creation (2:5-9). His humiliation, which under God's plan included suffering, made him like all men and his exaltation carries all mankind with him. Chapters 3 and 4 digress for a moment to warn all 'brothers in the family of God' (3:1) not to lose their privilege of entering into the final 'rest' of God.

Chapter 5 takes up a hint already dropped which is to be developed in full: Jesus is a high priest like Melchizedek (Gen

184

14:18–20), that is of mysterious origin, and not of the Aaronic but of eternal priesthood. Chapter 6 is an appeal inserted to beg the readers to follow the author into his deeper theology; Chapter 7 continues the argument about the superiority of Melchizedek over Abraham and the Levitical priesthood. The latter was imperfect and another priest, not from Levi, is necessary. 'The argument becomes still clearer, if the new priest who arises is one like Melchizedek, owing his priesthood not to a system of earth-bound rules but to the power of a life that cannot be destroyed' (7:15 f.). The author then refers to the necessity that

Every high priest is appointed to offer gifts and sacrifices: hence, this one too must have something to offer. Now if he had been on earth, he would not even have been a priest, since there are already priests who offer the gifts which the Law prescribes, though they minister in a sanctuary which is only a copy and shadow of the heavenly (8:3–5).

The argument then develops the theme that '. . . now Christ has come, high priest of good things already in being' (or 'destined to be'). 'The tent of his priesthood is a greater and more perfect one, not made by men's hands, that is, not belonging to this created world; the blood of his sacrifice is his own blood, not the blood of goats and calves; and thus he has entered the sanctuary once and for all and secured an eternal deliverance' (9:11 f.). Thus if he had been familiar with modern idiom, the author might well have said that Christ was a cosmic high priest the scene of whose sacrifice, in which he was both priest and victim, was not a shrine but the entire universe. Mediator of a new covenant (9:15), as high priest he

entered, not that sanctuary made by men's hands which is only a symbol of the reality, but heaven itself, to appear now before God on our behalf. Nor is he there to offer himself again and again, as the high priest enters the sanctuary year by year with blood not his own. If that were so, he would have had to suffer many times since the world was made. But as it is, he has appeared once and for all at the climax of history to abolish sin by the sacrifice of himself (9:24–25).

Chapter 10 applies this conception of the relation of the old to the new to Paul's problem which paradoxically saw the Law as of divine origin and authority yet powerless to effect its aim. The Law 'contains but a shadow, and no true image, of the good things which were to come' (10:1), but, consistently with the author's particular interest, this is illustrated in connexion with the sacrificial system; the daily service of sacrifice in the temple 'can never remove sins' – 'But Christ offered for all time one sacrifice for sins' (10:11 f.). The chapter runs on into an exhortation not to give way under persecution, for 'we have the faith to make life our own' (10:39). The mention of faith leads directly into chapter 11 which gives famous definitions and illustrations of faith. Two remarkable points are made. One is the notion of a people of God in different generations who worked and suffered united by a faith which looked forward to a goal not achieved in their lifetime: 'God had made a better plan, that only in company with us should they reach their perfection' (11:40). Thus the author reaches a conception of heaven which is less a place than an ideal society.

The other point is the inclusion of a number of unnamed martyrs who appear to include the Maccabees (11:33–40). Chapter 12 summons the readers therefore to endure with the same faith, 'our eyes fixed on Jesus . . . who, for the sake of the joy that lay ahead of him, endured the cross, making light of its disgrace, and has taken his seat at the right hand of the throne of God' (12:2) – thus unconsciously assimilating Jesus in part to the martyrs of his race. Chapter 13 mingles exhortation with ethics and closes with greetings.

The greetings ask the readers to be patient with 'this discourse of exhortation' and give them the news that 'our friend Timothy has been released' (13:23). The final greetings are from 'our Italian friends' (13:24). The 'letter' does not open with the usual statement of the name of the sender and addressee or addressees but plunges straight in with its effective and dramatic statement of doctrine. The style and vocabulary are not at all Pauline and the details about Timothy in the rest of the verse partly quoted above are mysterious. Although from the fifth century there has been a tradition which includes the work among the letters of Paul, it seems possible to argue that it is neither a letter nor by Paul. That it was addressed to

'Hebrews' is attested by the earliest manuscripts and by the whole writing; at the same time it is clear that the recipients were Christians, and it seems that in Hebrews we have an earnest sermon or tract appealing to Jewish Christians to abandon their reliance on the ordinances of the Law and to acknowledge Christ alone as necessary for salvation.

The 'greetings from our Italian friends' make our task more difficult; if this suggests that the writer was in Rome and Italy, it is perhaps consistent with the fact that the 'letter' was apparently well known in Rome very early, for it was extensively quoted by Clement of Rome c. 96 but not by anyone else until much later; but this implies a circulation in Rome, not despatch from it. Who then are the Italians? They are in fact described literally as 'those from Italy' and could therefore be companions of the author who had originally come from there but were with him somewhere else. They do not therefore help in identifying the circumstances of the 'letter'.

The date is a puzzling matter; the argument that the Jewish system of sacrifices has been rendered once for all obsolete by the sacrifice of Christ would have been greatly helped if the author had been able to say that Jerusalem had fallen and the temple been destroyed, and from this deduced (as we saw to be that habit of some Christians, when we were discussing the gospel of Matthew) that God had meant it to fall and therefore presumably its worship to cease. He does not use this argument and even seems to imply that the temple system may be still in being, if this is the right interpretation of the cryptic passage, 'Our altar is one from which the priests of the sacred tent have no right to eat' (13:10) — not 'have no possibility of eating'! This would mean before 70 and it is possible that the many references to possible and actual persecution refer to the woes thought to have begun with the events in Judaea which led up to the fall of Jerusalem. On the other hand the thought of the work as a whole is of the kind which one would expect to depend on some development of doctrine, and incidentally to be that of one who had, like Philo, some acquaintance with philosophical ideas stemming ultimately from Plato. If we think it must have been written a considerable time after the Fall of Jerusalem, we have to remember that it cannot be later than about 90; and we may have to add that it was probably written in a place where the Fall of Jerusalem made less impact than in some other places. This might be true of Alexandria, but also of some quarters in Rome. The reference to Timothy is no help; if to the Timothy we know as the close friend of Paul, it still tells us virtually no more about the circumstances of the actual composition of the work.

Although the argument is sensible enough that in spite of the lack of an epistolary beginning the work reads like a letter, since the recipients are obviously close to the author's mind all the time, we incline to the view that it is one of those writings (of which we shall hear more) which have been cast into the form of a letter and made to look like one of Paul's without the 'deception' being maintained in every respect. If this is right, we can call it a tract and imagine that it was for the consumption of Jewish Christians in general and not in any special place.

Of the author we know no more than we can deduce from the tract itself. In addition to what has already been said about his cast of thought, it must be observed that he was very well skilled in the use of scripture to explain scripture, sometimes in a way which seems very strange and arbitrary to us, in the manner of rabbinic exegesis. Like the author of Matthew he is a thoroughly Christian scribe, for whom the ancient scriptures *must* be about Jesus, for he is completely filled with the idea that Jesus is the promised Messiah and illuminates and is illuminated by the ancient heritage and wisdom. The ascription to Barnabas by Tertullian (*c.* 160–*c.* 220) may be due to Barnabas being a Levite and so credited with the elaborate doctrine based on temple usage, more probably to confusion with a second-century letter of Barnabas (no doubt pseudonymous) which is superficially like Hebrews. Luther's suggestion that it was Apollos has been, and still is in some quarters, very popular, for Apollos was an Alexandrian Jew who knew his scriptures well. There is really no reason to urge against this theory except that it is only a guess and that after all there must have been many others who would answer to the same description.

A Letter of James

To call Hebrews a tract addressed to Jewish Christians in general is the result of reason and to some extent speculation.

The opening of the letter of James almost openly proclaims that it is a work of this kind; here we have the stylised form of the opening of an ancient letter but in such words as preclude our thinking it was really meant to be a letter that actually went, so to speak, by post. The words, 'Greetings to the Twelve Tribes dispersed throughout the world' are clearly not a greeting to any person or people in a particular place; indeed, it is sometimes argued that the writing was originally addressed literally to the Diaspora or Dispersion, that is, to Jews living in other parts of the world than Palestine, for the explicit references to Jesus are confined to 1:1 and 2:1 and could have been added to an already existing tract. But it seems that the author refers clearly enough to Christianity when he describes and commends 'the man who looks closely into the perfect law, the law that makes us free, and who lives in its company, does not forget what he hears, but acts upon it' (1:25).

The relative lack of form and plan in this 'letter' have been the despair of commentators. It may well be that it should be regarded as a designedly miscellaneous composition to copy in a rather self-conscious way some examples of Wisdom literature, with their sententious ethical admonitions. Some have even ingeniously suggested that the author aspired to compose something to set alongside the Blessing of Jacob (Gen. 49) also addressed to the twelve tribes (or their heads) or the late Jewish work, the *Testaments of the Twelve Patriarchs*.[1]

In the miscellany there is one section which is of more obviously doctrinal importance, 2:14–26. Here the author uses some irony against those who rely entirely on faith. He urges that faith will do no good unless it is expressed in action. 'Was it not by his action, in offering his son Isaac upon the altar, that our father Abraham was justified?' (2:21). We are reminded of Paul's argument about the righteousness of Abraham and think that perhaps 'James' was contradicting Paul. This would be no more than a half-truth because Paul himself would have agreed with this notion, as many references would show, since he insists, for example, that judgment will take place according to deeds at the final reckoning (Rom 2:6 and 16) and commends 'faith active in love' (Gal. 5:6). But

[1] For an account of this theory see E. C. Blackman, *The Epistle of James*, The Torch Bible Commentaries, (S.C.M., 1957).

there may well have been people who misunderstood Paul, perhaps in a measure wilfully, and relied on grace and their own 'faith' in receiving it for their salvation. Such would not be true faith at all, but a bastard copy and a sham; divorced from life it would rely upon what Bonhoeffer has aptly called 'cheap grace', which simply does not exist apart from sincere discipleship.

Moreover, James is attacking in part the concept of faith which understands it as intellectual belief, in this instance monotheism. 'You have faith enough to believe that there is one God. Excellent! The devils have faith like that, and it makes them tremble' (2:19). Such faith was in fact necessary as a basis for Christian faith; and it was demanded by Paul and his fellow missionaries of pagan converts. But since James is writing to Jews he is warning them rather not to rely upon their monotheistic faith as a kind of badge of superiority over contemporaries who did not possess it. It is possible therefore that the controversy into which James was entering had nothing to do with Paul and his doctrine of justification by faith, but had much to do with Jewish pride in the purity of their belief which they retained even when they had become Jewish Christians.

The other features of this 'letter' may be brought out briefly by a swift analysis of its contents. Curiously enough, in view of the famous passage urging the uselessness of faith by itself, it opens with an emphasis on the need for faith in relation to God on the part of the individual believer (1:2–8). Next there is a short paragraph on the mortality of man (1:9–11) and then one rejecting the argument that God is responsible for a man's temptations (1:12–15, cf. Ecclus. 15:11). On the contrary, God is the source of all good things, and here follows a phrase or two of some significance for our judgment of the provenance of this 'letter'; for in 1:16 f. not only is this statement made about God but he is called 'the Father of the lights of heaven' with whom is found 'no variation'; and another technical astronomical term is used. This is something to which we shall return. 1:19–2:13 contain miscellaneous material of a most attractive practical nature on the theme of honesty and consistency in religion. Much of it may be summed up in '. . . be sure that you act on the message and do not merely listen' (1:22) and it includes the subjects of the difficulty of controlling the tongue, snobbery (including its invasion of Church life) and the necessity of keeping all of the 'law of liberty'. After the passage already noticed on faith (2:14–26), 3:1–12 consists of an extensive and imaginative diatribe against the unruly tongue, although it begins with a warning against the wish to become a teacher. It is not clear whether there is meant to be a connexion between the two. 3:13–18 distinguishes between wisdom from above and demonic wisdom and their fruit. 4:1–17 urges submissiveness before God in various departments of life, introducing this with a diagnosis of prayer left unanswered, which is due to its being uttered in order to fulfil selfish desires. The urge to patience is resumed, 5:7–11, but this is preceded by a tirade against the rich in 5:1–6 ending with some enigmatic words, 'You have condemned the innocent and murdered him; he offers no resistance.' It is a puzzle to know whether this is a general indictment or has a particular reference to the encompassing of the death of Jesus by the richer sections of the population of Jerusalem; if the latter, it is poignant because the same kind of people caused the death of James in 62, the brother of Jesus and traditionally regarded as the author of the letter. This again is something to which we must return. The letter ends with a mixture of admonitions including instructions for liturgical anointing of the sick for their recovery (5:12–20).

Let us pick up the points about the astronomical technical terms and the question of the authorship of the letter. The technical terms are not alone; in 3:6 occurs an unexpected phrase—the tongue 'keeps the wheel of our existence red-hot'. The wheel of our existence is literally 'the wheel of becoming' (or genesis) and is borrowed from Hellenistic philosophy of the kind which, perhaps derived ultimately from Pythagoras, taught that each individual soul was doomed to pass into a body which is born, dies and rots, to be released at death but to have to pass once more through this cycle. This cycle or wheel thus subjects the soul to the influence of corrupt matter and the tyranny of flesh. This is one of a few hints that the author had at least a smattering of Hellenistic culture, and it is therefore hard to believe that he was James the brother of Jesus.

This James did not believe in his brother during the latter's earthly ministry and nowhere in the New Testament is there an explanation why he becomes the head of the Church in Jerusalem during the imprisonment and perhaps prolonged absence of Peter. Acts 12:17 introduces him in his new authoritative position without explanation although there is a very old tradition that Jesus appeared to James after the resurrection in 1 Cor. 15:7, a tradition which is found with some elaboration in the *Gospel according to the Hebrews*. James shows no sign of being anything other than an Aramaic-speaking Jew and a conservative, for the tradition about him in Josephus, who also relates his death, is that he was popular with the moderate Jews (not Christians) in Jerusalem at the time of his death. His murder by a mob appears to have been engineered by the Sadducees and the high priest during the vacancy in the procuratorship after the death of Festus. Such a person is not likely to have written this perhaps superficially sophisticated 'letter', and arguments which have been urged in favour of such a theory crumble when they are examined.

For example, it is argued that the writer shows familiarity with the teaching of Jesus as it is known in the Sermon on the Mount, and this might be natural in a brother. Since James was not a believer at the time when this sermon was supposedly delivered, this is precisely what might be expected to be not the case. More important, the argument is very naive, for the form in which this teaching seems to recollect that of Jesus almost always reminds us of the gospel of Matthew which we have shown to be a late composition; and the most rational explanation of the likeness of the teaching is that the author of the letter and Matthew had access to the sayings in relatively late form, removed from their original utterance. The picture of the fond brother cherishing Jesus's sermon in his memory is absurd not only because he was not then a fond brother but also because the so-called sermon is really a collection of sayings, occurring in Luke in a different order, due to the zeal of Matthew or his source. If Pasolini's film about the 'Gospel according to Matthew' demonstrated anything it was that the sermon could never have been delivered as such.

The belief that James the brother of the Lord was the author arose largely from the name which the author gives himself at the beginning; yet there he describes himself as 'a servant of God and the Lord Jesus Christ', and does not claim to have been the brother of Jesus. If we are right in thinking that the argument about faith is due to a number of Churches or people misunderstanding Paul and relying hypocritically on what they called 'faith', this with other evidence may count for the letter being fairly late. It certainly belongs to the Jewish Christian sphere, and we may have here an example of pseudonymity with a fairly obvious clue to its point; the author writes what he would regard as a message from Jerusalem, still for him the divinely appointed centre of the world, to those Jews who had accepted Jesus as the Messiah. It is clear from several facts that the Christianity of the 'letter' is Jewish; often there is an attempt to make the writing sound like Wisdom literature, and the place of worship is not called *ekklesia* or church but synagogue. Above all the gospel and the way of life associated with t is a new Law. Thus is solved for this writer and his audience the question of the place of the Law in the new dispensation. There is a new Law for a new order, and it is continuous with the old.

Such features were common to many Churches in the early history of Christianity; this must be especially the case where and when the lengthening of the time before the coming of the Lord made necessary whole or partial abandonment of a life whose main characteristic was 'watching and waiting'. It was forced upon early Christians to adopt an ethic which was valid not for the time of waiting only but also for an indefinite period. Hence the turning to Judaism, Hellenised as it already was, for ethical ideals and rules; hence also the return of concepts which had been partially abandoned in early statements of Christianity. Adherents are bidden to copy the examples of men of the Old Testament who are regarded as 'righteous', and not simply to derive their way of life from the Spirit. Thus in Jas. 5:10 f. the prophets are examples of patient endurance rather than proclaimers of a gospel and Job is not the righteous man whose righteousness did not count before God, but an example of one who endured the trials which God allowed him to suffer and was in the end delivered from them. One senses an unconscious notion that Job's patience was the cause of his final deliverance rather than the fulfilment of divine promise.

It is hard to estimate the date of such a tract as the letter of James seems to be. If James the brother of Jesus wrote it, it must be so early that some of its features cannot easily be explained at all; if it is in any case a missive from Jerusalem, then it must seem that the city had not yet been destroyed and the tract must be dated before 70. The alignment with Matthew however would suggest a later date, and it is possible that the warnings against the rich are the result rather than the foreboding of disaster. In this case 'James' is not a symbol of Jerusalem but of the Christianity he and the city once exemplified, and the writer aspires to be or was recognised as someone, not otherwise identifiable, who held authority in this sphere. It is impossible to say where he wrote.

The First Letter of Peter

A very similar problem confronts us in 1 Peter; it seems to have been written by Peter the apostle but there are many reasons why it is hard to believe this. It begins as though written by Peter clearly enough and at the end greetings are sent from 'her who dwells in Babylon', which almost certainly means the Church in Rome. The greetings come from 'my son Mark' also, and this is consistent with what Papias tells us about the association of Mark with Peter in Rome. But what is Peter doing writing to 'God's scattered people who lodge for a while in Pontus, Galatia, Cappadocia, Asia, and Bithynia'? The conservative theory is that he wrote after the fire of Rome in 64, just before death at the hands of Roman persecutors engulfed him, Paul and other Christians. But in such circumstances was it natural that Peter should write a letter to Christians so far away in many of whose districts there apparently was no Church at this time, and to none of which we have any evidence that he ever went?

The main burden of the letter, 'Live in such a way as to remove prejudice against the Christian Church and you will probably escape persecution, especially if you show respect for civil authorities,' is again difficult. Certainly it was quite consistent to enjoin obedience to civil authorities in spite of persecution, for that was, as we have seen when describing Pauline teaching, part of the Christian life; but in the circumstances which the conservative view of the letter envisages we simply cannot make any sense of 'Who is going to do you wrong if you are devoted to what is good?' (3:13).

There are more sophisticated objections to Petrine author-ship. Once more we must refer to Acts 4:13. Peter was far from illiterate but he was not a scholar or expert. The letter however contains some of the best and most polished Greek in the New Testament; the thought is advanced, and easily and attractively expressed, even if we include the use of a rather technical term in 3:21, for this illustrates the relatively high culture of the writer even if it is not for us very easy to understand. Again, the situation seems to be that in which Christians are no longer merely waiting for the end of the age, though it is true that this thought is still very active, but have settled to a life alongside pagan fellow-citizens whom they are bidden to win over by good behaviour, and so escape threatened persecution. Some of these objections might be met, as has been urged by various editors, by supposing that Peter gave to Silvanus (5:12) the gist of what he wished to say and that his colleague worked up his thoughts into the impressive 'letter' which we know. The main objection to this theory is that the more it is relied upon the more clearly one admits that Peter wrote less of the letter than Silvanus and in the end one is left wondering why it is not known as the letter of Silvanus.

Of course the reason for this latter fact is that the letter begins firmly as though written by Peter; and we must find a theory which will account for a number of facts of which this is one. Another is that it was written at a time when persecution threatened Christians in northern Asia Minor. This latter point must be included in any reasonable theory of the origin of this writing. We look therefore for a time when persecution threatened Asia Minor, or some parts of it. This is not true of 64, for Nero's outburst was confined in its results to Rome. The year 96 is sometimes urged as a candidate, for a local persecution then threatened some of the inhabitants of this part of the world under the somewhat paranoiac Domitian, and this will be urged as the clue to the occasion of the book of Revelation. It does not seem likely however that this time of trouble affected people as far north as the parts of Asia Minor enumer-ated at the beginning of 1 Peter. For a persecution to fit these circumstances and places we have to wait for 112–3 when Pliny the Younger was Governor of Bithynia-Pontus and wrote to the emperor Trajan for guidance in dealing with Christians, about whom he confessed he knew very little and shows by his letter that even after questioning some Christians he understood rather less. It is interesting that he discovered some who had been but were not Christians any longer, some as many as twenty years before, which would bring us to near the time of the previous persecution under Domitian. This might be significant if we imagine that some who had recanted had also moved from one province to another within broadly the same area. These Pliny tested by trying to get them to curse Christ which he understands real Christians would not do, and if they obliged he let them go. He raises also the question with the emperor whether Christians are punishable for the name, that is whether the crimes of which Christians were suspected must be proved, or whether just to confess to being a Christian was enough. 1 Peter 4:16 seems to fit this situation well: '. . . if anyone suffers as a Christian, he should feel it no disgrace, but confess that name to the honour of God.'

It has often been noticed that the letter divides into two unequal parts; after the brief introduction of the first two verses, 1:3–4:11 reads like an effective sermon based on a reminder to Christians of their commitment in baptism, and to some this letter has seemed perhaps to be an actual baptismal sermon or even whole liturgy for that ceremony. In this first part the recipients are encouraged to avoid possible persecution by their exemplary lives. In the second part, 4:12–5:14 the writer addresses his friends as though a persecution was already raging. The two halves are further marked by the fact that 4:11 reads like a formal close to a sermon or apostolic letter. One way of accounting for this would be to say that 1 Peter is another example of a letter on the model of the ancient form according to which the real author gave general instructions to his amanuensis and added at the end something like a summary of what he wished to say, and wrote this part himself. This does not quite account for the facts here because of the change in situation which seems to be implied. It seems more reasonable to think of a writer sending an urgent message of comfort to those who were under persecution represented by 4:12–5:14 and enclosing the discourse reminding them of their duty as Christians which had originally been composed to meet another though not altogether different situation.

Let us see how such a theory works in relation to the contents of the writing. In 1:3–12 the writer expresses joy in the form of an extended *berakah* for the gospel which is characterised as the theme which 'prophets pondered and explored' (1:10) and which now 'has been openly announced to you through preachers who brought you the Gospel in the power of the Holy Spirit sent from heaven' (1:12)—apparently then not through the actual writer. It is also characterised as bringing eventual joy to those who accept it even if for a time they have to endure 'trials of many kinds', which would naturally refer to the general unpopularity of Christians rather than actual persecution. 1:13–21 exhorts to purity of life now that 'your days of ignorance' (1:14) are left behind, with a reminder that their freedom has been purchased by the blood of Christ. 1:22 contains a phrase which might suggest that those addressed had been very recently baptised for they are appealed to as those who 'by obedience to the truth ... have purified your souls'. This is made the ground for the practice of love towards one's neighbour of a real kind identified with taking part in the building of 'a spiritual temple' whose cornerstone is Christ and whose other stones are Christians. They can be considered also as now members of that 'chosen race' whom God designated in the past to make for himself 'a royal priesthood, a dedicated nation' (1:22–2:10). 2:11–3:12 exhorts the hearers powerfully to a lofty ethic; as in other letters, some by Paul, citizens as such, servants, women, husbands are in turn instructed. But here there is a remarkable emphasis peculiar to this letter: the servant who suffers unjustly is made a sort of type of Christ. Elsewhere in the New Testament it may well be that the idea of the Servant of the Lord found in Second Isaiah inspired the writers in their account of Jesus and perhaps Jesus himself; but this author takes a figure from everyday— the humble slave, known all too well in the surrounding civilization, who was punished unjustly.

3:13–18, beginning with the unexpected remark which we have already noticed, 'Who is going to do you wrong if you are devoted to what is good?', proceeds in fact to entertain the possibility that a Christian might 'suffer for your virtues'. If so, he should count himself happy. The teaching necessary after such a hard saying tells the Christian in circumstances of persecution how to be like Christ. 'He, the just, suffered for the unjust, to bring us to God' (3:18). Thus the argument that Peter could not have written the optimistic prophecy in 3:13 is weakened, though other arguments against the Petrine authorship remain. In 3:18-22 it appears that the author envisages the activity of Christ when 'in the body he was put to death; in the spirit he was brought to life'. He 'made his proclamation to the imprisoned spirits', probably all those who had died before this time, and even including disobedient 'angels'. In 3:21 baptism is explicitly defined, but unfortunately in such a technical metaphor that it is not easy to take the point: 'baptism is not the washing away of bodily pollution, but the appeal made to God by a good conscience.' Thus the New English Bible, but the second sentence may be translated otherwise, perhaps, 'the assurance before God of a loyal attitude of mind'. In 4:1-11 exhortation to a consistent life is based on what Christ has suffered for the Christian, and this section ends with a paragraph which opens with, 'The end of all things is upon us' (4:7).

Whoever was the author of 4:12-5:14, he might clearly enough have prefaced his letter to the persecuted with such material as this; nor is it at all obvious that the two parts of the letter must belong to a different author, though this is possible. He was expecting the end of the age, and seems to have regarded the trials which Christians have to endure as a sure sign of the impending judgment (4:17); it is fairly safe to say that he wrote from Rome ('Babylon') when a persecution was afflicting Christians in northern Asia Minor. That this may well have been in 112-3 is probable but not certain. It is possible that the author was Peter but unlikely, and of course impossible if we favour the date 112. In that case the name Peter at the beginning may be used much as the name of James may have been used at the opening of that letter — in this case it is a sympathetic letter from the Church of Rome.

Jude

In the course of time the Christian Church suffered from at least two difficulties within itself; one was a corruption which sprang from the selfish outlook of those who had not really committed themselves to the service of Christ and their fellow-men but had embarked on what they took to be the way to their own private salvation. Such could represent some particular kind of teaching, in reality their own invention, as the true version of Christianity. They would call this the only 'spiritual' version or the 'true' gospel. Often they wove around their views a fantastic doctrine concerning celestial beings by which they explained the universe and how it could have been brought into existence ultimately from a wholly spiritual God though itself material and beneath the contempt of those who had 'risen above it all'. Possibly this last description fits some people known to the reader. However that may be, such were the gnostics and other false teachers in the days of the early Church.

The other difficulty arose from a strand within the orthodox pattern, a strand once very prominent in that pattern; this was the oft-quoted belief in the end of the age to be ushered in by a returning and triumphant Lord whose character became in the imagination of some people more and more assimilated to the stern judge than to the loving redeemer. As time went on and this return did not happen, 'transmutation' of eschatology sometimes characterised the thinking of rebellious rather than of sympathetic souls.

Such was the situation with which the author of a brief tract or letter who calls himself 'Jude, servant of Jesus Christ and brother of James' had to deal. The writing is interesting because it uses late Judaistic literature, including the influential book of Enoch (1 Enoch) which was evidently at this time, and (as we know from some of the ancient manuscripts) for several years to come, regarded in some Christian quarters as canonical. It also evidently regards a similar book, the *Testament of Moses* or a part of it almost wholly lost usually called the *Assumption of Moses*, as authoritative; for the author appeals to the example narrated there of the archangel Michael not daring to rebuke Satan (because the latter was a spiritual being rebuking of whom must be left to the Lord).

These are some of the features of this strange composition. Others include fierce rebuke of those who mislead their fellow-Christians in the ways described in the opening paragraphs of this section. The main message even through all this strong reproach of 'certain persons who have wormed their way in, the very men whom Scripture long ago marked down for the doom they have incurred' (4) is to stand fast by the expectation of 'the day when our Lord Jesus Christ in his mercy will give eternal life' (21). The attitude to scripture here is but one of a number of hints that the author cannot have been Jude the brother of Jesus (Mark 6:3) but must belong to a much later generation when so many developments, many of them injurious, had occurred within the Church. The situation becomes even clearer when we turn to 2 Peter which, as we shall see, goes naturally with Jude.

2 Peter

This letter claims to be from 'Simeon Peter, servant and apostle of Jesus Christ' but even in early times its authenticity was doubted. Its occasion was exactly like that of Jude, and it is a natural theory to hold that the author in fact used Jude as a basis for his own composition. Besides more minor examples, 2 Peter 2:1–22 recalls Jude 4–16 and the false prophets and false teachers denounced in 2:1 are the same as those in Jude 18. 2 Peter then can be regarded as an enlargement of Jude; it exhorts also to virtue in the manner of Hellenistic piety. Virtues are virtues and not fruits of the Spirit (1:5–7); though they are conventionally called 'gifts' in the New English Bible, the Greek word does not occur in the original. The author knows of 1 Peter and refers to it (3:1); and he seems to use the gospels to create the impression that he is really Peter by referring to the Transfiguration as a historical event at which he was present (1:17 f.). He uses an interesting argument about the inevitability of God's judgment. This is due not only to the wickedness of those who are to be condemned but to the fact that scripture shows that God has at various times undoubtedly acted as judge, as when he overthrew Sodom and Gomorrah. On this subject of judgment also he expands Jude, adding a Stoic view of the end of the world (3:7, 10).

The most famous argument in 2 Peter is that 'with the Lord one day is like a thousand years and a thousand years like one day' (3:8) — which may be true as a general statement, but hardly the point; for the promise of the Lord's coming was obviously at one time for a date unknown indeed but definitely within the lifetime of many of those being addressed, a date which therefore could be conceived of only on the human time-scale. Any other way of thinking makes the promise to mere men absolutely pointless, and the argument used by 2 Peter nothing but dishonest. One further indication that this tract must have been written comparatively late in the history of the New Testament and perhaps confidently regarded (as it is by most scholars) as the latest book in it, comes from a remark usually prized by the student who explores this rarely read work. After referring in an admiring way to Paul 'with his inspired wisdom' he has to admit of his letters that 'they contain some obscure passages' (3:15 f.). But Paul's writings are already scripture and all such writings are liable to wilful misinterpretation (3:16).

Jude and 2 Peter then are fictitious testaments; just as there were such writings in late Judaistic literature, so in this very Jewish Christian material there are fictitious testaments, not of patriarchs but of apostles. Nothing could show more clearly that the Church has moved into an era when touch has been lost with the historical Jesus and an institution looks back to the apostles as founders of itself. In this strange way these writings, whose provenance is otherwise mysterious, provide an indication why those who wish to understand the original message of Christianity must study the New Testament, because even there they will find that obscuration of the original gospel has in some places already begun.

Chapter VII

The Book of Revelation

Nero goes down to history as a monster of tyranny, but his effect on the Christian Church was for the most part confined to the local persecution in Rome after the fire there in 64. His reputation as a madman ruling by terror was so great throughout the Roman Empire that fear of him continued after his death. Such irrational yet understandable fears cannot believe that the author of the original terror is dead; if so reported he is still feared as able to return reborn in another shape to continue his cruel activity. Thus arose the notion of Nero *redivivus* (Nero 'returned to life'), the fear that Nero would return, wreak vengeance on his enemies, and begin again a reign of terror. It was widespread in the Empire.

The next persecution of any substance which befell the Christian Church was again a local one; it arose in Asia Minor and was caused ultimately by the ridiculous vanity of the emperor Domitian (81–96). This Caesar liked to receive the honour due to a god. Many emperors rationally enough accepted the fiction that they were gods with cynical opportunism but without any sign that they believed the nonsense. It was the peculiar vanity of Domitian that he liked to be referred to in official edicts as 'our Lord and our God', a conceit which must have excited the horror of many minds, especially Jewish or Christian. Compliance, which could be as external as you wished, might well stave off any punishment or unfavourable notice. The main thing was to appear politically innocent. This last was difficult for Christians who were early accused of grave crimes behind closed doors, and these calumnies made possible the irrational and cruel persecution in Rome in the time of Nero. It became impossible unless one recanted: then for the sake of political peace it was necessary to subscribe to some ceremony which was religiously abhorrent, when the claim to divinity appeared to be made to the dishonour of God himself, whom

Christians called 'our Lord and our God'. Such claims were in Roman days, and indeed are now, easily possible for the cynic who does not find it hard to deny the majesty or even the existence of God himself.

For the earnest and brave Christian such idolatry was and is impossible. A situation in which this earnestness and courage were put to the test appears to have arisen in Asia Minor, especially in Phrygia, about 96, for in that region the cult of the goddess Cybele and her attendant Attis was assimilated to the cult of the emperor, which was usually reserved for state ceremonial occasions and then taken seriously by nobody. In this cult Domitian was worshipped in real earnest and it was served by a number of priests who were called 'kings'. It is easy to see that such a situation might well be used for the testing of Christians in their loyalty to the Empire and that this might easily become little less (or more) than a sport for the spiteful. It is probable that Jews in the district who were fanatically opposed to the Christian claims supplied many of the informers who brought to punishment those who would not comply with official regulations by joining in this worship.

Punishment in the Roman Empire for this kind of crime was graded according to the status of the accused. The guilty, if persons of lower rank, were often sent to the Sicilian saltmines. The more prominent in society might be exiled. Such a persecution as we have described and at the date given seems to have involved a man called John who was evidently quite an important person in society and as such bore high office in the Church. To this circumstance we owe one of the most puzzling and controversial books in the New Testament. In this book, The Revelation of John, the author tells his readers, 'I was on the island called Patmos because I had preached God's word and borne my testimony to Jesus' (1:9).

The book, odd as it is, when one learns to understand it a little, reveals quite a reasonable amount of data about its origin and occasion. Take for instance the date; in 17:8, in the course of explaining a fantastic vision there is a reference to the Nero *redivivus* myth: 'The beast you have seen is he who once was alive, and is alive no longer, but has yet to ascend out of the abyss before going to perdition.' The author goes on about other details of the vision which included seven heads also regarded as hills (monsters assimilated to Rome, which was famous for being founded on seven hills). The book goes on further:

> They represent also seven kings, of whom five have already fallen, one is now reigning, and the other has yet to come; and when he does come he is only to last for a little while. As for the beast that once was alive and is alive no longer, he is an eighth—and yet he is one of the seven, and he is going to perdition (17:10 f.).

To shorten a long argument—let us suppose that the kings are emperors and that the numbers of them relate to the series from Augustus onwards, but omitting the three who were emperor for only a short while in 68 after the death of Nero, each being ousted by a rival until finally the last of these three is ousted by Vespasian (69–79) who returned from his campaign in Judaea to take the throne. Let us further suppose that the writer of the book is adopting a device often used by apocalyptists and is pretending to write at a certain time which he makes identifiable but is in reality writing at a later time. This enables him to appear to prophesy so that credence is given to the part where he is really prophesying. In this case the author is living in the reign of Domitian who is the eighth, 'and yet he is one of the seven'; thus Domitian is also Nero *redivivus*, and Nero was one of the seven who preceded him. The emperor who is to last for a little while is Titus, son of Vespasian, known to have reigned only 79–81. On this theory we can make excellent sense of the otherwise obscure verse which follows (17:12): 'The ten horns you saw are ten kings who have not yet begun to reign, but who for one hour are to share with the beast the exercise of royal authority.' These are the priest-kings of the cult whose authority is limited to the brief hour during which they work their pagan idolatrous magic.

The title of the book can easily be explained although it might seem puzzling to those who think that the New Testament is all revelation of Jesus Christ in the sense that it is a revelation by him. We have had occasion often to correct this and to show that the sense in which the New Testament writings are a revelation of Christ is that they show forth

Christ himself, whether by a picture of his activity or by presenting the doctrine of the work of Christ or by some way akin to these. The books are not for the most part a revelation of secrets which Christ revealed, even if the Fourth Gospel is rather an exception. For there it is hinted that he had some secrets he could reveal if he could find the right listeners (see John 3:12). For the most part what we have affirmed about Christ and revelation in the New Testament is true, and the only exception is the book we are now considering. This proves to be almost the exception which proves the rule, for it is a record of what purports to come from the risen Christ and comes under suspicion as largely due to invention by the author. Here Jesus Christ is set alongside figures of the Jewish past who acted, according to the claims of their human scribes, as deliverers of supernatural messages concerning the outcome of immediately pressing events, and added much information about the supernatural sphere as well as about what was going to happen in earthly history. Such were for example Enoch and the angelic guide of Daniel, and now Jesus himself is taken to be a revealer of the same kind, albeit a supreme example. Reverence puts him at a remove: 'He made it known by sending his angel to his servant John, who, in telling all that he saw, has borne witness to the word of God and to the testimony of Jesus Christ' (1:1 f.).

The author calls himself by what was probably his own name John, and claims nothing further. He is not an apostle but addressed his readers as 'your brother' (1:9). He does not claim to be an *episkopos* (bishop) or even a presbyter, although he seems very familiar with the way in which presbyters were disposed at the eucharist and uses this memory as a basis for his picture of the worship of God himself in heaven (4:4 f.). He claims to have received the revelation which he writes on a special occasion: 'It was on the Lord's day, and I was caught up by the Spirit' (1:10) when in exile on Patmos. He writes to seven Churches in the province of the Roman Empire in the west of Asia Minor, which included Lydia to the north and Caria to the south of Asia proper. They are Ephesus, Smyrna, Pergamum, Thyatira, Sardis, Philadelphia and Laodicea (1:11), and to each there is a special message indicating clearly enough that he knew the conditions in each place well, though he disguises them, as all underground writers must do when they write about matters which may be disapproved by the oppressing power.

In this book woes are pronounced, a fact to which we shall return. One who tries to give a brief account of the book and its contents may feel that he is subject to one of them, but the task shall be attempted. It ought to be observed at the outset that the book is odd in that it uses words to describe what is better seen in images, and would be ideally set before the eyes by cinematic art. For the visions are cinematically conceived and absurdity results when this is forgotten. (This warning is not anachronistic for 'cinematically' means no more than in a fashion involving *kinema* or movement.) If the warning is remembered a book of genius is recognised, even if it is the genius of a very odd mind indeed.

The author is devoted to series of sevens: (1) Chs. 1–3, Letters to Seven Churches; (2) 4:1–8:5, Seven Seals; the seven seals are introduced in 5:1 as the seals of a scroll; only the Lion of Judah, the conquering Messiah who is identified with the sacrificed Lamb of God, can open them (i.e. declare the revelation). In chapter 4 the scene is set in heaven and appears to be modelled with a touch of genius on the disposition of a Church met for the eucharist in which the throne of God takes the place of the seat of the presiding elder or presbyter and the table is the altar. In slightly greater detail the seals are arranged thus: 6:1–8, seals one to four, horsemen; 6:9–11, seal five, martyr souls; 6:12–17, seal six, portents of judgment. Here ch. 7 'intrudes' with its dramatic presentation of the Christian holy ones who alone 'will be able to stand' (6:17). 8:1–5, seal seven, silence and incense, probably reflecting a solemn moment in worship on earth.

Our cinema director must now fade into a great picture of angels with trumpets (need we say seven trumpets?) which should be easy for him on the basis of a verse just before this, 8:5, which says, 'Then the angel took the censer, filled it from the altar fire, and threw it down upon the earth; and there were peals of thunder, lightning, and an earthquake.'

(3) 8:7–11:19, Seven trumpets sounded by angels; trumpets one to five in 8:7–9:11 comprise the first woe consisting of portents. Trumpet six in 9:13–11:13 comprises the second

woe consisting in the end of the age; and trumpet seven proclaims clearly the Messianic kingdom in 11:15–19 (cf. 1 Cor. 15:24).

There is an interlude before the fourth set of sevens; it comprises three chapters which may be briefly analysed thus: 12, the vision of the woman who is evidently the Church as a continuation of Israel; accordingly she bears the Messianic child. The chapter includes also the event of Satan cast down (12:9) as adumbrated also in Luke 10:18 and John 12:31. Chapter 13 concerns the beast from the abyss which is an archetypal monster of destruction charged with the horror of the persecutor, and chapter 14 balances chapter 7 with its moving vision of the Lamb surrounded by those who had his name written on their foreheads. The Lamb appears to preside over a number of portents initiated by angels.

(4) 15:1–18:24, seven plagues from seven bowls, with which 'the wrath of God is consummated' (15:1). In this section chapters 15–16 describe the pouring out of the bowls and in chapters 17–18 the fate of 'Babylon', that is Rome, is described. Chapter 19 shows the clash of the gospel with Rome, for, 'Then I saw the beast and the kings of the earth and their armies mustered to do battle with the Rider and his army' (19:19). From 19:13 we find the clue to the Rider: he is 'the Word of God'. Here is an echo of the concept met in discussing 2 Thessalonians, the opposition of the gospel by its enemies and the simultaneity of this contest with the era of woes or persecutions.

The series of sevens is now finished and treatment is given to the subject of the demonic forces behind the terrestrial events, chapter 20 telling of the thousand years which are to separate the original triumph of the Lamb from the final conquest of the devil at the end of the reign of the Lamb. The beginning of this thousand years or millennium is marked by the first resurrection to which only martyrs are admitted: they reign with him for a thousand years, the period being ended by the second death which has no power over these martyrs. The second death engulfs all evil forces and hurls them to destruction. They are engulfed in 'a lake of fire' (20:15) which would give the film director another easy task. Easy also for the cinema would be the dramatic replacement of this lake of fire and all that has preceded it by the final vision, 'Then I saw a new heaven and a new earth' (21:1). Chapter 21 describes the new Jerusalem and 22:1–5 a restored creation whose central feature is 'the river of the water of life, sparkling like crystal, flowing from the throne of God and of the Lamb down the middle of the city's street' (22:1 f.). The book closes with a final instruction to the author emphasising that the end is near (22:6–21).

The radical cause of this colossal outburst of image-making is the basic conviction of John that the persecution from which he and many of his fellow-Christians are suffering (and he seems to expect them to be a very great number, perhaps all Christians), coupled with the appalling blasphemy of the worship of a man who called himself Lord and God, signals the end of the age, the Messianic woes presaging the final deliverance. He thus interprets his own experience on the basis of his belief in standard Christian apocalyptic, very much as Paul some sixty years earlier had interpreted his experience against the background of his own Pharisaic eschatology. The clue therefore lies in such a short standard apocalypse as has been preserved in Mark 13:5–37, where the words are represented with scant historical probability as coming from Jesus himself.

It is such an apocalypse that John the author of Revelation has elaborated. Over all his composition hover two main thoughts or feelings; the first is that of the already accomplished victory of Christ, the triumphant note of which is sounded for example in chapters 7 and 14. The second is the sense of horror expressed by the phrase in Mark 13:14, 'the abomination of desolation' which we have already seen to be a quotation from Daniel and 1 Maccabees (p. 94). In Revelation the abomination is identifiable not exactly as a thing, but as the emperor putting himself in the place of God before the world at large.

In addition to these notes other more detailed features of the Marcan Little Apocalypse can very easily be identified. Mark 13:1 f. warns against false messiahs, and the whole book of Revelation may be said to be a warning, or rather an expression of loathing about the entire situation of false Messianism. Mark's wars, earthquakes and famines are found throughout the book. Again, as we have remarked several times, during the time when these troubles are taking place the Lord's witnesses will be persecuted and judged. With this compare Rev. 6:9 f.:

'When he broke the fifth seal, I saw underneath the altar the souls of those who had been slaughtered for God's word and for the testimony they bore. They gave a great cry: "How long, sovereign Lord, holy and true, must it be before thou wilt vindicate us and avenge our blood on the inhabitants of the earth?"' – a cry echoed in Luke 18:7. During the same time they are to preach the gospel to all nations (Mark 13:10; cf. Rev. 6:2 and 19:11, 13, 21 where the Word of God rides forth). No less characteristic are the cosmic portents in Mark, and these again need no special references for anyone willing to read even superficially the book of Revelation, for here their description is developed to the utmost.

The artistry of John lies in the elaboration with which he has set out his convictions, using material from Exodus, Ezekiel and Daniel and from other parts of the Old Testament. The book is best appreciated as a bizarre masterpiece in the art of reusing imagery and one of the most percipient of critics has called his book about this work *A Rebirth of Images*.[1] It is therefore all the more regrettable that Revelation is the natural prey of cranks. These refuse to see the historical circumstances of the author's heritage and of his own day as sufficient for understanding it. Such cranks have used it as the astrologer uses the stars; despite all scientific explanation, they see, the one in the book, the other in the heavens, hidden prophecies of things to come. They fail to see that this was not the strength but the weakness of the author, that he really thought that the cosmic disasters which he described were about to befall the earth and to be succeeded by the vindication of the righteous. He is at his loftiest when he forgets himself and describes not what is to be, but what is, though in this he is naturally still bound by the terms of his own heritage; it is then that he carries conviction with his profound vision of the reality behind the shifting scene of creation. He paints there not a strange picture of a God who cannot be described but 'a Lamb as it had been slain' and we hear a poetic echo of the utterance which expresses the heart of Christian theology.

[1] A. M. Farrer, *A Rebirth of Images* (Dacre Press, 1949).

Chapter VIII

The Formation of the 'New Testament'

JEREMIAH 31:31 is perhaps the most obvious example of the promise of God to make a new covenant to take the place of the old which he had made through Moses and which his people had broken. It is part of the earliest Christian teaching that God made this promised new covenant through Christ. Often 'the old covenant' is, in linguistic usage, scarcely distinguished from the books in which it is contained or which describe the way in which it was made, and how it was kept by God, broken by man and renewed on many occasions (as for example in Nehemiah 10). Thus the part of the Bible which relates all this became known as the Old Covenant, although this strictly means the covenant itself, an invisible entity, rather than the writings about it. In 2 Cor. 3:14 Paul already refers to the old covenant as though its day were over, and in Gal. 4:24 he says that Sarah and Hagar 'stand for two covenants'. One of these is the new covenant made through Christ who in his 'institution of the eucharist' is reported as saying, 'This cup is the new covenant . . .' (1 Cor. 11:25; Luke 22:20). Tertullian (*c.* 160-*c.* 220) was the first to translate the Greek by the Latin phrase *novum testamentum* which has given us 'New Testament'. As the scriptures of the old covenant came to be called by that name or 'the Old Testament', so the scriptures of the new covenant came to be called 'the New Testament', the phrase (in Greek) being used for the writings first by Clement of Alexandria about 200.

We have to trace in outline how the books now accepted as the New Testament came to form this collection and how others were rejected. The process was gradual. At first the scriptures acknowledged in the Churches were those of the Old Testament; it was an essential part of the teaching for former Jew or former pagan that Jesus fulfilled these scriptures, so that all converts whatever their background, took over the Jewish scripture and claimed that they alone had the right interpretation of

them. As late as Papias we find this bishop of the Church pre-
ferring the oral tradition (as we should now call it) to any
written material about Jesus. He shows great respect for information which can be shown to have derived ultimately or
reasonably directly from the apostles even though he knows of
written gospels. This was in Asia Minor; in Rome a decade or
so later (i.e. about 150) Justin writes as though he knew possibly
of a greater number of gospels than four, but he speaks of
'memoirs of the apostles which are called gospels'. In his day
therefore at Rome it seems that some documents about Jesus
were beginning to enjoy some, though not complete, authority.
For Justin also it is the Old Testament which comprises the
'scriptures' — the things which 'are written'.

If we go back to the earliest writings of the New Testament,
those of Paul, we find the Old Testament treated as scripture
but no other written works such as might later have become
parts of the gospels or other New Testament writings. But there
is ample evidence of oral tradition such as the passages in 1
Cor. 11 concerning the eucharist and 1 Cor. 15 concerning the
resurrection, to which we have often referred; we may add some
references in 1 Cor. 7, a chapter in which Paul explicitly distinguishes what he says on his own authority from anything
which he says on the authority of the Lord. This latter material
seems to be oral but may have been in part noted down, and to
be of the character which ultimately provided sayings sources
for the synoptic gospels.

Paul did not think of himself as writing scripture but the
Churches which received his letters evidently treasured them
and kept them carefully, though perhaps not so carefully that
they avoided muddling one letter with another, if the theories
of some critics are to be believed. We have already seen that
in his own lifetime Paul seems to have sent a copy of Romans
to Ephesus, perhaps to other places also. In addition to this and
to such hints as that in Col. 4:16 that letters from him were
read in other Churches besides that to which they were originally sent, we know from Paul himself as well as from Acts of
the manifold activity of messengers plying between one Church
and another. These facts provide a ready explanation for the
phenomenon of Paul's compositions becoming known quite
early in cities other than those to which he first sent them. No

doubt also his reputation was enhanced some time after his death when in 70 Jerusalem fell and with it went much of the influence of non-Pauline Jewish Christianity. Since Pauline influence can be traced in all Christian writings likely to have been composed from about 90 onwards, many think that about that time a deliberate effort was made to form a corpus of Pauline writings and to have them copied and distributed.

This is the era when the formation of a body of recognised literature for the Church emerges and begins to come into focus. Mark had probably written his gospel a good deal earlier, in about 65; but the later period of 70–90 saw the creation of Luke-Acts and Matthew, the latter virtually swallowing up Mark and for a time reducing the importance of the first and shortest gospel to a drastic extent. At first some writings, perhaps all, were used and venerated only in particular districts, Matthew for instance having a relatively wide circulation in Syria and Asia Minor where it was 'the gospel' and so known probably for quite a long time, gaining much later its title as the Gospel according to Matthew (see p. 46). But the extent to which Christians travelled and thereby shared their writings had not diminished since the apostolic age ended in about 70. Indeed the subsequent era saw not only the composition of Luke-Acts and the Fourth Gospel, but also of sub-apostolic writings such as the Pastorals and the General Letters (James, John, 1 and 2 Peter, and Jude).

The 'body of recognised literature' formed what came to be called the 'canon', or list; we possess a number of such lists or canons, and these illustrate several facts which have already received some notice. Prominent among these facts are two: the first is that in the earliest days a number of works not finally accepted and therefore unfamiliar to us were included. Some of these belong to the intertestamental period and cannot therefore be regarded by later Fathers of the Church as part of the New Testament canon although they might well be willing to see them as part of the Old Testament or Apocrypha, that is scripture of greater or lesser authority. The second fact is perhaps equally unfamiliar to the average enquirer: these early lists or canons give clear evidence of doubt of the authenticity of a number of writings in general use and acceptance. Such doubt is not therefore the invention of modern critics.

The earliest canon is odd. It has a great interest of its own because it is not only the earliest list we know but is that of a heretic. His name is Marcion and he came from Pontus to Rome about 140. He was very pro-Pauline and is the classical example in antiquity of the man who can do without the Old Testament. He misunderstood his hero's attitude to the past tradition and welcomed his struggle to free Christianity from Judaism. As Luke had been a helper of Paul his gospel was welcome, though Marcion edited his own version of it. He added to this, the only gospel which he accepted, his own editions of Galatians, 1 and 2 Corinthians, Romans, 1 and 2 Thessalonians, 'Laodiceans' (i.e. perhaps Ephesians), Colossians, Philemon, Philippians.

This would not do for the Roman Church, nor for Irenaeus who recognised all four gospels, Revelation, 1 John, 1 Peter, and two other writings illustrating the points recently made above. One of these was the book called The Wisdom of Solomon (often referred to simply as Wisdom) which is part of the Apocrypha; the other was a curious work called the *Shepherd*, combining allegories about the Church and ethics, and including a passage on post-baptismal sin. Of great importance is the canon called after the scholar who found it in Milan in 1740, L. A. Muratori. This Muratorian Canon is in Latin and probably represents the canon of the church of Rome about 200. It rejects the *Shepherd* whose author Hermas, it says, wrote it recently and was the brother of bishop Pius I (140–155). The manuscript of this canon is in a fragmentary condition but evidently had the gospels in the order familiar to us followed by Acts. The letters of Paul follow in a different order from that to which we are accustomed, and they include the Pastorals as Pauline. Other books included are Jude, 1 and 2 John and Revelation. Before the last Wisdom is listed and after it a work which was included in the canon for some time, an *Apocalypse of Peter*, though with a qualification about its authenticity. It is not perhaps so striking that Hebrews, James (though both these were known in Rome a century earlier) and 3 John are missing, but most significant that 1 and 2 Peter are not found in a canon apparently representing the choice of the Church at Rome.

The Egyptian Church was apparently more hospitable, for

the canon of Clement of Alexandria in about 200 included the four gospels and fourteen Paulines, Hebrews having been absorbed into this list, Acts and Revelation. Jude and the other general letters, along with the undoubtedly spurious *Letter of Barnabas* and the *Apocalypse of Peter* are put into a 'disputed' class. He does not quote 3 John, 2 Peter or James, but accepts 1 *Clement*, the *Shepherd* of Hermas, and a writing of uncertain date but not later than about 150 usually known as the *Didache* or *Teaching of the Twelve Apostles*. (1 *Clement* is a letter to the Church of Corinth from Clement, bishop of Rome about 96.) The Church historian Eusebius, following the great Alexandrian scholar Origen, tells us frankly of different opinions concerning some of the books. Thus the four gospels, Acts, Paulines (incl. Hebrews) with 1 John and 1 Peter are accepted, but Revelation only 'if you like'. Disputed are James, Jude, 2 Peter, 2 and 3 John and definitely unauthentic the *Acts of Paul* (part of a considerable body of unquestionably spurious literature about the apostles), the *Shepherd*, the *Apocalypse of Peter*, *Barnabas*, the *Didache*, Revelation ('if you like'), and the *Gospel of the Hebrews*. He adds a number of books which are heretical. The details need not concern us but it should be noticed that Eusebius finds it worth while to condemn these latter and thereby reveals that they were read by some Christians.

Eusebius was bishop of Caesarea and lived *c.* 260 − *c.* 340. This just brings us into the period of the earliest surviving manuscripts of New Testament writings. We shall see presently that they are themselves sometimes witnesses to a comprehensive canon including books now rejected. It will be as well to explain the conditions which have determined the character of the text of the New Testament in relation to the originals. In the ancient world an author would probably have a book which he intended for general circulation copied by several scribes immediately. This meant that a number of copies, inevitably differing a little through errors and unconscious alterations, circulated at once. The search for the autograph (the copy written by the author or the person to whom he dictated) is therefore virtually doomed to failure from the outset. Such conditions probably applied to all the gospels and almost certainly to Luke. They applied with some modification to Paul who can only in a particular and more restricted sense have intended his letters for 'general' circulation. Such language may seem contradictory, but we may say that Paul intended them for 'general' circulation if by that we may be allowed to mean for a wider circulation than the particular Church which he was addressing, though not for the entire world. That kind of circulation was in his case to come later, after his death. We may suspect that some of the compositions which, as we have seen, probably copy the style and matter of apostolic writings but do not really belong to them (notably the general letters), were written in such a way that indefinite or general circulation was intended for them from the outset.

When the canon begins to be formed, the material most used was papyrus and the writings were made up in what at the time was a fairly new form – that of the codex or primitive book. Two main collections called after their owners, the Bodmer and Chester Beatty papyri, give texts of much of the New Testament, but only the Chester Beatty collection provides substantial and continuous material. These papyri represent the earliest form of the text, of which the Egyptian manuscripts, which must be briefly described, are a kind of revision.

These Egyptian manuscripts enjoy some fame because they include some which are on fairly constant show to the public. One of these is the Codex Sinaiticus in the British Museum and another the Codex Vaticanus in the Vatican. These two are examples of 'uncials', that is, roughly speaking, manuscripts written in capitals and without ligatures to join up the letters, very attractive calligraphically. The Codex Sinaiticus (designated by the Hebrew letter 'aleph (א) but latterly more often by S) once contained the whole Greek Bible, and is the only uncial to contain the whole of the Greek New Testament. In addition it contains of the Apocrypha, Wisdom, Ecclesiasticus, Judith, Tobit and 1 Maccabees – with also 4 Maccabees which is not in the Apocrypha of the western Church. Of what are usually called New Testament apocryphal books it contains *Barnabas* and the *Shepherd*. The Codex Vaticanus (B) is not now complete but once contained the Old and New Testaments and the Apocrypha. These and other important representatives of the text in Egypt are interesting witnesses to the activity of the Church there, especially as we know so little about the latter in its earliest years from any direct evidence. It is in the second and third centuries that the scholarly activity of Christians in Alexandria comes into great prominence, especially through Clement and Origen. The evidence of Clement and of these uncials shows that in Egypt in the fourth century there was rather a broad canon and that it was not so fixed in the minds of Church officers that every manuscript of the New Testament contained all the same books; but all those now comprising the New Testament are represented in Sinaiticus and Vaticanus, and in others related to them.

The Egyptian uncials are the result of great scholarly activity, especially in Alexandria in the years 100–450. After the fifth century books became comparatively rare, but a kind of renaissance produced more writing and copying in the eighth century, not only in Alexandria but in many places in the eastern Mediterranean area. The period from 835 onwards is that of the production of a large number of minuscules, that is manuscripts in minuscule or small letters. These are much harder for the non-expert to read because the letters are joined and the writing runs on. Hence this writing is sometimes called cursive. The sack of Constantinople in 1204 reduced much of the work of scribes but the making of manuscripts went on with some energy for another two hundred years.

We can see a kind of descent table emerging: the papyri (now very thinly and fragmentarily represented) provided the archetype for the great Egyptian manuscripts, and this text was edited to provide the Byzantine text represented by a vast number of minuscules. ('Byzantine' because Byzantium was the original name of the city which Constantine renamed after himself when he made it his capital.) The character of these texts differs, though only slightly, in the sense that exceedingly small variants are common to the Byzantine text, as they are to the Egyptian or Alexandrian text. It was for a long time customary to distinguish another and much smaller group of manuscripts and regard them as representatives of the Western Text. The most famous of these is the Codex Bezae (D), given in 1581 by the French scholar Beza to the University of Cambridge; it has some remarkable variants, in the form sometimes of whole sentences, especially in its texts of Acts. One reason for designating this form of text 'Western' was the support which D receives for its left-hand pages written in Greek from its opposite pages, which are in Latin (d). It was thought therefore that D originated in the West, perhaps in Africa.

This introduces us to the versions, that is translations of the New Testament into other languages, many of which were made so early that they are valuable witnesses to an early form of the original text. The Latin is usually called the Old Latin to distinguish it from the recension made by Jerome in the fifth century to make a standard Latin text. This latter is called the Vulgate. Other important versions are Syriac, Coptic, Ethiopic, Armenian and Georgian.

The Western group included one form of the Syriac and for this and other reasons it is only as a convenient habit that the title 'Western' is now used. The Byzantine text contains a number of manuscripts which form sub-groups, and these in turn seem sometimes to have characteristics in common with a further small group of more ancient manuscripts. For a time it was usual to designate this group 'Caesarean' since it seemed to be partly represented by manuscripts which originated in that city. But it is now recognised that this latter group is too wide and heterogeneous from the expert's point of view for this name to be useful. Nevertheless many of these manuscripts may well owe their origin to the library at Caesarea known to Origen and to which Armenian and Georgian scholars referred when making their translations.

Such an outline as we are able to give here must mention, if no more, the fact that early Fathers of the Church also provide interesting witness to the form of the text when they quote it, as they frequently do, and sometimes discuss, as Origen did, the manuscripts which they used.

It remains to explain one or two general points. The first is that for the great majority of readers the differences between manuscripts and patristic quotations in their versions of any passage are tiny, and there is no question of there being in any modern everyday sense more than one 'version' of the New Testament. The whole sentences mentioned as occurring in D, especially in Acts, are exceptional; and D is unique in this respect. Even here there is no real departure from the main story. The variants are interesting and may be significant but they do not alter what Acts tells us in any important degree.

We shall see presently an illustration of this. The differences between manuscripts or versions are of a subtler kind, and interest the theologian from a doctrinal or historical point of view rather than the average reader for whom they would convey little. This also will be illustrated.

The second point is that the Byzantine (or 'Koine') text, attested as it is by the vast majority of (though not by the oldest) manuscripts, was used by the editor and printer Stephanus of Paris, based on the work of Erasmus, in the sixteenth century. This, until very recently, was that printed in all editions of the Greek New Testament in England, those on the continent following almost exactly the same text. This procedure has the merit of representing in the main text printed the largest number of manuscripts, so that less space is taken up in the *Apparatus Criticus* at the foot of each page which gives as many variants as the editor of a particular edition thinks right. Nevertheless such a text is almost certainly further from the earliest form of the original than one good ancient manuscript would give us. The great scholars of the nineteenth century in England, on whose work the Revised Version was based, namely Westcott and Hort, thought it best to base their text on the Vaticanus and Sinaiticus. Their reasons were however more complex than this and involved a theory of manuscript grouping which is being continually criticised. In particular, their idea that the great 'Alexandrines' represented a neutral, that is correct and unbiased text, nearly perfectly has been shown to be erroneous, since there is no such thing, and in any case we now have papyrus evidence for an earlier state of the text than even these fine uncials can give us. The situation therefore in a modern edition of the Greek New Testament is usually either that the old 'received text' is printed or an eclectic text which the editor thinks is the nearest to the original. And at the foot of the page he shows as honestly as he can what alternatives exist.

We may now give a few examples of the use of textual criticism in study of the New Testament. One obvious example is the ending of Mark, for this will illustrate a little the character of the evidence. Mark 16:9–20 appears to a student who gives attention to this question at once to be spurious. These verses are absent from a number of early witnesses, including Vaticanus and Sinaiticus. A shorter alternative ending appears in some rather later uncials, and this is printed in a note at the end of the gospel in R.S.V., but only referred to in a note in the Revised Version. It is printed in the text in a small paragraph by itself in the New English Bible just after verse 8. An enormous number of manuscripts contain verses 9–20 but this does not make up for their omission in significant numbers by important early witnesses. These latter include several Church Fathers who mention the lack of an ending in Greek copies of Mark known to them. The inclusion of 16:9–20 in the Authorised (or King James) Version is due to their presence in the received text. Armed with the textual evidence the student can then consider the character of verses 9–20 and the significance of there being an alternative ending in some manuscripts. It then becomes fairly apparent that this longer ending (verses 9–20) has been made up from knowledge acquired from other gospels and Acts. Thus we reach the inescapable conclusion that Mark as we now have it ends abruptly with 16:8, and the rival arguments that Mark may have so ended it in this way intentionally, and that he cannot possibly have intended to do so, may still be heard clashing in the corridors of scholarship.

1 John 5:7 provides an illustration of doctrinal interest, which may be very easily inspected simply by comparing the Authorised and Revised Versions of the English Bible, when it will be seen that verse 7 was regarded by the Revisers as unauthentic. The matter is not in fact confined to verse 7 but to save complicating the discussion it may be simply stated that words which involve verse 7 and a few more in verse 8 amount to a statement about the Trinity which is a glaring anachronism at this time in the development of doctrine. Erasmus could not find the passage in any Greek manuscript and it seems as if in his day it did not exist in any, although it was written into the margin of an old Greek manuscript since his time. Of Vulgate manuscripts only some of about 800 or after contain the passage. Though much more might be said about this strange fact, enough of the facts have been given to show the value of knowledge of the text. In this instance very elementary knowledge would suffice to convince a student that the author of 1 John did not write a passage like this, which seems to imply a developed trinitarian doctrine.

Our next two examples concern places, and the first illustrates the vagaries of D. Acts 11:28 narrates the prophecy of Agabus, and the D version of this includes the words, 'when we had gathered together'. This would add to the 'we-passages' of Acts (see p. 59) and imply the presence of the author. This is very interesting since Luke according to some external evidence was a native of Antioch, which is the scene of this event. The other is of interest in establishing the theory that Paul wrote two recensions of Romans; in that letter 1:7 and 15 make it hard to believe this part of the letter was intended for anywhere else than Rome since in the first of these two verses 'in Rome' qualifies the phrase, 'all those whom God loves', and verse 15 has a phrase which will translate literally into 'you who are in Rome'. However, it will readily be seen that other place-names could be substituted for Rome here or the phrase which makes specific reference to any place might be omitted. One single manuscript makes these very omissions, and this by itself might be thought rather thin evidence. No doubt it is, but it is interesting that in the margin of two others at 1:7 a note has been inserted by the same hand as wrote the manuscript to the effect that Origen in commenting on the passage omitted any reference to the place both in his citation of the text and in his comment. There is also some rather complicated evidence which strongly suggests that the letter ended differently in two separate recensions.

Our last example is Matt. 27:16 f. In this passage Pilate asks the crowd whether he is to release to them Barabbas or Jesus; but this is not the full text. The choice is between Barabbas and 'Jesus the so-called Christ'. In some of the witnesses which many would still sum up as Caesarean the famous robber is called Jesus Barabbas in both verses, thus providing a pointed choice between two men called Jesus, but with different additions to their names. For the rather obvious conclusion that Barabbas also was called Jesus there is no evidence in the parallel verses, Mark 15:7 and 11. If then there is to be a theory that Mark suppressed the fact out of reverence for Jesus, we should have to credit Matthew with two characteristics not usually thought to be his: he possessed another source than Mark here which gave him this extra bit of information, and he was determined to preserve it in the teeth of the objection that it detracted from the dignity of Jesus to share a name with a criminal. This is the less likely in that for Matthew the name Jesus is invested with special significance (Matt. 1:21; contrast Luke 1:31). We are left with the conclusion that the addition of 'Jesus' to the name Barabbas is not authentic to Matthew's text, but also without any ready explanation of its appearance.

From this outline of the subjects of canon and text of the New Testament it is possible to see the nature of New Testament study in one of its most useful aspects: the concept of the canon by which it was possible to say that a particular writing had authority or lacked it is seen to be less sharply defined than at first sight appears. The early Church cheerfully read books shunned by later ages or more distant fellow-Christians. Again, there can be no finding the 'true text'. Study of the manuscripts and other witnesses is excellent evidence for the way in which scribes make mistakes and for the preoccupations of a doctrinal nature or in the realm of historical conviction which cause conscious or unconscious alterations. Such study is part of the historical investigation of a still-living text.

Chapter IX

The Relevance of New Testament Studies

At the opening of the first chapter it was claimed that the significance of the New Testament lay in Jesus Christ. An increasing number of thoughtful and sympathetic people find the traditional explanations of his significance entirely unsatisfactory. They therefore find themselves faced with the necessity of explaining in some other way the vast complex of results arising from the life of Jesus. The matter is more pressing than it may seem at first glance. For centuries the Christian religion has provided the sanctions for the inhabitants of a large part of the globe, certainly for those of our western civilisation. Behind many of our laws, behind the most important of our social *mores* lies the unspoken often quite unarticulated belief that these rules are the will of God which he has revealed in Christianity. In our time the reality of God for many has faded or vanished, while the character of Jesus has been almost universally so caricatured that it has been very properly rejected.

In spite of this we have abundant evidence that the figure of Jesus continues to attract and to mystify. Who or what was he? Son of God? The phrase is meaningless! An early Maharishi? Then how did he get crucified? A Chè Guevara? Then what was he doing commending in that nationalist situation obedience to Caesar? These are awkward questions. Never mind. No one believes this Son of God idea and we need not worry about it. He *was* a man of prayer, perhaps he was a kind of Maharishi and — sublime thought — his contemporaries did not understand him. Yes, that might be it. Then of course he may well have been a nationalist leader, and that is why he was put to death by the occupying power. This is what his disciples thought, after all. As for the evidence that he would not agree to this interpretation of his own work and destiny — well, he wouldn't, would he?

Even when the figure of Jesus does not attract at all, the

results of his life have been so enormous that anyone with any interest in understanding how things are, and how we got to this place, will leave him out of their investigations only if they are willing to falsify the results. Clearly one of the phenomena which must be explained is the rise of the claim itself, the claim that Jesus was God as well as man. Not, if you like, by taking it seriously but by showing why and how it arose. For the belief has been itself so enormously influential that it might be regarded as the western historian's prime concern, more obviously than an investigation into Jesus himself. Whether you are sympathetic or hostile, the facts demand that you take the historical phenomenon of the person of Jesus seriously and find out what it is all about. Is it not time the matter were settled? Then we can get on with a new civilisation based on some really rational principles.

It appears to me that this last task — to determine the principles by which we are to live — is the most pressing problem of our times, far more important in the longest run than any of the 'practical' problems. For these — the population increase, the pollution and threatened slow death of our planet, the constant horror of war and vile oppression, and many others of an even more pressing nature to many individuals — all depend in the end on our attitude towards them. It is common ground that mankind possesses the knowledge and technical ability to deal with many of these problems but there is no common ground as to how to apply solutions or, in the case of some of them, whether they ought to be applied. This situation also includes a deep moral and spiritual dilemma. Indeed, it goes beyond the question of morality and embraces the whole matter of the nature of man himself. And these pressing questions are all affected by the historical question, Who or What is Jesus? Is it right, for example, to say 'is' or ought we to say 'was'? These matters are all so inevitably bound up with one another, through the nature of our history, that there cannot be any more relevant study than a thorough critical and, at the same time, sympathetic investigation into the New Testament. History, philosophy, psychology, sociology, politics and many other more traditionally labelled 'scientific' subjects all have their obvious relevance. But nothing can be more relevant than New Testament studies.

I use these phrases advisedly. I do not say that there can be nothing more relevant than a study of Christianity. For Christianity itself falls in our day under a huge question mark. What is it? Almost every day television and journalism, from time to time supported by the cinema, conspire to demonstrate that what most people think it is bears no relation to what it is for those whose task it is to study it (and whose opinion is therefore not consulted). In any case, Christianity has suffered no less than the civilisation to which it has so abundantly contributed a change almost equivalent to a *Zusammenbruch*. What else can one say when those who inherit a religion containing the reminder, 'You died, and your life is hid with Christ in God' can in all seriousness speak about the death not of man (which is assured) but of God (who by definition cannot die)? We need therefore not only on behalf of civilisation but on behalf of Christianity itself an investigation into its origins and thereby into its real character.

We have introduced two inseparably related subjects: Jesus and Christianity; we must now say a little more about them even though our treatment within the space possible can be only scanty and allusive. We will begin with Christianity and see where this takes us.

Let us start with something quite simple, albeit of the utmost importance. Not long ago a writer in the *Observer* said of Paul that he was so impressed by the teachings of Jesus that he devoted his life to spreading them throughout the then civilised world. In fact, Paul hardly ever quotes the teaching of Jesus, and when he refers to it he says things with the authority of Jesus which are rather unexpected, and for which sometimes there is no support elsewhere, though never things which contradict what Jesus says according to the gospels. But this is not quite the point. Whether Paul knew little or much of what Jesus taught (and this is in fact one of the most teasing and fascinating problems of New Testament study), this is not what *Paul himself* taught.

Paul was preoccupied in heart and mind with an interpretation of his own experience which his past and religious background afforded him; Jesus had been raised by God from the dead. This meant that he was after all the Messiah and this in its turn meant that as Messiah he was awaiting the time when he should return to earth, to inaugurate the Messianic kingdom which was to precede that of God himself; God would become king when the Messiah had brought into subjection all the forces in rebellion against God. This gospel, expressed in these entirely mythological terms, was believed by Paul as the sober and pressing historical truth, and it was this that he travelled the world to announce, and with the announcement to warn in time all who would listen, of the impending judgment involved in the series of events which he believed to be imminent. Not unnaturally he thereby created a problem when some of those whom he had converted and persuaded to this expectation died: would those who had died be left out of the kingdom to whose Lord they had committed themselves by baptism? The matter is interesting not only for itself, fantastic though it is, but for the fact that in connexion with his answer to this dependent question Paul quotes the authority of Jesus. He says that he has it on the word of the Lord that the living will not forestall the dead when the Lord comes, for then the Christian dead will be raised. Paul thinks he has the authority of Jesus for this, but I do not think this is what Philip Toynbee meant by 'the teachings of Jesus'.

We may be tempted to say that if this is the main Christian message of the main Christian missionary, we ought to abandon Christianity altogether. This eschatology, as it is called, the doctrine of the last things, the association of the coming of the Messiah with the end of the age, is neglected in the pulpit but occupies the study and the lecture room. There have been many attempts to explain away the apparent promise or threat — there are passages to support either way of putting it — that the end of the age would come with the return of Christ as judge. There are attempts in the New Testament itself; one is in the odd work called 2 Peter, which inspired the rather obvious remark addressed to God that 'A thousand ages in thy sight are like an evening gone'; which is not at all the point since the promise was for fulfilment in a *human* lifetime. More modern is the arresting attempt of Schweitzer, who thought that Jesus was a thoroughgoing eschatological teacher and died a broken man because his risking death on the cross had not at the last moment brought the kingdom by divine intervention. We cannot stop to discuss this now but it illustrates the relevance of New Testament studies very well: Schweitzer can be shown to be faulty only if you understand the background of gospel criticism, which he wrested to support his own theory.

By contrast others, notably C. H. Dodd (famous now for the part he played in the translation of the New Testament in the New English Bible), believed that Jesus taught that he had brought the kingdom of God *now* and that his followers misunderstood him enough to reduce this 'realised' eschatology to the old familiar Jewish futuristic eschatology, which we find accordingly in the gospels put into the mouth of Jesus. As a kind of variant, Bultmann and his many followers believe Jesus used the language of the kingdom which was necessarily eschatological, to challenge his contemporaries existentially with the gospel, which was not. But while Mark understood this well enough (and would presumably on this theory have been surprised if anyone had taken him literally), Luke committed the unpardonable error of thinking that the eschatology *was* to be understood in historical terms, thus falsifying the gospel. Now in these last days we have a kind of reinstatement of the original simple eschatology which appears to take it literally while protesting that of course it doesn't. My own view, for what it is worth, will be expressed best if we return to Paul, who started all this.

Paul certainly held a doctrine of simple futuristic eschatology such as Schweitzer described; perhaps Jesus did, but for the moment we are concerned with Paul's gospel about Jesus. None of the theologies just described are at all impressive. They all suffer from acute dishonesty, albeit often unconscious. The whole of the New Testament taught a naïve eschatology, even if—and this is the point—they made great efforts to bring out the reality of Christ, not 'up there and coming back' but 'here among us for ever', which is the other truth about him which was forced on them by their experience. Indeed, Paul taught a great deal more than this main eschatological framework. In doing so he penetrated so deeply into the heart of man's predicament that one is bound to ask whether this framework, so vital to Paul, was not in fact the accidental means of concealing Christ's real significance. For Paul claimed also that it is by a living relation with Christ that man's search for right standing with God was fulfilled, that right standing of which he despaired when he struggled to establish it by his own right living. This longed-for 'righteousness' was granted to man by God himself through the acceptance of Christ as a means of redemption. Indeed God showed his character as eternal redeemer in what he did for man through Christ. The use of these terms demands some interpretation of the concept of redemption: in essence it claims that there is a benign power available in infinite measure for righting the wrong, and that it is operative not only in individual minds but in the universe at large. And if we do not think something like this, why do we bother? Why do men acquire surgical skill, make demonstrations and protests, devote themselves to hard and intractable causes, and investigate the character of the planet so that (given the goodwill) it may be saved for other generations of not only men but animals?

Paul then discovered in his own experience and in that of his fellow-Christians a living faith which was capable of surviving the dispensable shell enclosing the real truth.

For a long time it has been clear to New Testament students that its message (if that is the right way to speak about it) is couched in mythical language and written by first-century men for first-century man. To interpret it into other terms is a colossal task, involving understanding the language (in both literal and metaphorical sense) in which the New Testament is written, and translating it, so to speak, into a modern idiom. Origen thought like a Neoplatonist, Augustine like Plato, Thomas Aquinas like Aristotle. These and many others have tried their best to reclothe Christianity in a dress fashionable in their own day. With our own comes the manifold phenomenon of existentialism; and one of the most fascinating and interesting aspects of the modern learned world is the very intelligent attempt by the German veteran *Neutestamentler* Bultmann and his followers not only to state the gospel existentially but to show that it is in origin and essence existential. Maybe it is, but so far success eludes these thinkers, perhaps because of the unnecessary alliance with an extreme and probably illogical historical scepticism.

Let this suffice for a mere indication of how Paul and with him the gospel is often grievously misunderstood, and how this is if one may say so, partly his own fault; and we may take it as an indication of how relevant New Testament studies are if we embark on the task, perhaps now appearing more formidable than we thought, to understand, and—as we find necessary—to reappraise—Christianity. We may turn to another and connected question, the common image of Jesus himself. In a television broadcast some time ago I heard an intelligent journalist say to a divine, 'After all, Christ came on earth, saying, "I am the Son of God—you must believe me".' What is sad about this is not that the journalist made this statement, for which he can be readily justified, but that the divine in question did not immediately—or indeed at all—explain that the journalist was giving a rough and ready summary of the Christ of the Fourth Gospel. Now here is where New Testament studies come in again. We may not say straightaway, as I would like to do, that this Fourth Gospel portrait is unhistorical, for it has been regarded in past ages as the most reliable historically. I would rather say immediately that such a Jesus as is portrayed here, *if he is to be regarded as the historical Jesus*, cannot be commended as a divine being whom it is proper to worship. How can one admire and love, how can one even like a person who in the Fourth Gospel indeed does much as the journalist said? Until the early nineteenth century it was regarded as probable that this gospel provided the account nearest to history of all the four, because it was traditionally written by John the apostle, son of Zebedee, who therefore was, as the author claims for himself in the gospel, an eye-witness. These questions have been fully discussed in Chapter Five. We recall not only the contrast with the other gospels, but a few facts which we need not here develop: nowhere does the author say that he is John but carefully disguises who he is by a long periphrasis as if he did not wish us to know who he was. If we consider also that his theology is remarkably advanced and subtly expressed, and betrays the preoccupations of an age rather later than any years immediately subsequent to the time of Jesus, we begin to suspect that the feature which repelled us at first is due to the author's manner in making the Jesus whom he portrays speak as if he were the Christ whom he worshipped. In this gospel the Jesus featured speaks what the author believed about him, not what the historical Jesus said or could have said. This is made a great deal more probable when the story of the external evidence is unfolded and we see that the gospel was certainly not accepted at first, especially not by those who might be glad to have the memoirs of an eye-witness; and that it was the favourite not of orthodox Christians but of gnostic heretics.

When the historical authority of the Fourth Gospel was seen to be suspect, attention was drawn to the three synoptic gospels which present a much more probable historical figure. But they in their turn have come to be recognised as theological documents, presenting a person in such a way that he is seen to be what the post-resurrection Church claimed for him — the Messiah or Son of Man or Son of God destined to return to inaugurate the kingdom of God. In spite of the undoubted theological character of these writings, they possess far more claim to include historical sayings and incidents either than the Fourth Gospel or than is sometimes allowed to themselves by contemporary critics. Since this subject has already been discussed (Ch. Two), we may pass on to a few examples in this sphere; for here New Testament studies have a particular and indispensable contribution to make towards the understanding of a problem important for the Church and indeed for the world of the present day.

Take for instance the Messiahship. Institutional Christianity is dominated by the assumption that Jesus not only was the Messiah (which if you insist on talking this sort of language he may well have been) but himself regarded it as the indispensable clue to understanding himself and his mission; further, that he greatly commended Peter for perceiving this and as a reward promised him that he would be the rock on which the Church was to be built, an utterance which virtually invested Peter with the status of the first Pope. I am quite sure myself that there is not the slightest chance that this passage in Matthew's gospel is historical. It is a commonplace of gospel criticism that Matthew is, in spite of its position in the New Testament, a relatively late work, bearing many signs of this and no signs which even try to disguise it. Compared with Mark at the point where the dialogue is introduced Matthew is seen to have inserted it into his Marcan outline (for he was following Mark here). Matthew is certainly not Matthew the apostle, and his gospel did not go by that name when it was first published. The passage itself bears many signs of lateness. It is then very unlikely that it was uttered by the historical Jesus. Nor does it bear the meaning usually attached to it, for in the Jewish manner the 'rock' is the Messiahship which Peter the Rock typifies, and it is on the rock of the fact that he is himself the Messiah that the Jesus of Matthew's gospel will build his Church — that Church which Jesus never mentions in any other source, no not even in the Fourth Gospel.

Such opinions, whether assented to or not, are the common coin of discussion among all denominations when the New Testament is discussed by experts. Yet in debates on the unity of the Church and the possibility of uniting the whole Church of the entire world under one polity, it is often suggested that the Pope in some form must be retained; and the fact that the most important grounds for this assumption have for many serious theologians been entirely removed by criticism is not even mentioned.

We may in passing ask and answer the question, What then was the attitude of the historical Jesus to the Messiahship? The short answer to this is of course that we do not know; but we can extend it by pointing out that in Mark, the oldest account of this incident, Jesus does not fully accept Peter's insight but at the most treats it with caution and regret, some would say with positive repudiation.

It is then impossible to found the unity of the Church on the notion of a dominical edict given to Peter. We can go even further and call in question another assumption with very practical consequences — that the Church presented at first a wonderful unity which was intended to be maintained when it expanded over all the world, that Jesus himself foresaw this expansion and prayed before his death for the unity of his apostles and the Church which they were to build. In my view the historical Jesus would have been surprised at the very idea that he was to found or cause or encourage anyone else to found a new institution. He was a Jew, and I do not think his own outlook can be understood without realising that he was very conscious of the fact, and that he cared ardently for the people of God to whom he belonged. He may well have foreseen that the 'Kingdom of God' would pass as a judgment to another people, but he made no claim to found a *new* Kingdom. The prayer for the Church so often quoted is in John 17, and has no claim to be

regarded as historical. There was never any unity in the Church
from the time that Stephen and the other Hellenists split off
from the Jerusalem Church of the apostles, if indeed they had
ever been part of it. One is tempted to say there was never any
unity in the Church, risking the anachronism, since the sons of
Zebedee asked for the first seats in the kingdom.

In fact the book known as the Acts of the Apostles and the
letters of Paul bear eloquent witness not only to the way in
which apostles could quarrel but to the way in which severe
differences arose between Paul and the much more conservative
'Hebrew' Church in Jerusalem, and in which very severe
differences amounting to hostility arose between him and the
judaisers who followed him about, and who, if they themselves
were to be believed owed their authority to those conservatives.
Again, the witness of early Church history is to a number of
different Churches with strikingly different customs and even
beliefs, looking to widely different centres. But was not the
Church as part of the gospel implicitly and sometimes explicitly
urged to unite? Indeed it was. Its task was not however to
unite itself—such ultimate unity as it had in Christ was enough
to be going on with—but to unite mankind. Those who claim
that Christian unity consists in a conformity of doctrine can
find little support in the New Testament, but those who claim
that all men and women are 'one in Christ'—politically and
socially one—are echoing the spirit of the gospel.

We have then to question whether Jesus thought of himself
as Messiah, and we deny absolutely the possibility that he
sought to found a Church, still less a monolithic structure with
a uniform doctrine about himself. You may be tempted to rejoin at some point, but does not the New Testament contain the
doctrines of the Virgin Birth and of the resurrection, and do
not these claim to establish the unique divine status of Jesus?
And does not this make him *either* an incredible figure, *or*
someone to accept in despite of all the rest of our experience,
trusting that he is a miracle and as such immeasurable by any
usual standards?

There is much that might be said about the Virgin Birth.
Here we must be content with a few points which will outline
the answer which New Testament studies must give. First of
all, it is not wholly a New Testament doctrine, but is confined

231

to the comparatively late gospels Matthew and Luke. It is unknown to Mark, the earliest gospel, and unknown to Paul and the rest of the New Testament. Paul spread his gospel over much of the Roman Empire without showing any sign of knowing it. In Luke it is part of a story which patently exhibits two sources, one of which apparently knows nothing of the virginal conception; in Matthew it is an obvious piece of *haggadah*, or story-telling inspired by thinking about scripture. I do not think there is any chance at all that it is historical. And this is ironical in the extreme, for a complete misunderstanding of its purpose (which was to relate the story of the divine care of God for his apparently neglected people who are personified in Mary) has bid fair to turn Christianity into a cult of the virgin goddess, as the architecture of the cathedrals of medieval Europe still clearly testifies.

With the resurrection it is different. Without it there can be no Christianity at all, and this fact is proclaimed and echoed on every page of the New Testament. But some very important points need to be made, in making which the relevance of New Testament studies may be once more illustrated, even though space necessitates leaving out a great deal, perhaps often just what others would think most essential to the problem.

First we have to distinguish between what the resurrection meant to its first proclaimers and what it means to us now. Then it meant that *the* resurrection had begun, Christ being the first example. You will see how your interpretation of that eschatological problem will affect vitally what you think about what it means now. If you belong to the 'thousand ages in thy sight' school perhaps you are still prepared to wait for the Second Coming. In that case you may still expect *the* resurrection to be completed as Paul did, but with more delay than he anticipated. But if you belong to those who regard eschatology as only a way of putting an existential demand, the resurrection means the presence *now* of this demand of 'Christ crucified' in your life. It means that Christ may have died a death like other men and to lie still in his 'Syrian grave' but that the challenge of his death and the life it offers you is *not* buried, that the Spirit of God is now and always challenging you to the new life in Christ.

There is great truth in this latter outlook. For what it asserts of the demands of the gospel of Christ crucified is true to that gospel. The resurrection, whatever else it means, must mean the continuing life of Christ in and for his followers, even those who do not believe in his own literal resurrection. Of course there are many who see no truth in this at all; but I am assuming the existence, on the basis of observation, of the continued power of Jesus Christ to attract and to summon to discipleship. This one might almost equate with the resurrection as we understand it now. Almost, but not quite. For if there is truth in it, then the earliest preachers of the gospel presumably thought about it and above all experienced it in the same way. Once again New Testament studies become relevant; for they reveal what the believer might expect and the unbeliever be surprised to find. There is indeed evidence offered of a strange and if you wish unacceptable character, to the effect that Jesus appeared to his followers and thereby assured them he was alive; but in every instance such an appearance was for more than that purpose. Careful investigation shows that in every case it was for the purpose of commissioning the person thus assured and sending him to do something connected with the gospel, usually to proclaim it. The result is a number of people, their sorrow turned to joy, living and working *in the power of* the resurrection. This is what we discover to be the heart of the matter if we investigate the New Testament critically and thoroughly. To give but one example, Mark obviously writes in this way though the authentic version of his gospel (which lacks the last twelve verses in the Authorised Version) contains no story of appearances at all.

The Fourth Gospel, the Virgin Birth and the resurrection are all in their turn seen to render testimony of a different kind from that which appears at first sight. By looking at these subjects we touched on the great problem of the historical Jesus. We have shown a willingness at least to admit that he was not as he is represented in the gospels.

The problem is this: in all the gospels, including the three which are at present occupying us, Jesus is represented as working miracles. In the synoptics he is also shown as receiving a vision (or hearing a divine voice) at his baptism, as walking on the water, as multiplying bread, as being strangely transfigured, and as the centre of other events incredible to us.

233

Every instance tells us something very significant about the
Christ worshipped in the Church but at the cost of historical
credibility. In these circumstances we must ask, what was Jesus
really like? A common answer is to make an almost total dis-
junction between the Jesus of history and the Christ of faith,
adding as though it were obvious that the historical Jesus has
been presented as though he were the Christ of faith, but of
course he was not like this at all. He was not, because no one
could have been. No doubt we must concede that the gospels
give us only accidental glimpses of the historical Jesus and that
their portrait of him is coloured at every point by their convictions about him. We possess neither a biography nor the means
of constructing one. But is it true that Jesus was not at all like
the Christ of faith because no one could be?

It seems to me that this is precisely what New Testament
studies and logic render us incapable of saying. The Christ of
faith was in the first instance preached by those who had known
the historical Jesus and then by some, including Paul, whom
they could and apparently did instruct. It would be open to
them to preach in such a way that they falsified the character
of Jesus, but is it probable that they could then have preached
him at all, that is if they knew he was substantially different?
What would have been their object? Clearly in such a case to
deceive the world; logically this remains a possibility, and some
may choose it. But it is a more probable theory that they
preached Christ because they had been impressed by the man
he was, that they said he was the divine redeemer because they
had found him to be such a person, that this was *for them* the
natural way in which to express it. They had formed this
impression through their earthly acquaintance with him. Allow
for all sorts of different impressions. Allow for the exaggeration
or even the invention of many wonders. It still remains the
most feasible explanation of the gospels that they present the
Jesus of fact, even if the presenters, being first-century men,
did it in such a way as hides the historical truth *from us*.

Just above was mentioned the possibility that the first
proclaimers of the gospel proclaimed more than the bare fact
of the resurrection. Luke comes to our aid here. He makes the
risen Jesus say to his apostles of the Messiah that 'in his name
repentance bringing forgiveness of sins is to be proclaimed to

all nations'. And we saw that perhaps the most durable of the insights of Paul, separable from eschatology and the attitude to time which it involves, was that Christ was the embodiment of the divine operation of redemption. It is precisely this that every Christian finds to be his experience. We can prove nothing by these facts, but we can see a possibility for a new statement of Christianity which takes note carefully of the fullest criticism and remains true to the gospel which was preached from the first. For in the excitement generated by a long period of scepticism we have failed to notice the extraordinary correspondence between the experience of the scholar and the worshipper. Recognition of the fact that he knows Christ, yet must in another way admit that Christ remains totally unknown to him is not only the despair of the scholar, it is also the boast of the Christian. In a famous passage Paul made the same point: 'we see only puzzling reflections in a mirror.'

Study of the New Testament will then lay open to view some radical difficulties in accepting the gospel as it is often conceived, and above all as it was originally conceived and is recorded in the New Testament itself. It will however also disclose means of discovering the permanent element in that gospel, the recognition of Christ as God's act of redemption. This is enhanced when it is no longer tied as it was originally by historical accident to an eschatological framework; but it will imply a doctrine of God which may be unfamiliar, that God is met and known not primarily as creator, but as the redemptive force in the world of man. Whether this concept can be made viable through philosophical treatment so that the whole concept of God can be so understood, operative at all levels of creation, is a question outside my province. This very fact may serve to indicate another relevance of New Testament study—it is clearly not fully relevant by itself to our situation. It demands the full attention of biblical scholars, historians and philosophers.

It may well seem that the Church as an institution has been given short shrift. Paradoxically the Church is all-important. For if the New Testament calls in question one idea of it, it is to establish another, one capable of being very clearly envisaged. The picture which we should have in our minds is that of the faithful gathered round a table for the celebration of the eucharist, the fellowship meal at which they believe Christ to be present. Again, it probably needs some New Testament studies to bring home that we are not here speaking only of the eucharist as it was 'instituted' at the Last Supper, an event which obviously associated it with the death of Jesus, but also as the continuation of those fellowship meals which seem to go back to the Galilean days and which are illustrated by what are in the gospels presented as miraculous feedings of a multitude. There is abundant evidence in the gospels, in Paul and in early Church history for the paramount importance of this act of communion. It is sad that there has been so much controversy about the eucharist. It may be that in the future all shades of thought among believers will unite their views about this solemn action by accepting the entirely Catholic doctrine that at the eucharist the true celebrant is Christ himself.

We pass on to two final examples of relevance. We live, it would be said, in a permissive society, which by its very title sounds nervous of its right to exist. Ought it not to be called 'the spoilt-child society'? Probably a scientific study would show that it is not really a majority of our contemporaries who live in it; but we hear enough about it to be compelled to answer the challenge which may be expressed something like this. Jesus stands for freedom, for forgiveness, for the underdog, above all for love. There is truth in these assertions but not if they fail to be qualified by some solemn reflections. For Jesus, those who are free are free only to serve God. What other freedom is there in 'taking up a cross'? Certainly *all* should have forgiveness but this is as much a command to those who need it as to those inclined to withhold it. Jesus did not address those on whom he showed mercy with the words, 'Your sins are forgiven so it does not matter that you committed them' but something expressed either in words or in attitude which said, 'Your sins are forgiven—begin again your life of real service to God.' The Prodigal Son was welcomed not as prodigal but as returning. As for love—it is not *eros* but the divinely given *agape* which is commended in the New Testament, and if in it man is urged to love his fellow-man, he is also urged to love God in terms whose meaning study reveals: he must acknowledge the sovereignty of God. And this is the first and great commandment, not merely an odd way of saying the second.

Moreover, when the Christian needs to be told exactly what he is to do every day (other than watch and wait for that dénouement which did not come) if he is to live as a Christian, he is told in very certain terms, mostly borrowed from Jewish ethics, to observe some very old-fashioned virtues. If New Testament studies make anything plain about Christianity in its essence, it is that according to it there can be no trifling with morality, and that the morality on which it insists is very old and not a bit trendy. But it would be false to the New Testament if that were represented as all. The strict morality enjoined is to flow from divine love and divine grace. It is merely the day-to-day clothes of the glorious body within, the body which is 'alive to God' and which has discovered that this apparent slavery is in reality the very co-ordination of instincts and aspirations and desires which brings fulfilment not to them each by each but to the whole personality.

In this connexion it is hardly possible not to mention marriage. It is extremely ironical that a saying of Jesus which makes a statement about the ontic union of man and wife is usually lost in the discussion about divorce which is attached to it; this whole passage illustrates very pointedly the relevance of New Testament studies, and incidentally just as clearly the *relevance* of such study, and not that it settles the matter in debate by itself. The passage is one in which it would be normal among the vast majority of New Testament students to say that Matthew was using Mark. Now it is one of the characteristics of Matthew that at various points when following Mark he adds a scarcely noticed phrase to bring out what is implicit in Mark, in order to make a matter perfectly clear. In the passage in question Mark 10:11 reports Jesus as saying, 'Whoever divorces his wife and marries another commits adultery against her' — and the same is said to be true of the wife divorcing her husband. On the background of Judaism this would be startling if previous adultery were not regarded as the one exception, the one valid reason even for a strict adherent of the Law to divorce his wife. In his parallel passage Matthew adds the necessary phrase, 'except for adultery'. Very strict Churchmen who wish to argue that there can be no cause for divorce whatever which is valid for a Christian sometimes argue that this is an addition by Matthew and not authentic. So far as

I know, this is the one and only instance where modern critical knowledge of the New Testament is ever used in debate, and that by a section of the public not otherwise eager to accept as probable or as relevant such expertise. I have never seen it mentioned that there is a very probable explanation for the phrase in Matthew here, namely that here as elsewhere he is doing no more than bring out for the sake of clarity what he took to be implicit in Mark. I repeat that this cannot be regarded as more than a passing comment on a difficult problem; but it may suffice to show that quite technical study of the New Testament, while not decisive, may be of vital relevance to a debate on matters of deep concern to many people.

The saying to which we have just referred is in some ways far more important if we ignore what it says about divorce and attend to its assertion about marriage. The concept of a man and woman making 'one flesh' is an excellent example of the fact that the ethics which Jesus himself appears to have taught can hardly be welcomed by those who wish to interpret him as in every sphere a rebel who out of pity for the oppressed would relax all the rules of the 'establishment'.

These and similar considerations provoke the debate whether it is possible to accept the principles derivable from the teaching of the gospels for whole civilisations: are they not impossibly high and remote from what can be expected from mere humanity? The two main answers to this very pertinent question can be held together only by entertaining and seeking to resolve a paradox. They are the principles of the Christian life and this according to the New Testament can indeed be lived only by grace, the special gift of God. On the other hand if they are true for man's nature, if they are the best for his best, they could hardly be other than those best suited to man as such. The 'amphibious' nature of man has often been observed. Perhaps one can do no better for a conclusion than to express the hope that the great contemporary discovery of our kinship with the animals will not lead us to abandon the insight whose expression is writ large on every page of the New Testament, that we cease to be what we are if we fail to acknowledge our membership also of a quite different world.

SELECT BIBLIOGRAPHY

Select Bibliography

(Additional to those books already mentioned in the footnotes)

FOR GENERAL CONSULTATION

The Westminster Historical Atlas, ed. G. E. Wright and F. V. Filson (S.C.M., 1953).

L. H. Grollenberg, *Atlas of the Bible* (Nelson, 1956).

D. Guthrie, *New Testament Introduction* (Tyndale Press, 1970).

A. Wikenhauser, *New Testament Introduction* (Herder Nelson, 1958).

K. H. Schelke, *An Introduction to the New Testament* (Mercier, 1969).

W. Marxsen, *Introduction to the New Testament* (Blackwell, 1968).

W. D. Davies, *Invitation to the New Testament* (Darton, Longman and Todd, 1967).

A. H. McNeile (2nd ed., C. S. C. Williams), *An Introduction to the Study of the New Testament* (O.U.P., 1953).

W. G. Kümmel, *Introduction to the New Testament* (S.C.M., 1965).

O. Cullmann, *The New Testament, an Introduction* (S.C.M., 1968).

R. H. Fuller, *The New Testament in Current Study* (S.C.M., 1963).

—— *A Critical Introduction to the New Testament* (Duckworth, 1966).

F. V. Filson, *A New Testament History* (S.C.M., 1964).

F. F. Bruce, *New Testament History* (Nelson, 1969).

L. Goppelt, *Apostolic and Post-apostolic Times* (A. & C. Black, 1970).

G. B. Caird, *The Apostolic Age* (Duckworth, 1955).

COMMENTARY SERIES DESIGNED TO COVER THE WHOLE NEW TESTAMENT BY SEPARATE BOOKS

The Interpreter's Bible, (N.T. Vols. VII-XII).

Peake's Commentary on the Bible, ed. M. Black, (Nelson revised edition, 1962).

The Torch Bible Commentaries, S.C.M. Press (N.T. complete) based on R.V.

The New Clarendon Bible, Nelson, based on R.S.V.

The Cambridge Bible Commentary, C.U.P., (N.T. complete) based on New English Bible with companion volumes, *Understanding the New Testament* (ed. O. J. Lace) and *New Testament Illustrations* (C. M. Jones).

The Pelican New Testament Commentaries.

A. & C. Black's New Testament Commentaries with companion volume, C. F. D. Moule, *The Birth of the New Testament*, 2nd ed. 1966.

The Anchor Bible, Doubleday, New York.

Tyndale New Testament Commentaries.

GOSPELS AND ACTS

F. C. Grant, *The Gospels, their Origin and Growth* (Faber, 1959).

W. R. Farmer, *The Synoptic Problem* (Macmillan, 1964); a historical review critical of the usual conclusions.

R. Bultmann, *The History of the Synoptic Tradition* (Blackwell, 1963).

M. Dibelius, *From Tradition to Gospel* (Nicholson and Watson, 1964).

H. J. Cadbury, *The Making of Luke-Acts* (S.P.C.K., 1927 and 1958).

C. K. Barrett, *Luke the Historian in Recent Study* (Epworth, 1961).

N. Perrin, *Rediscovering the Teaching of Jesus* (S.C.M., 1967).

H. Zahrnt, *The Historical Jesus* (Collins, 1963).

G. E. Ladd, *The New Testament and Criticism* (Hodder and Stoughton, 1970).

W. Barclay, *The First Three Gospels* (S.C.M., 1966).

S. Johnston, *The Theology of the Gospels* (Duckworth, 1966).

N. Perrin, *What is Redaction Criticism?* (S.P.C.K., 1970).

E. C. Hoskyns and N. Davey, *The Riddle of the New Testament* (Faber, 1931, revised 1936).

X. Léon-Dufour, *The Gospels and the Jesus of History* (Collins, 1968).

O. Betz, *What do we know about Jesus?* (S.C.M., 1967).

I. H. Marshall, *Luke: Historian & Theologian* (Paternoster, 1970).

C. H. Dodd, *The Parables of the Kingdom* (Nisbet, 1935; also Fontana paperback).

A. M. Hunter, *According to John* (S.C.M., 1968).

PAUL

C. H. Dodd, *The Meaning of Paul for Today* (Allen and Unwin, 1920; also Fontana paperback).

A. M. Hunter, *The Gospel according to St. Paul* (S.C.M., 1966).

D. E. H. Whiteley, *The Theology of St. Paul* (Blackwell, 1964).

For all other books of the New Testament, and indeed for those specially mentioned in the above list, it is best to consult one of the commentaries devoted to the particular book in question. There is always an introduction explaining the problems connected with its origin and meaning.

Index

Index of Scripture References

INDEX OF SCRIPTURE REFERENCES